THE LIFE
AFTER

1

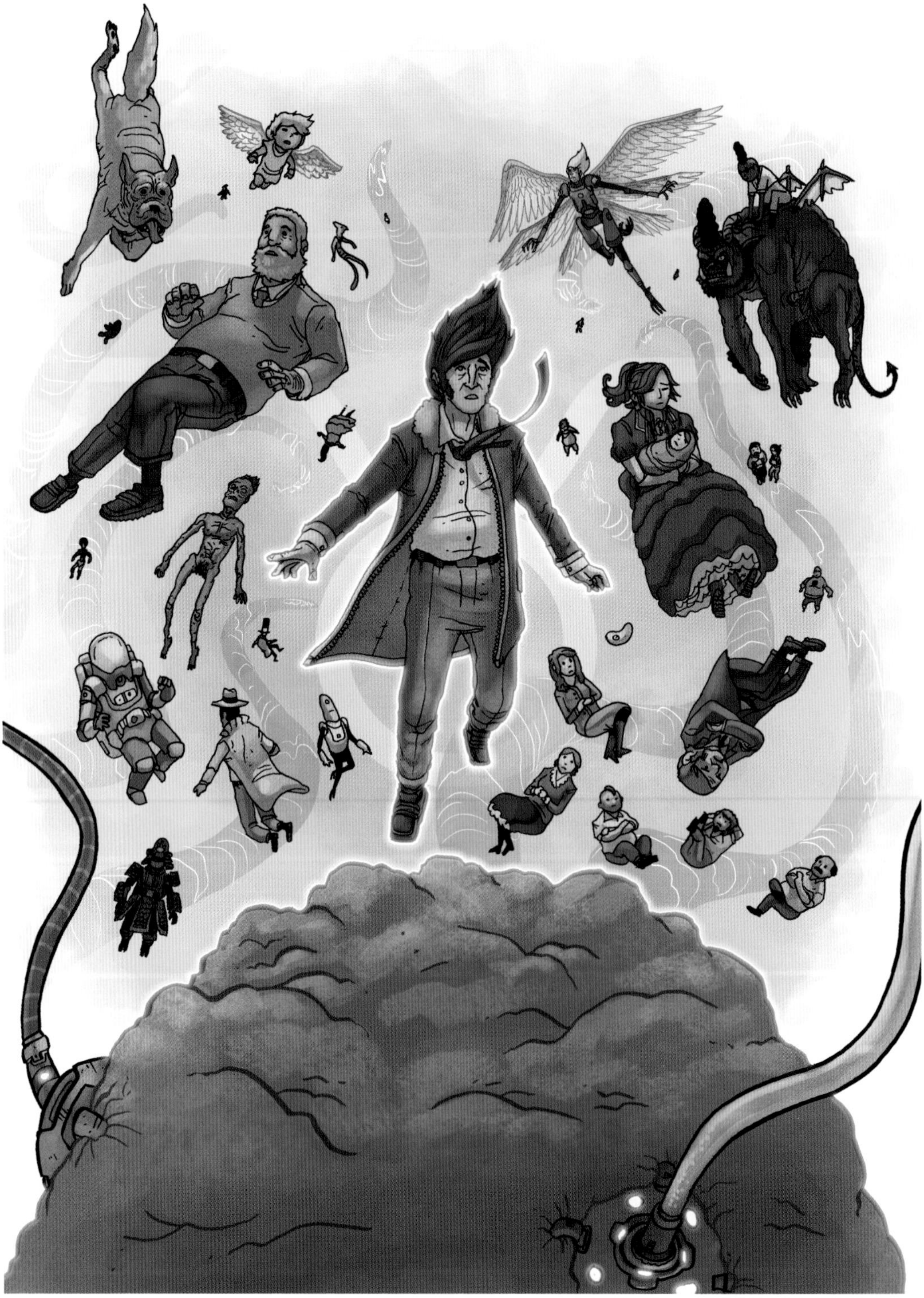

The Life After

THE LIFE AFTER

1

Written by

JOSHUA HALE FIALKOV

Illustrated and colored by

GABO

Lettered by

CRANK!

Designed by

KEITH WOOD

Edited by

JAMES LUCAS JONES &
ARI YARWOOD

AN ONI PRESS PUBLICATION

PUBLISHED BY ONI PRESS, INC.

Joe Nozemack publisher

James Lucas Jones editor in chief

Andrew McIntire v.p. of marketing & sales

David Dissanayake publicity coordinator

Rachel Reed director of publicity

Troy Look director of design & production

Hilary Thompson graphic designer

Angie Dobson digital prepress technician

Ari Yarwood managing editor

Charlie Chu senior editor

Robin Herrera editor

Bess Pallares editorial assistant

Brad Rooks director of logistics

Jung Lee logistics associate

onipress.com • facebook.com/onipress
twitter.com/onipress • onipress.tumblr.com

thefialkov.com • @joshfialkov
yogabogabo.com • @galvosaur

This volume collects issues #1-5 of the
Oni Press series *The Life After*.

Chapter breaks by

Nick Pitarra & Megan Wilson and Gabo.

Oni Press, Inc.
1305 SE Martin Luther King Jr. Blvd.
Suite A
Portland, OR 97214
USA

First edition: January 2015
Square One edition: March 2017

ISBN 978-1-62010-389-0
eISBN 978-1-62010-198-8

Library of Congress Control Number: 2014944756

1 2 3 4 5 6 7 8 9 10

PRINTED IN CHINA.

To the great potato in the sky, and
the sweet potato in my home.
- Joshua

To Leah, for helping me break
out of the cycle.
- Gabo

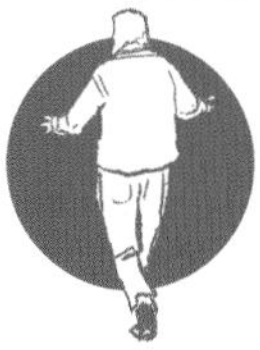

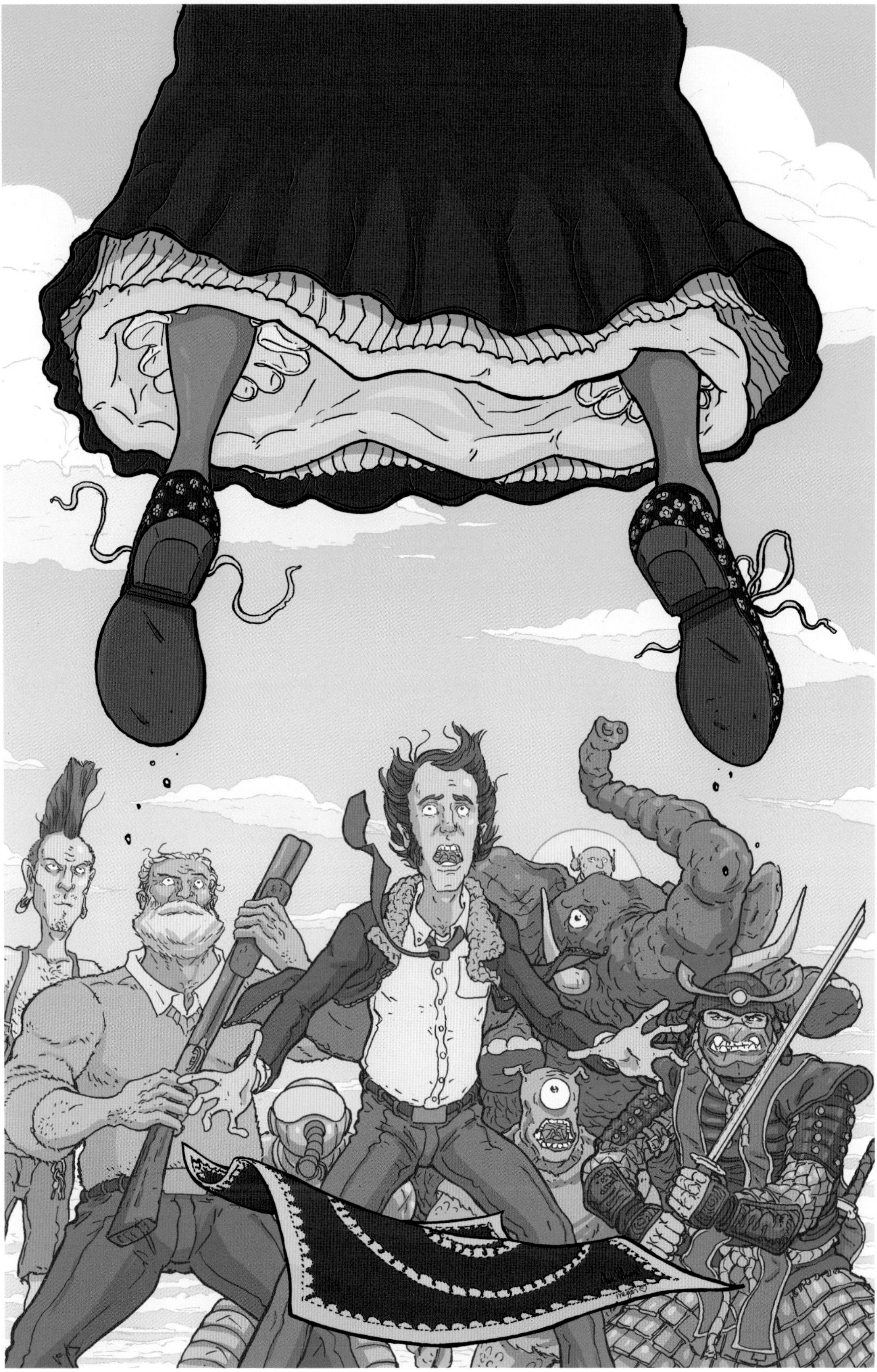

Chapter One

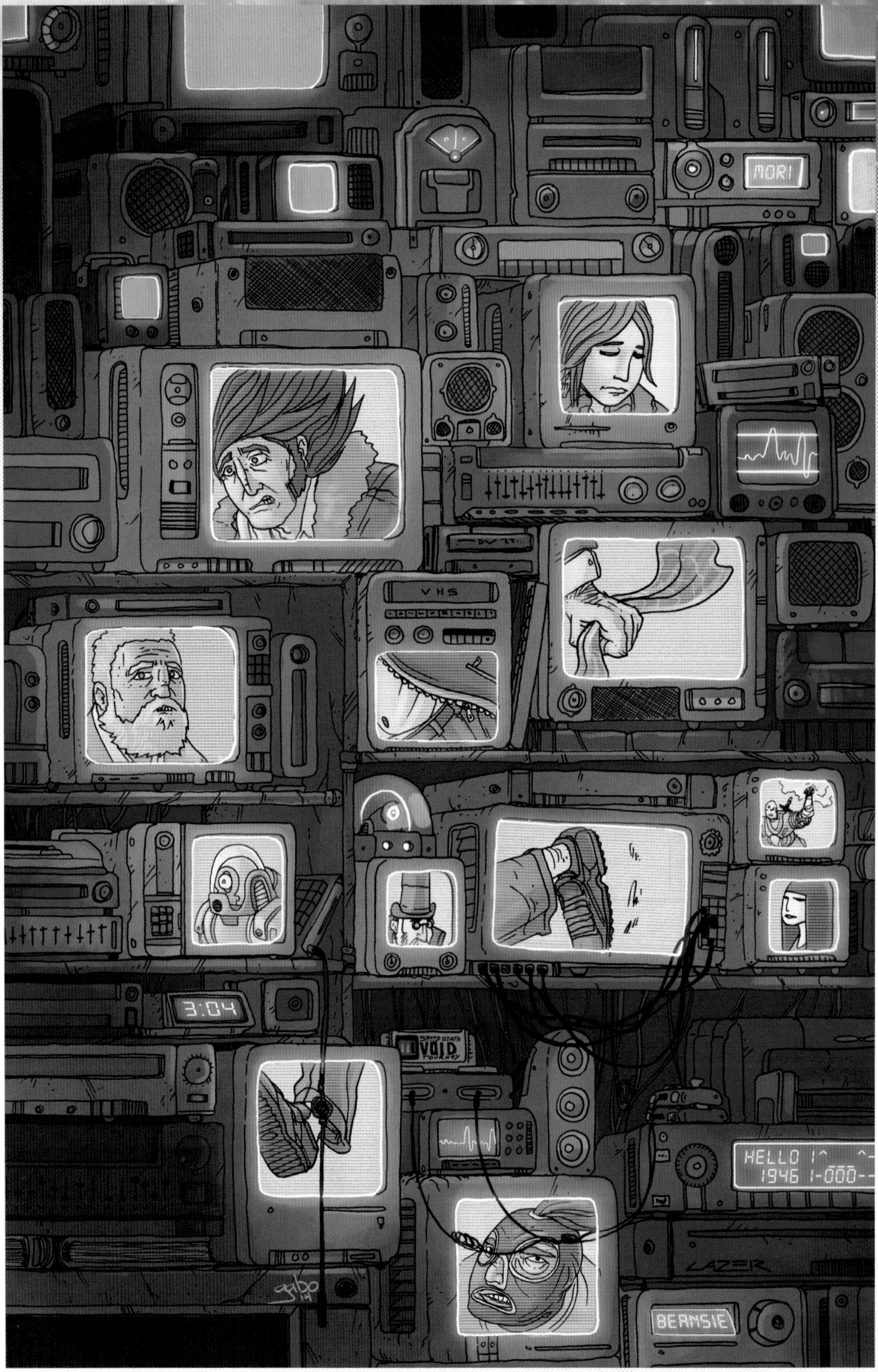

MORI
VHS
3:04
VOID
HELLO
1946
LAZER
BEANSIE

THE LIFE AFTER

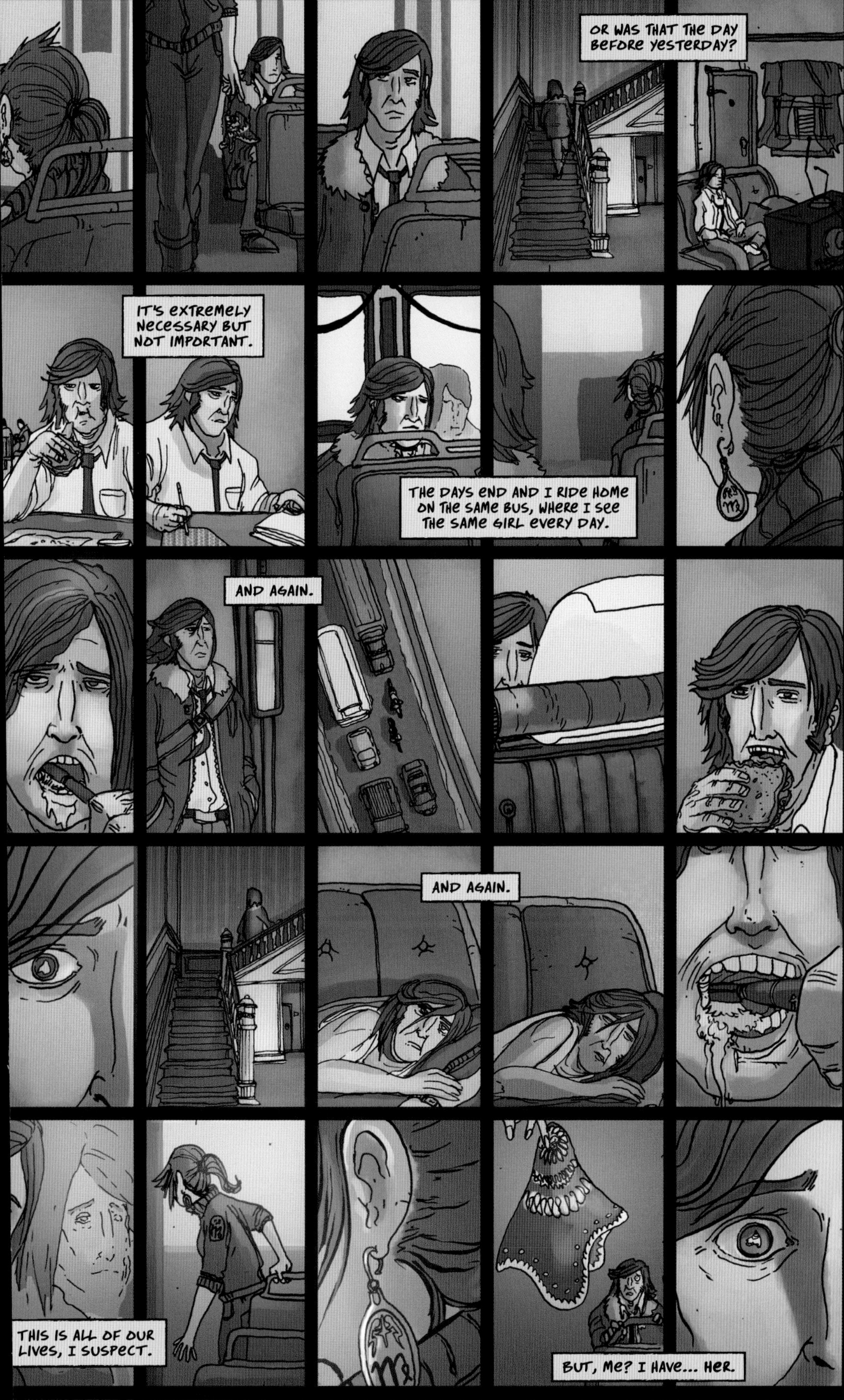
OR WAS THAT THE DAY BEFORE YESTERDAY?
IT'S EXTREMELY NECESSARY BUT NOT IMPORTANT.
THE DAYS END AND I RIDE HOME ON THE SAME BUS, WHERE I SEE THE SAME GIRL EVERY DAY.
AND AGAIN.
AND AGAIN.
THIS IS ALL OF OUR LIVES, I SUSPECT.
BUT, ME? I HAVE... HER.

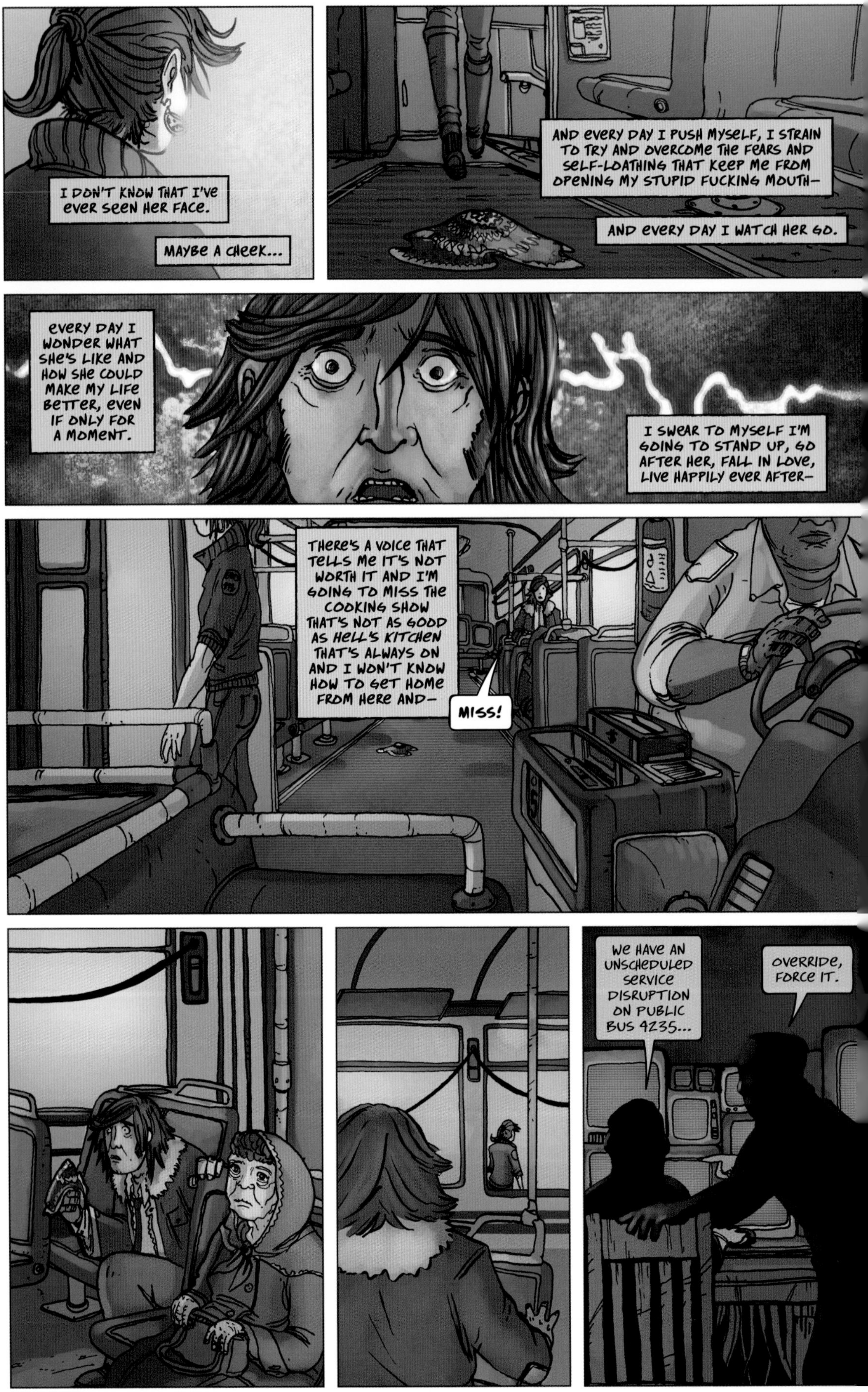
I DON'T KNOW THAT I'VE EVER SEEN HER FACE.
MAYBE A CHEEK...
AND EVERY DAY I PUSH MYSELF, I STRAIN TO TRY AND OVERCOME THE FEARS AND SELF-LOATHING THAT KEEP ME FROM OPENING MY STUPID FUCKING MOUTH—
AND EVERY DAY I WATCH HER GO.
EVERY DAY I WONDER WHAT SHE'S LIKE AND HOW SHE COULD MAKE MY LIFE BETTER, EVEN IF ONLY FOR A MOMENT.
I SWEAR TO MYSELF I'M GOING TO STAND UP, GO AFTER HER, FALL IN LOVE, LIVE HAPPILY EVER AFTER—
THERE'S A VOICE THAT TELLS ME IT'S NOT WORTH IT AND I'M GOING TO MISS THE COOKING SHOW THAT'S NOT AS GOOD AS HELL'S KITCHEN THAT'S ALWAYS ON AND I WON'T KNOW HOW TO GET HOME FROM HERE AND—
MISS!
WE HAVE AN UNSCHEDULED SERVICE DISRUPTION ON PUBLIC BUS 4235...
OVERRIDE, FORCE IT.

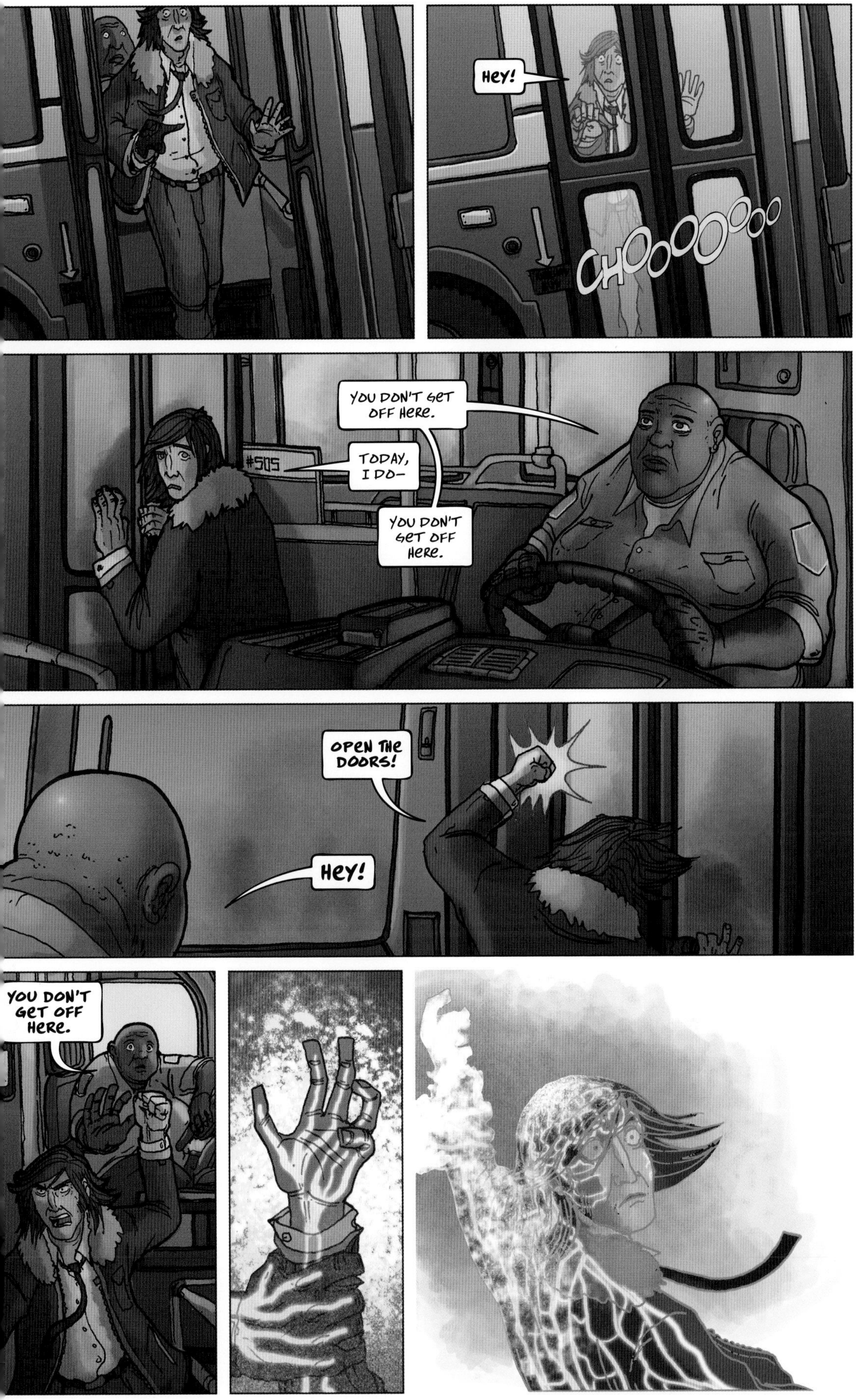
Hey!
CHOOOOOOOO
YOU DON'T GET OFF HERE.
#505
TODAY, I DO—
YOU DON'T GET OFF HERE.
OPEN THE DOORS!
Hey!
YOU DON'T GET OFF HERE.

LAST STOP. EVERYBODY OFF.
ANYBODY ELSE?
HURM.
Rx
FUCK 'EM.
WHAT THE HELL WAS THAT?!
YOU DON'T GET OFF HERE.

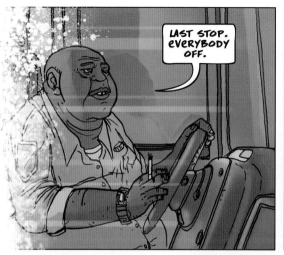

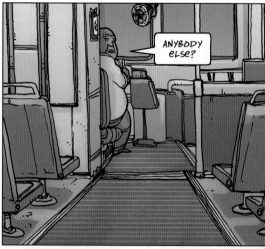

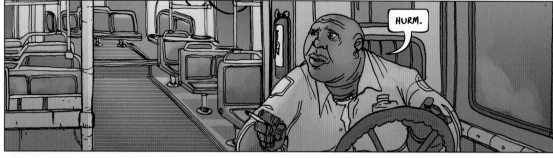

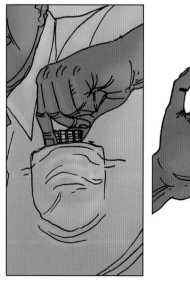

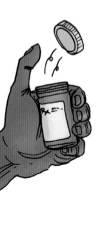

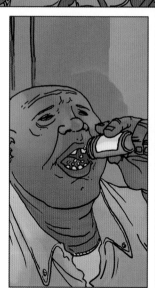

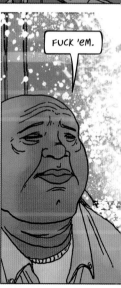

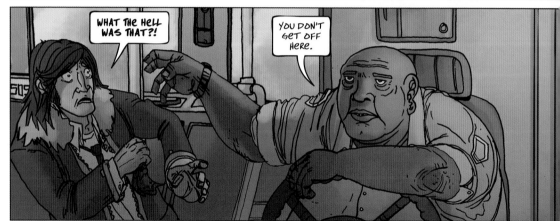

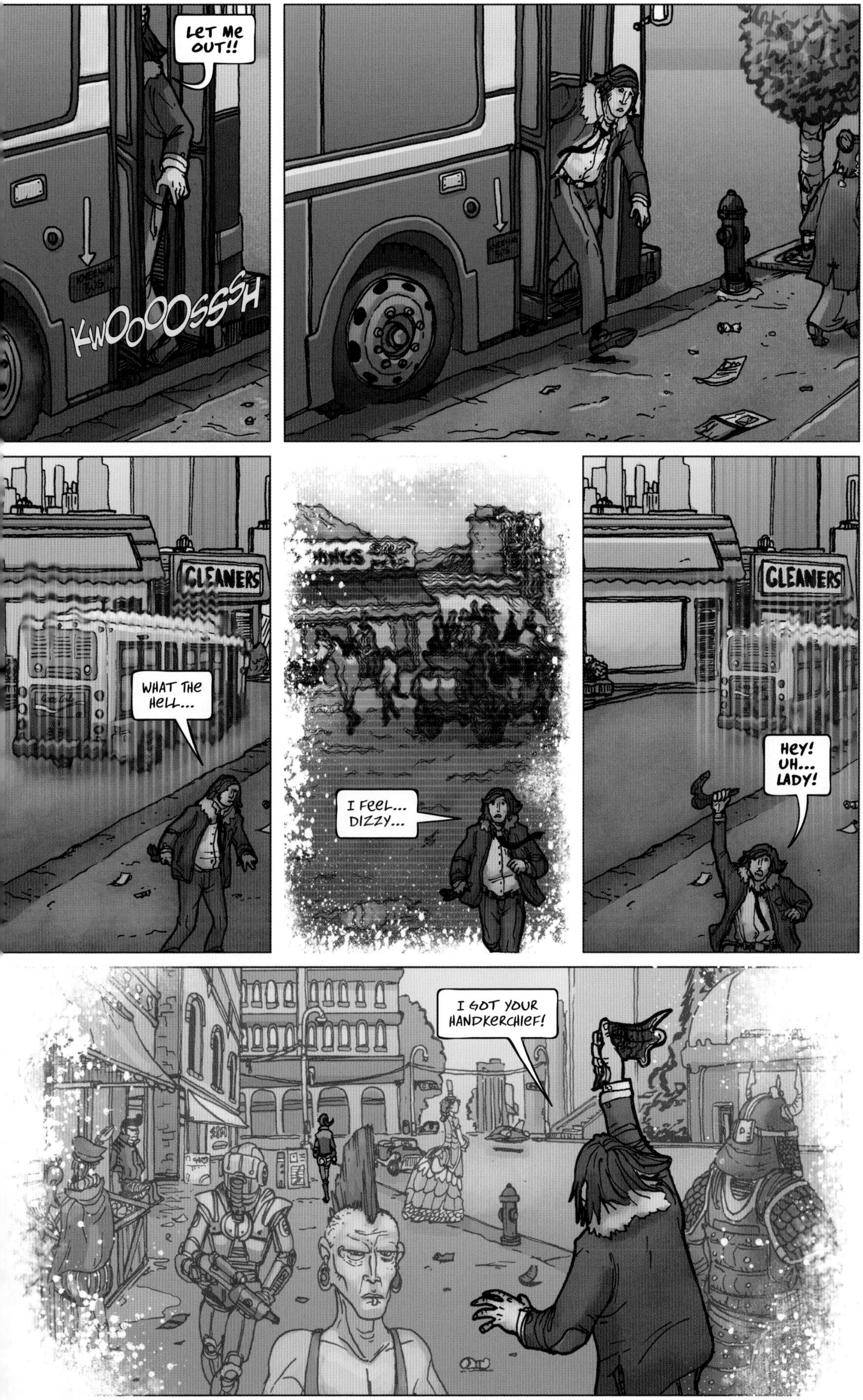
LET ME OUT!!
KWOOOOSSSH
WHAT THE HELL...
I FEEL... DIZZY...
GLEANERS
HEY! UH... LADY!
I GOT YOUR HANDKERCHIEF!

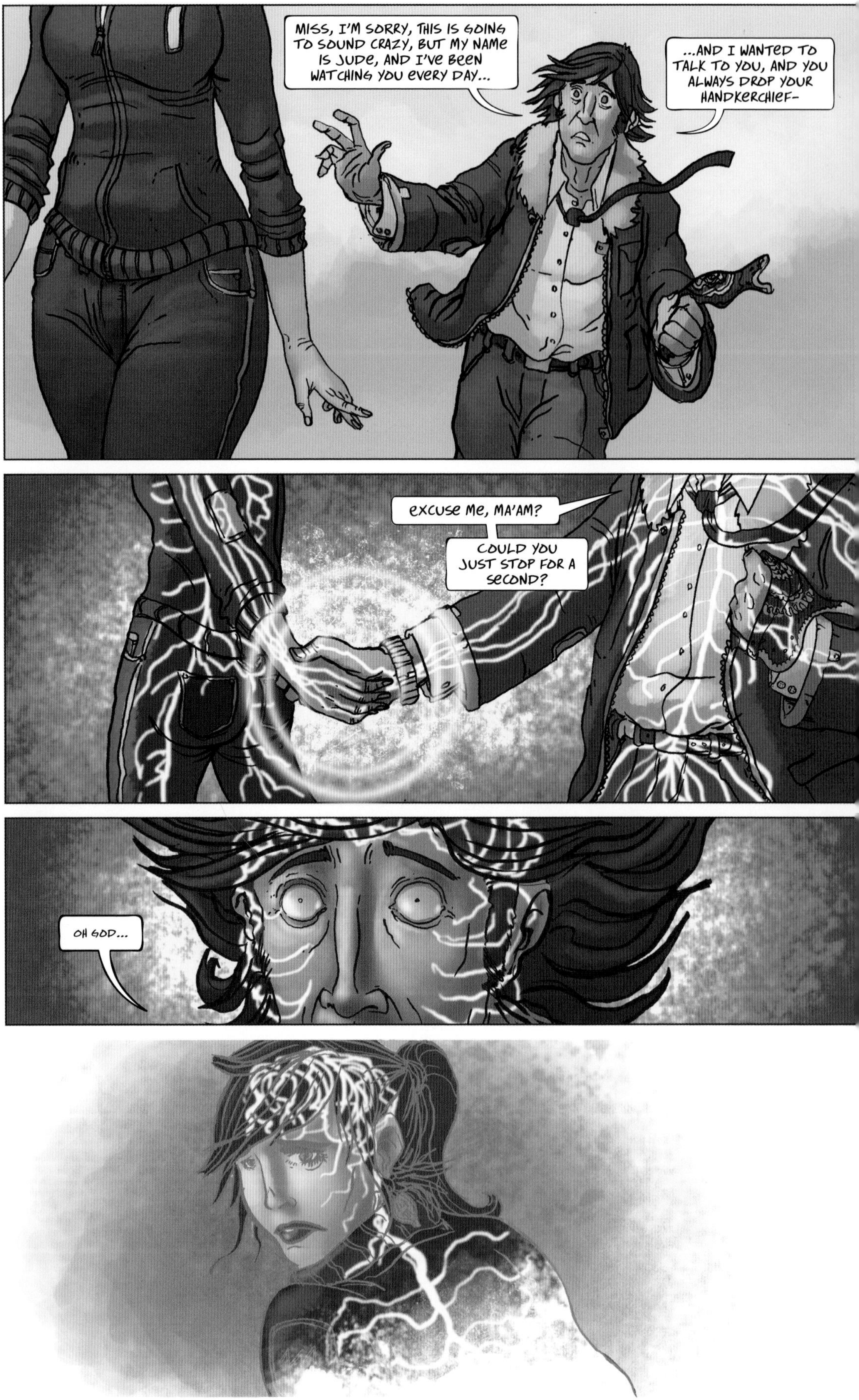
MISS, I'M SORRY, THIS IS GOING TO SOUND CRAZY, BUT MY NAME IS JUDE, AND I'VE BEEN WATCHING YOU EVERY DAY...
...AND I WANTED TO TALK TO YOU, AND YOU ALWAYS DROP YOUR HANDKERCHIEF-
EXCUSE ME, MA'AM?
COULD YOU JUST STOP FOR A SECOND?
OH GOD...

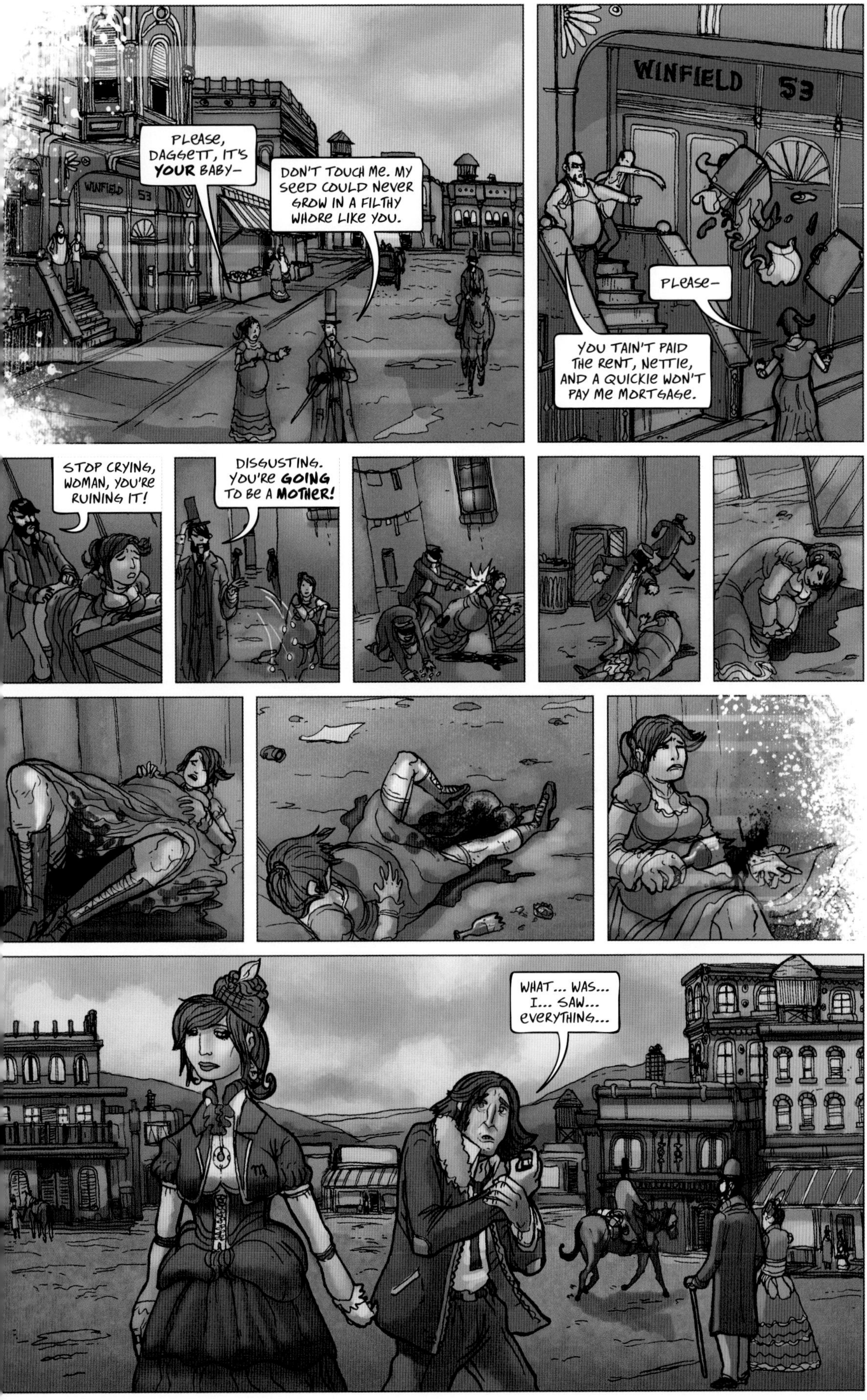
PLEASE, DAGGETT, IT'S YOUR BABY—
DON'T TOUCH ME. MY SEED COULD NEVER GROW IN A FILTHY WHORE LIKE YOU.
WINFIELD 53
PLEASE—
YOU TAIN'T PAID THE RENT, NETTIE, AND A QUICKIE WON'T PAY ME MORTGAGE.
STOP CRYING, WOMAN, YOU'RE RUINING IT!
DISGUSTING. YOU'RE GOING TO BE A MOTHER!
WHAT... WAS... I... SAW... EVERYTHING...

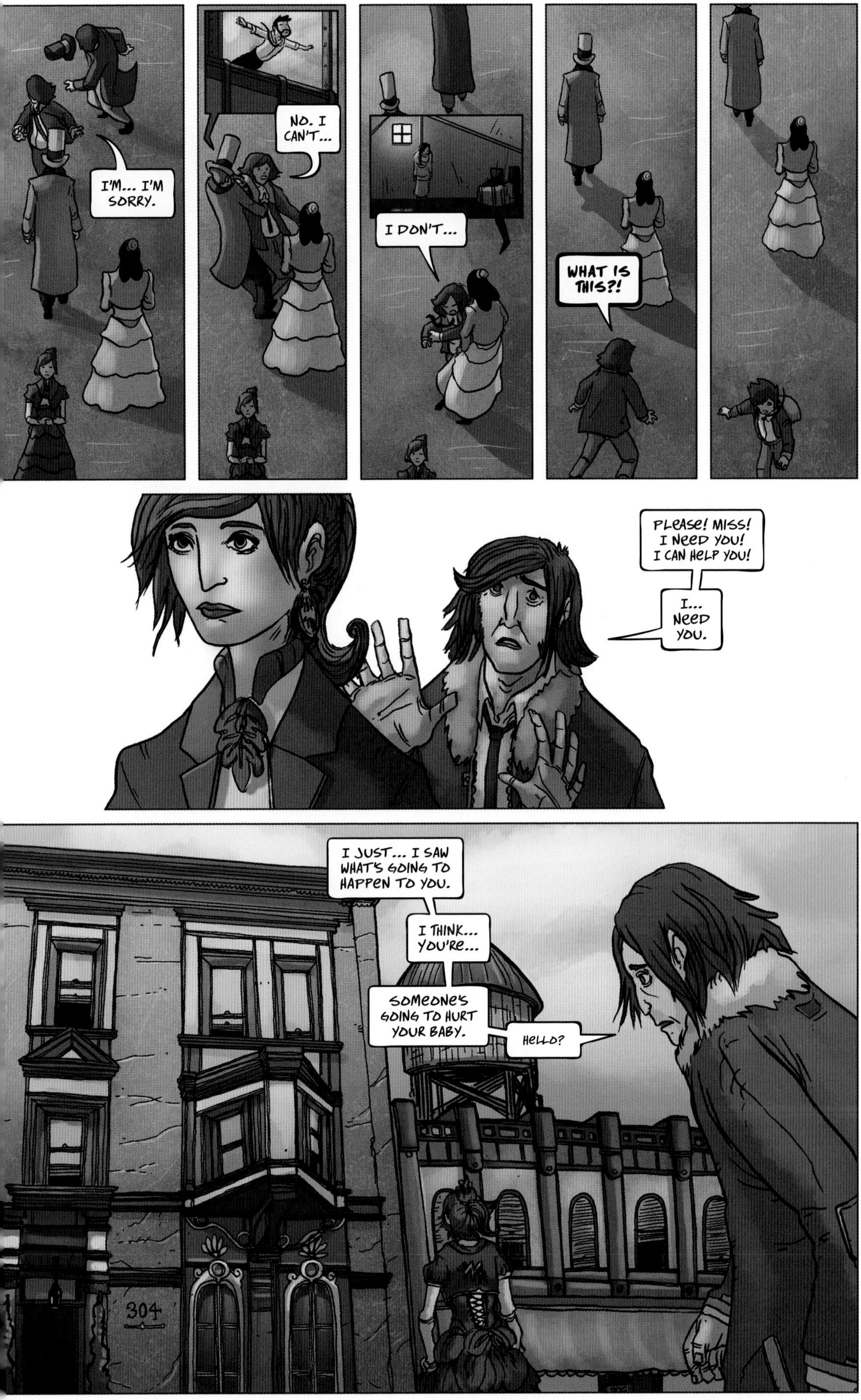
I'M... I'M SORRY.
NO. I CAN'T...
I DON'T...
WHAT IS THIS?!
PLEASE! MISS! I NEED YOU! I CAN HELP YOU!
I... NEED YOU.
I JUST... I SAW WHAT'S GOING TO HAPPEN TO YOU.
I THINK... YOU'RE...
SOMEONE'S GOING TO HURT YOUR BABY.
HELLO?
304

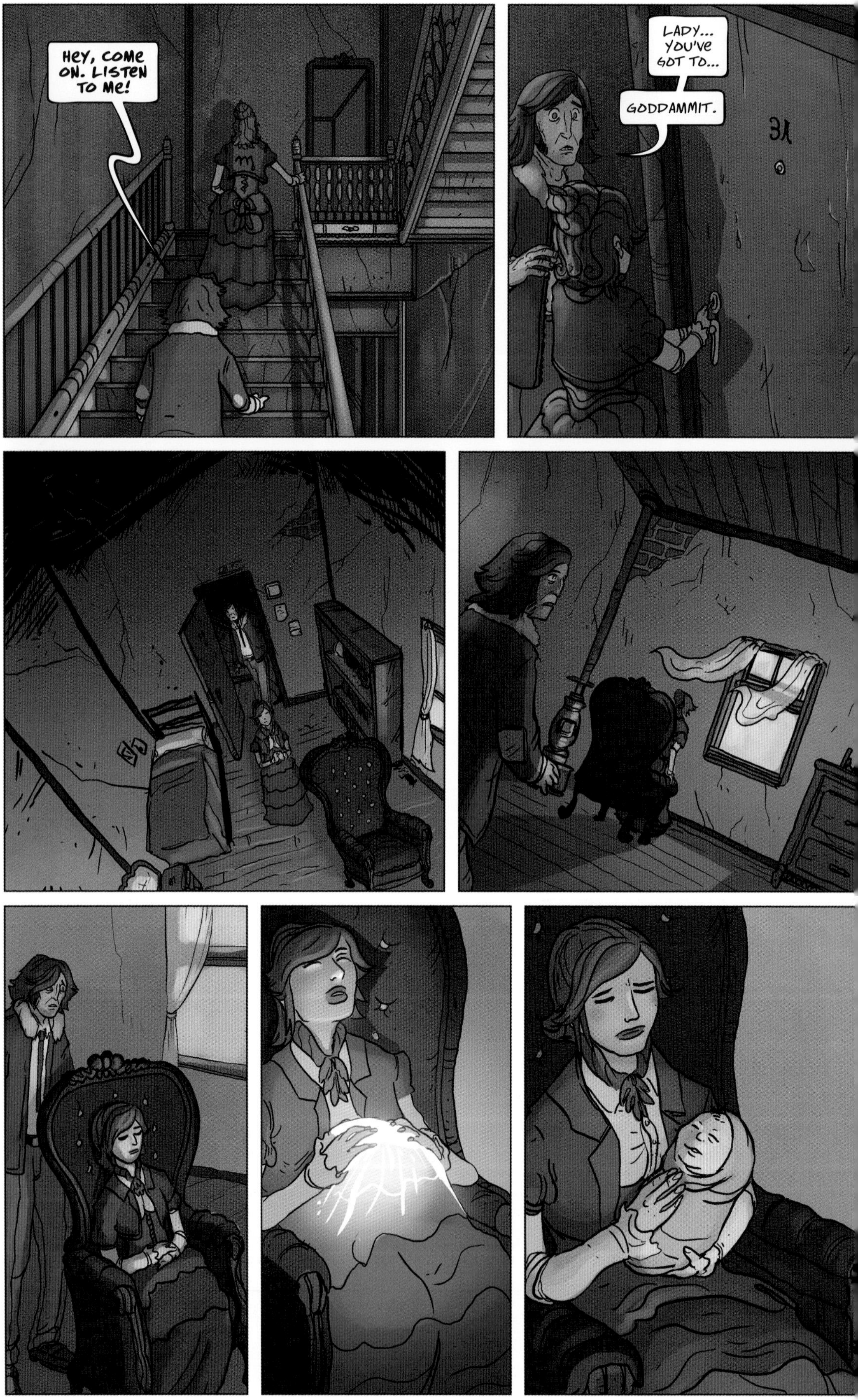
HEY, COME ON. LISTEN TO ME!
LADY... YOU'VE GOT TO...
GODDAMMIT.

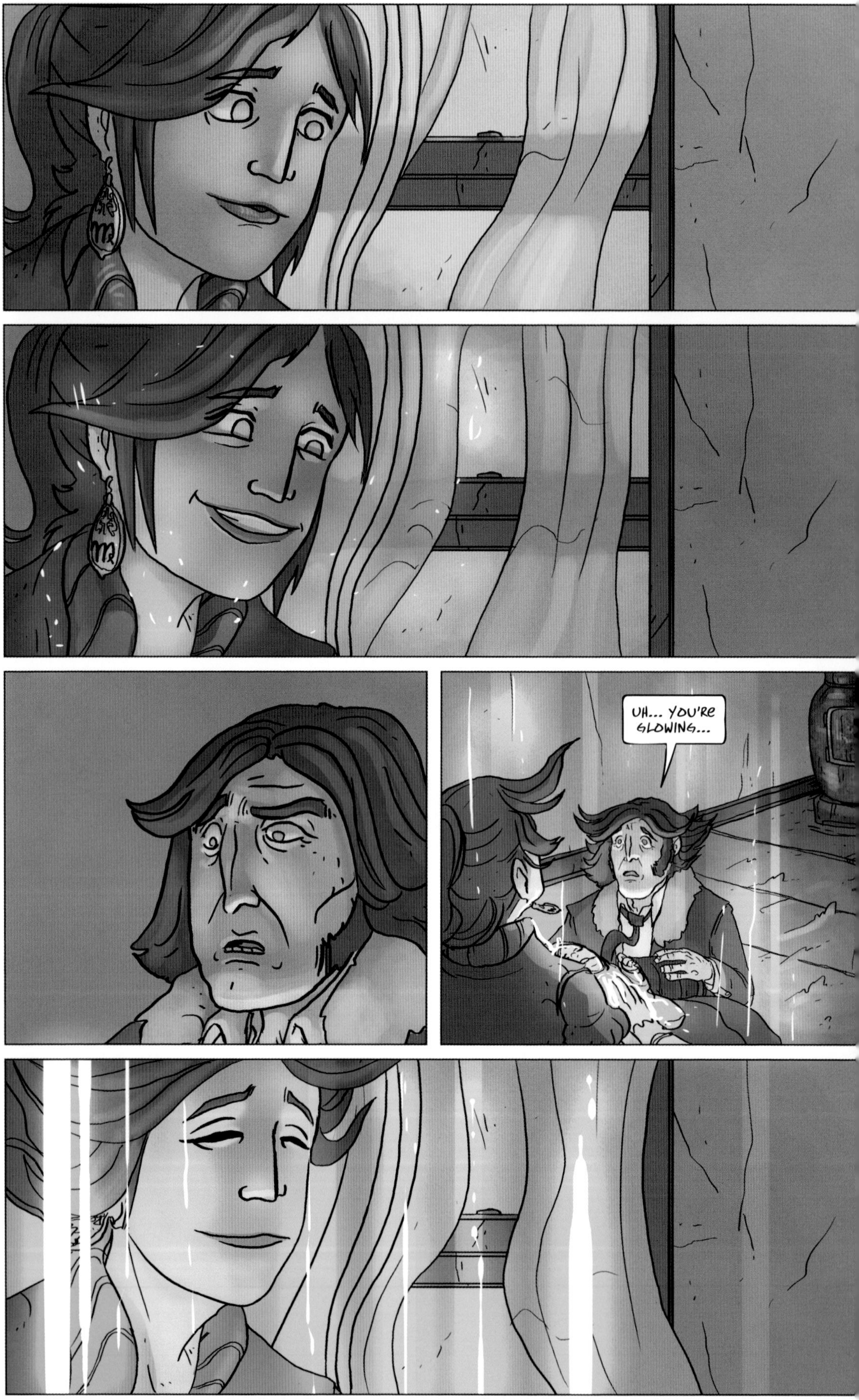
UH... YOU'RE GLOWING...

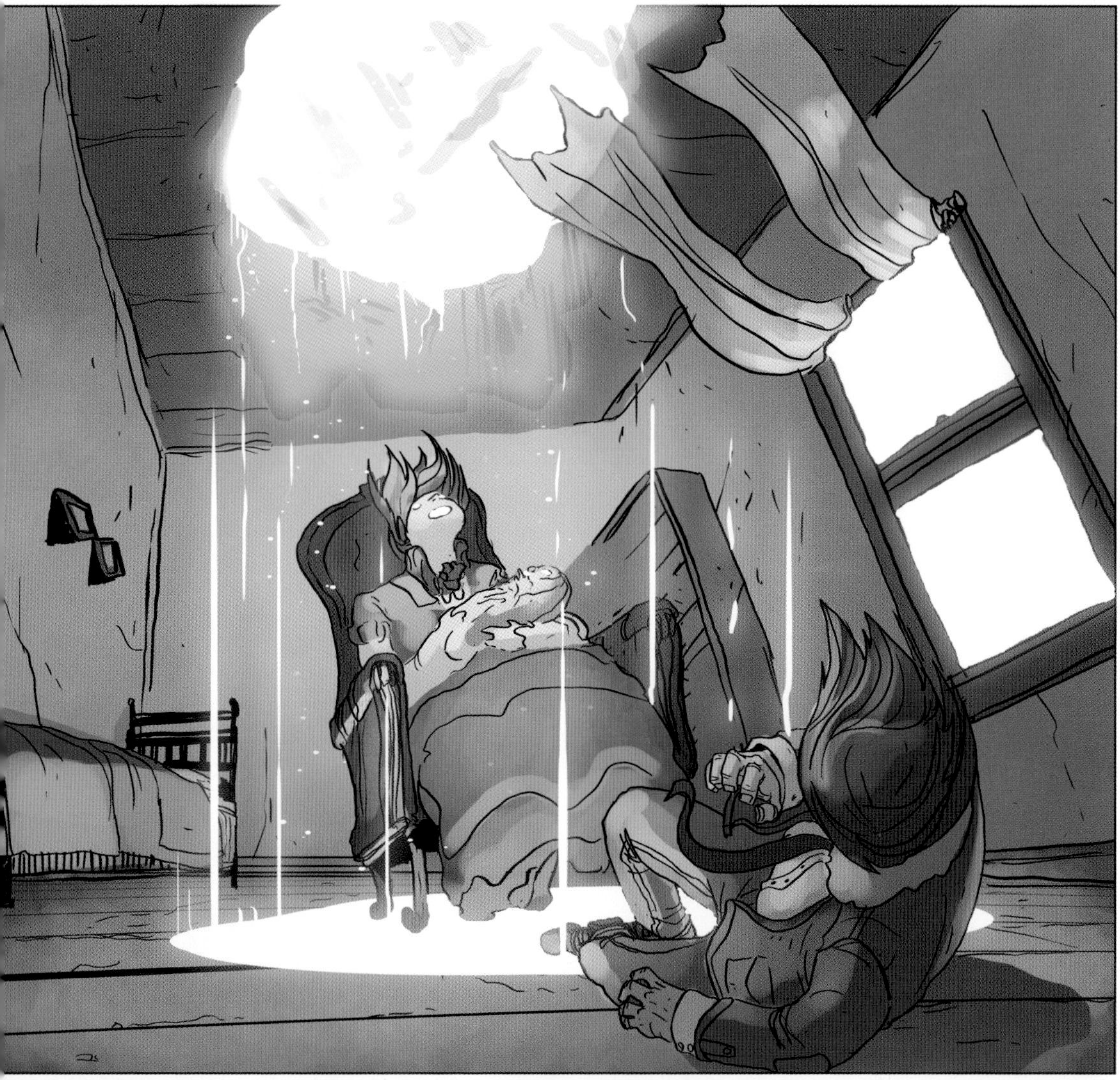

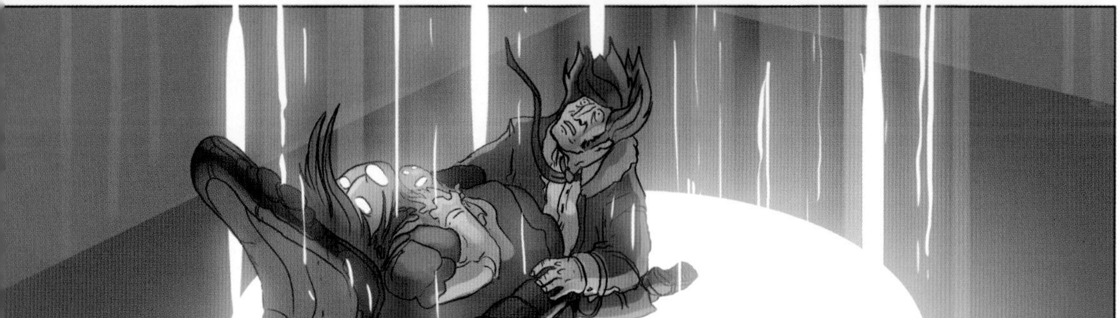

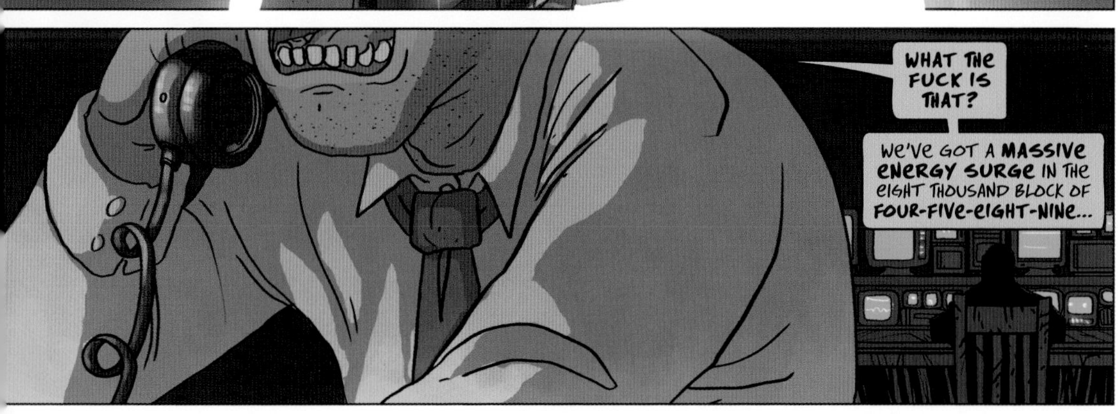

WHAT THE FUCK IS THAT?
WE'VE GOT A MASSIVE ENERGY SURGE IN THE EIGHT THOUSAND BLOCK OF FOUR-FIVE-EIGHT-NINE...

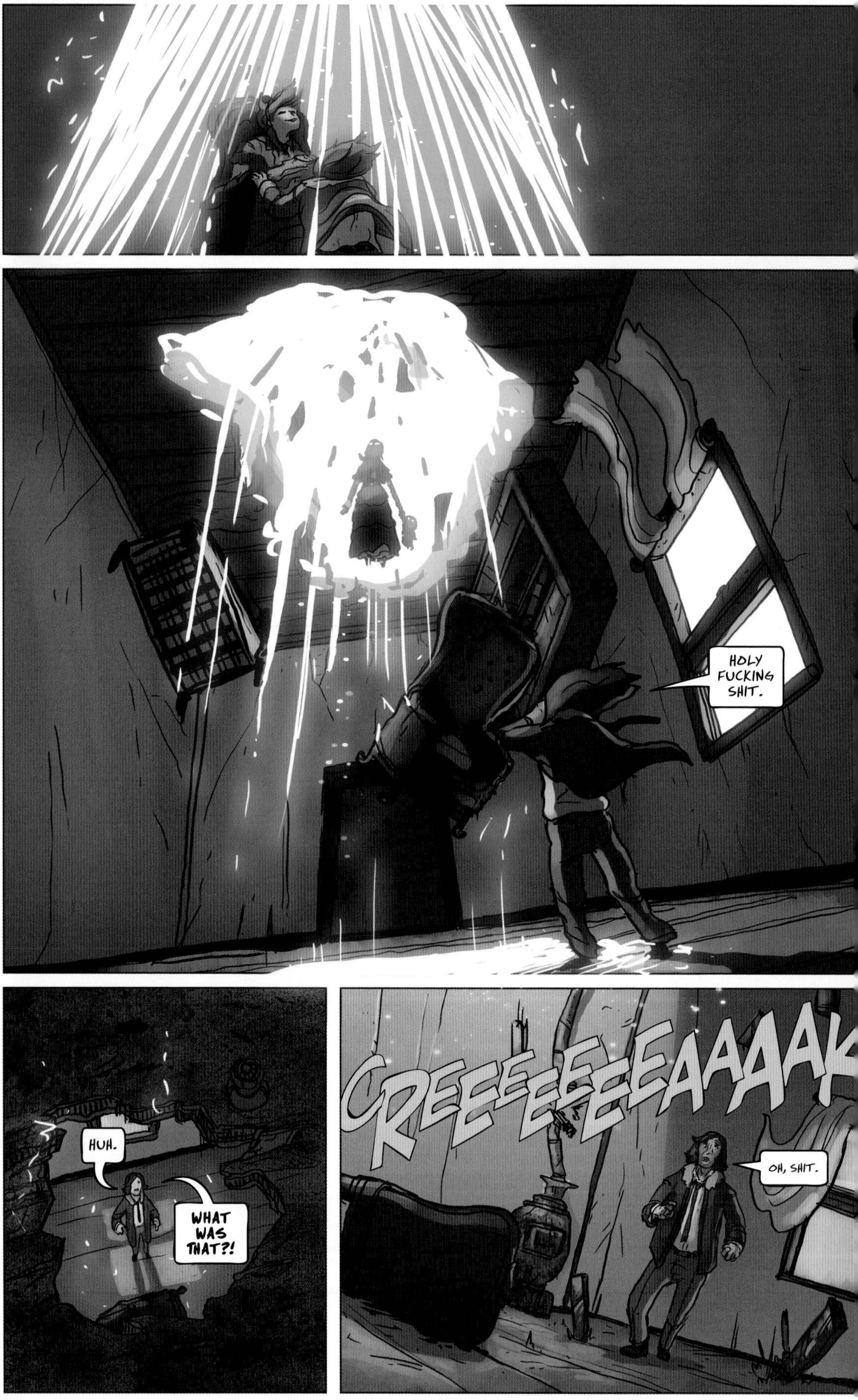
HOLY FUCKING SHIT.
HUH.
WHAT WAS THAT?!
CREEEEEEEEAAAAK
OH, SHIT.

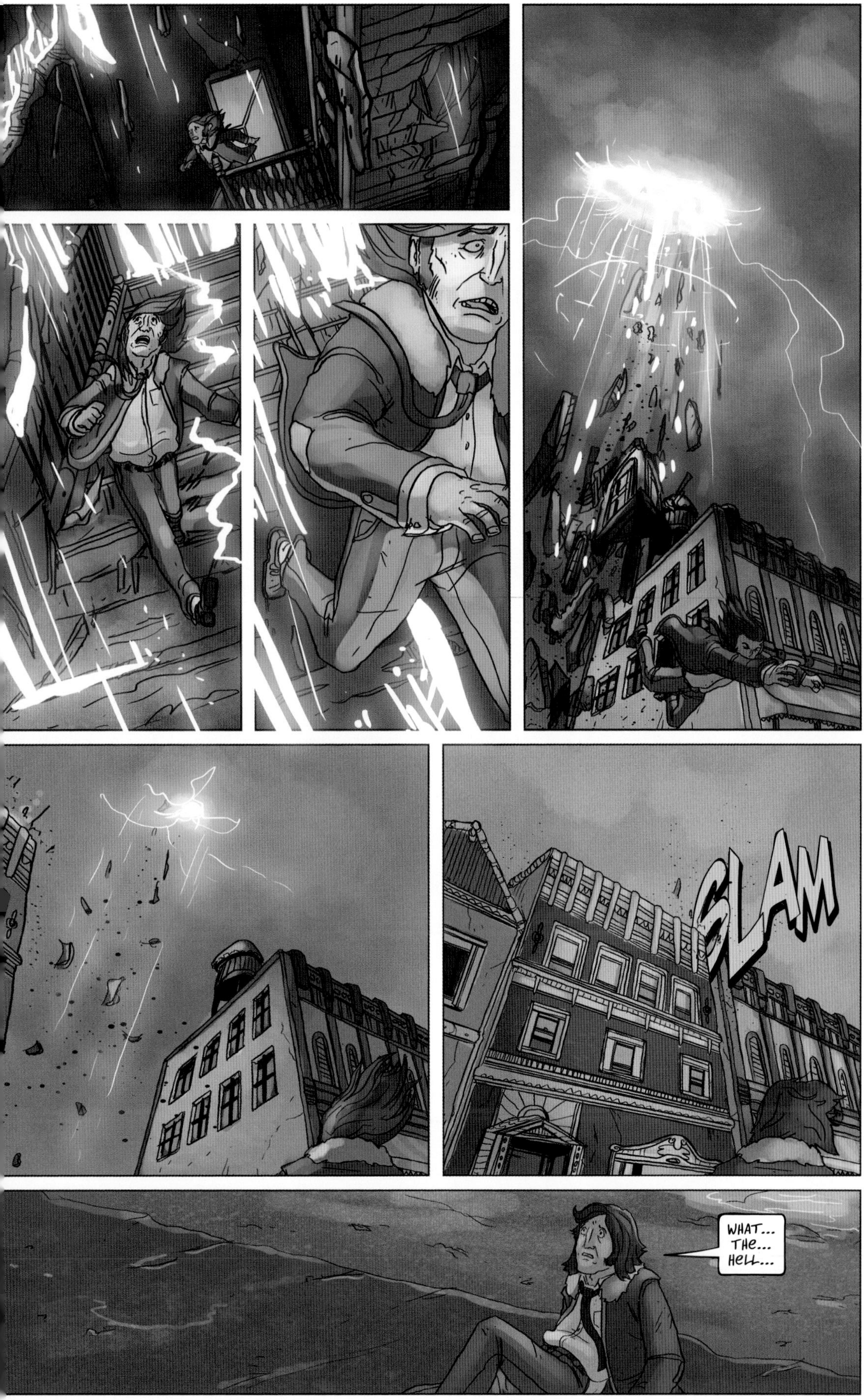
SLAM
WHAT...
THE...
HELL...

AM I... DEAD?
WHERE AM I?
SECTOR 4589
ALPHA CENTAR
ERROR...
CLASS UPPER LEFT
CRASH SECTOR AL
HUH.

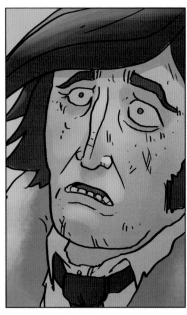

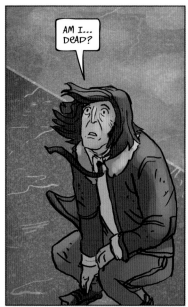

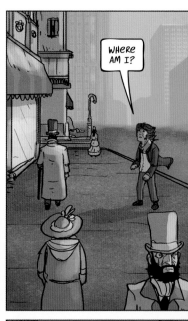

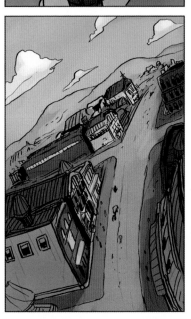

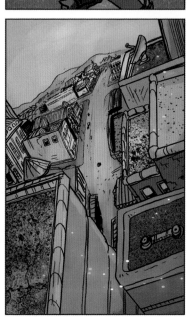

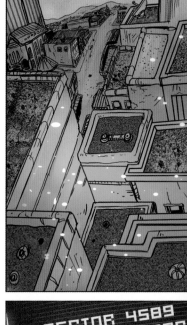

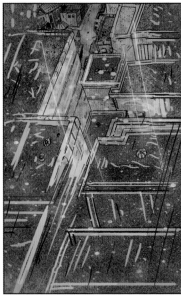

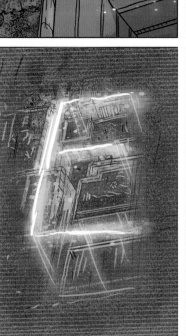

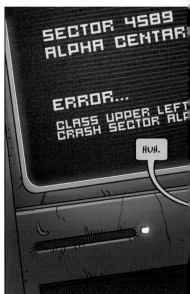

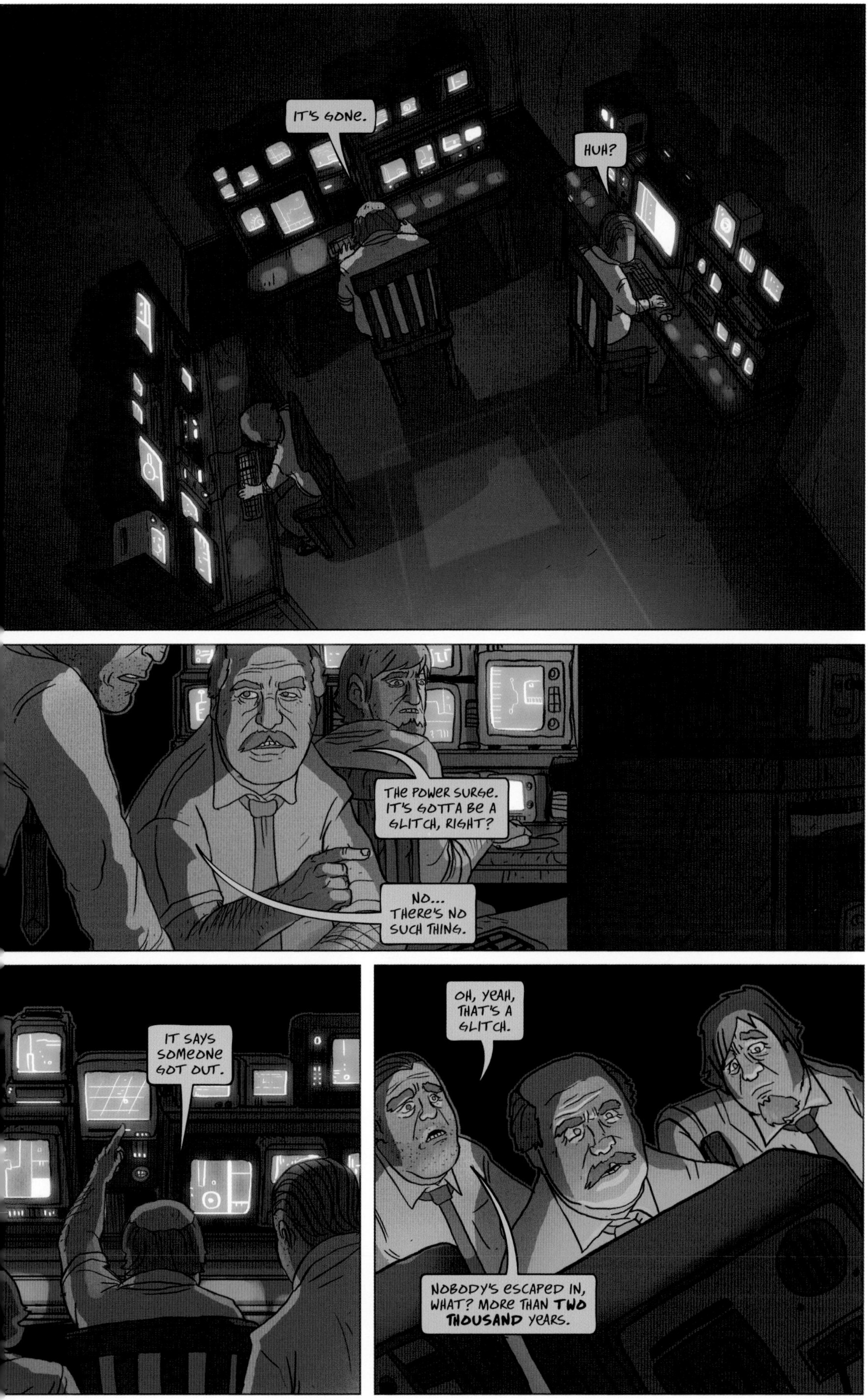
IT'S GONE.
HUH?
THE POWER SURGE. IT'S GOTTA BE A GLITCH, RIGHT?
NO... THERE'S NO SUCH THING.
IT SAYS SOMEONE GOT OUT.
OH, YEAH, THAT'S A GLITCH.
NOBODY'S ESCAPED IN, WHAT? MORE THAN **TWO THOUSAND** YEARS.

I... AM I DEAD?

I REMEMBER...

"EXCUSE ME..."

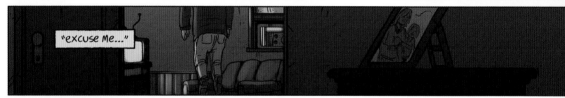

GAH!

I JUST... I HAVEN'T MET SOMEONE ELSE WHO'S AWAKE IN... HELL, I HAVE NO CONCEPT OF TIME.

LITERALLY.

WHO...

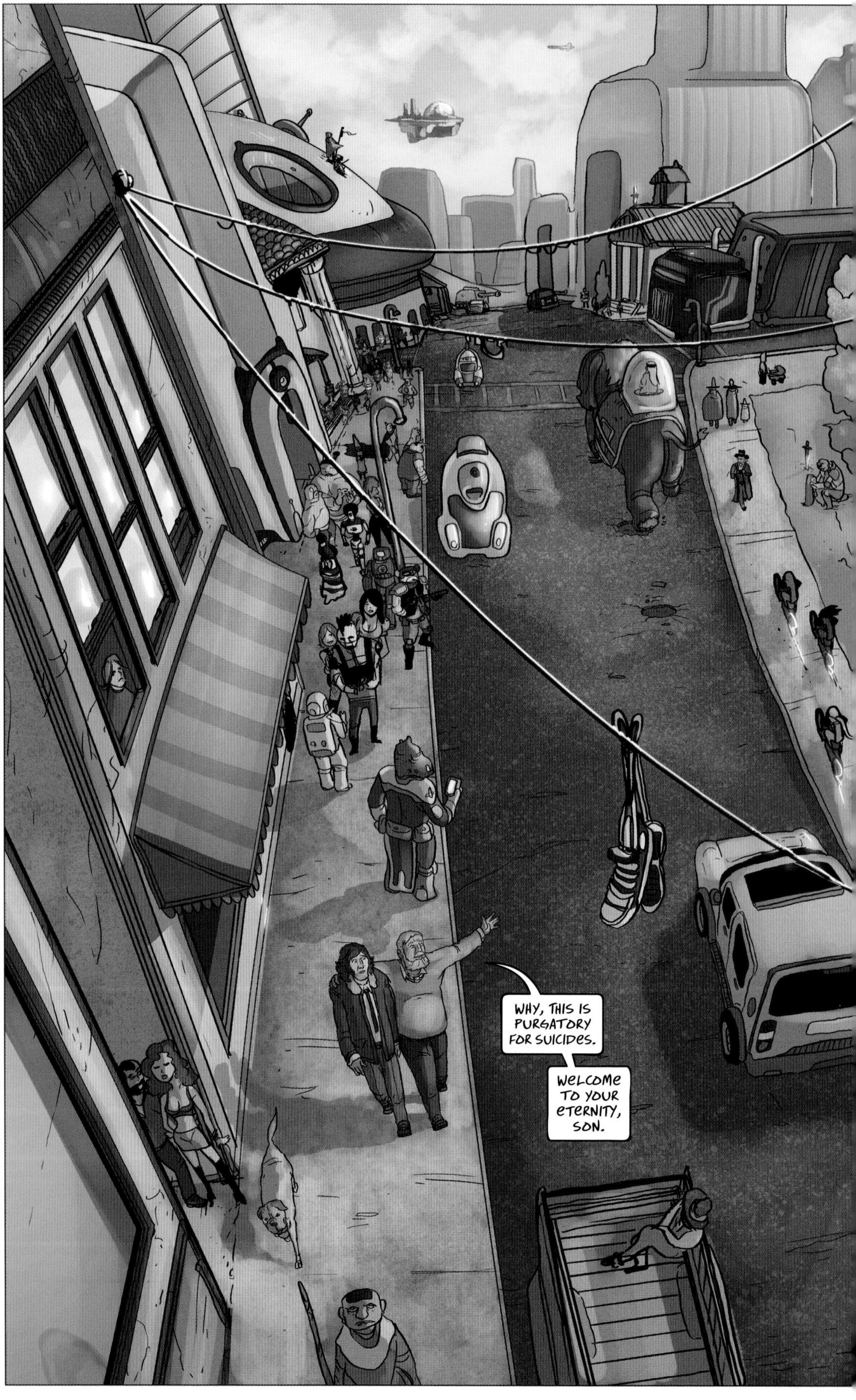
WHY, THIS IS PURGATORY FOR SUICIDES.
WELCOME TO YOUR ETERNITY, SON.

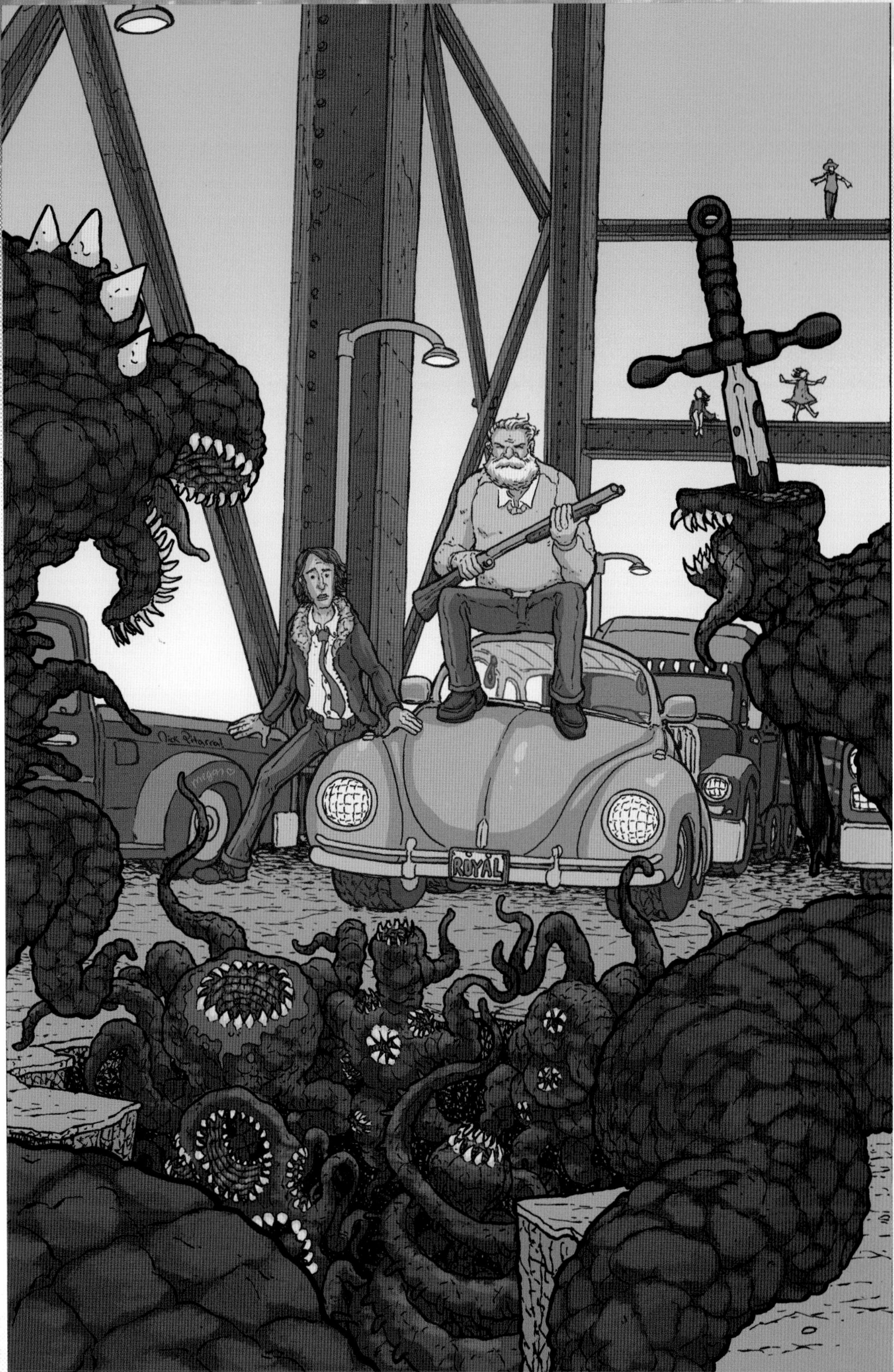
ROYAL

Chapter Two

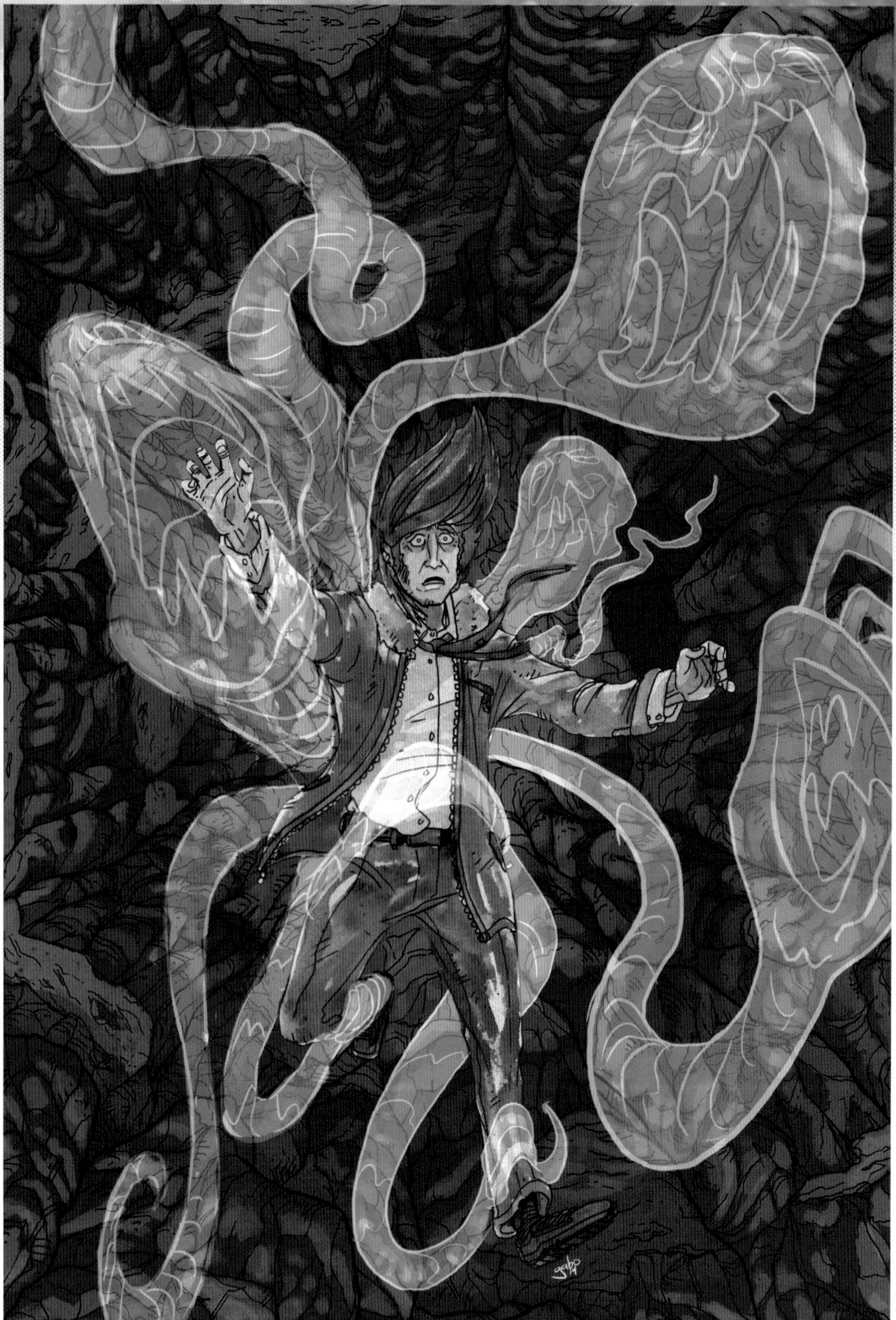

THE LIFE AFTER

X-MAS

FUCK IT.

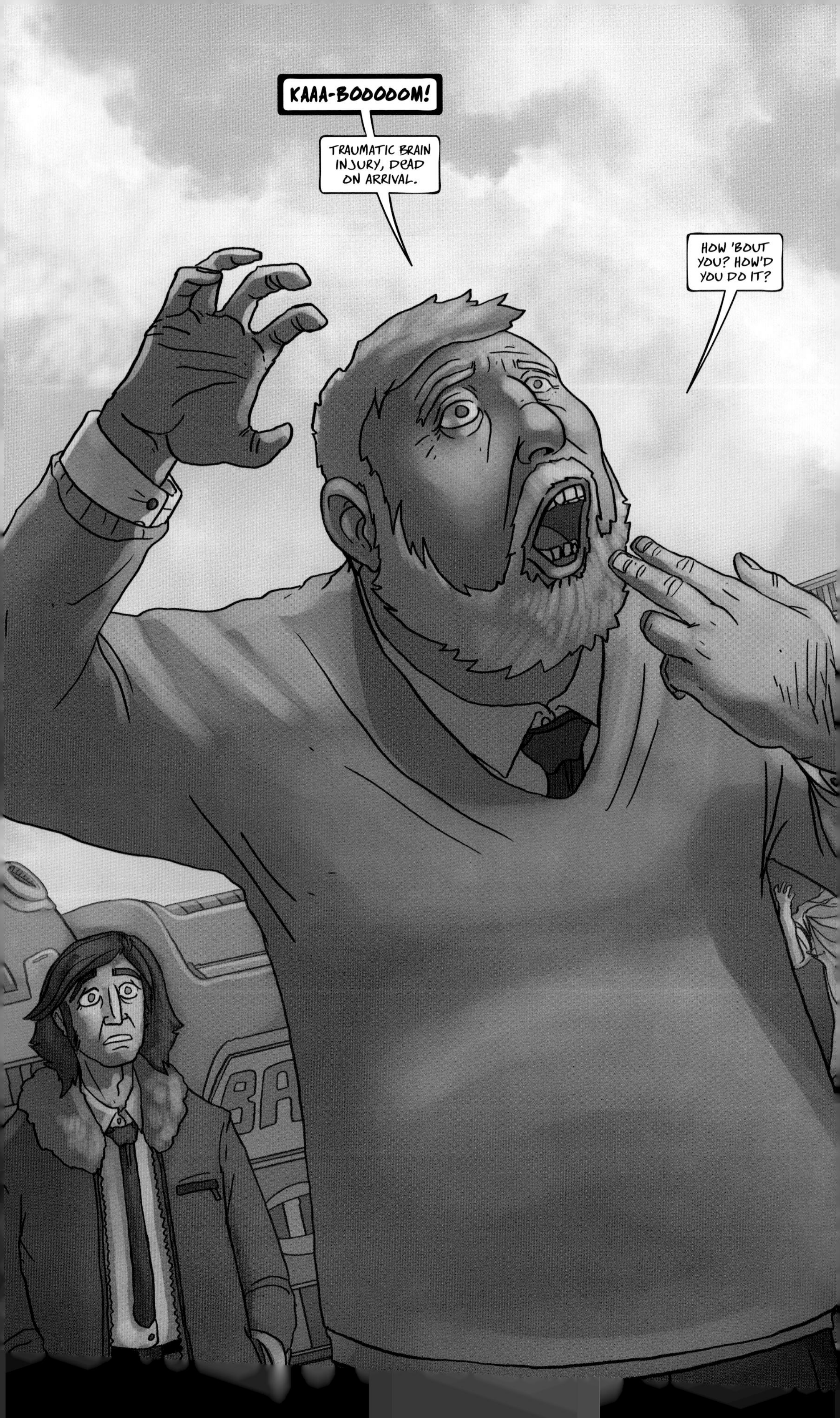
KAAA-BOOOOOM!
TRAUMATIC BRAIN INJURY, DEAD ON ARRIVAL.
HOW 'BOUT YOU? HOW'D YOU DO IT?

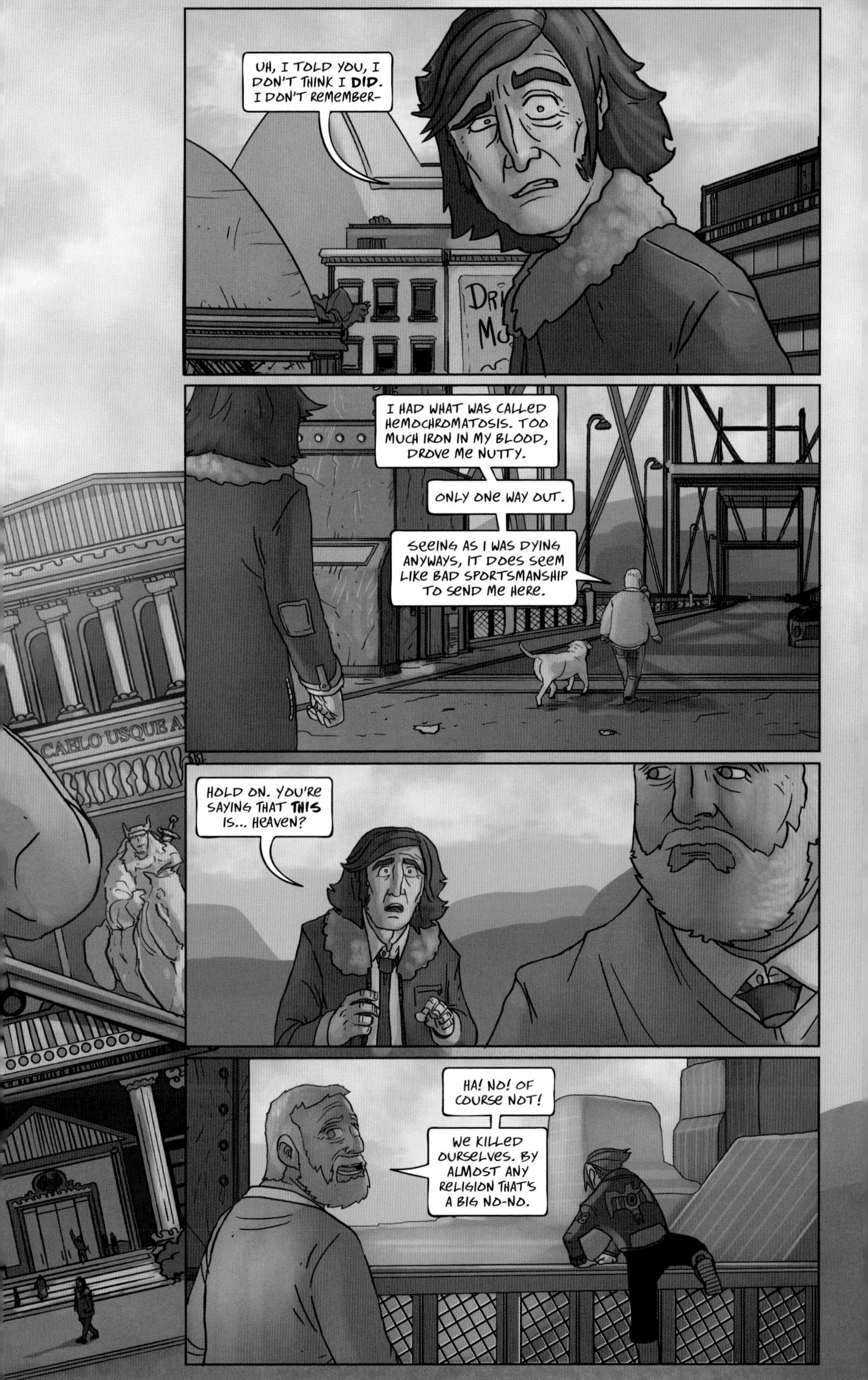
UH, I TOLD YOU, I DON'T THINK I **DID**. I DON'T REMEMBER-
I HAD WHAT WAS CALLED HEMOCHROMATOSIS. TOO MUCH IRON IN MY BLOOD, DROVE ME NUTTY.
ONLY ONE WAY OUT.
SEEING AS I WAS DYING ANYWAYS, IT DOES SEEM LIKE BAD SPORTSMANSHIP TO SEND ME HERE.
CAELO USQUE A
HOLD ON. YOU'RE SAYING THAT **THIS** IS... HEAVEN?
HA! NO! OF COURSE NOT!
WE KILLED OURSELVES. BY ALMOST ANY RELIGION THAT'S A BIG NO-NO.

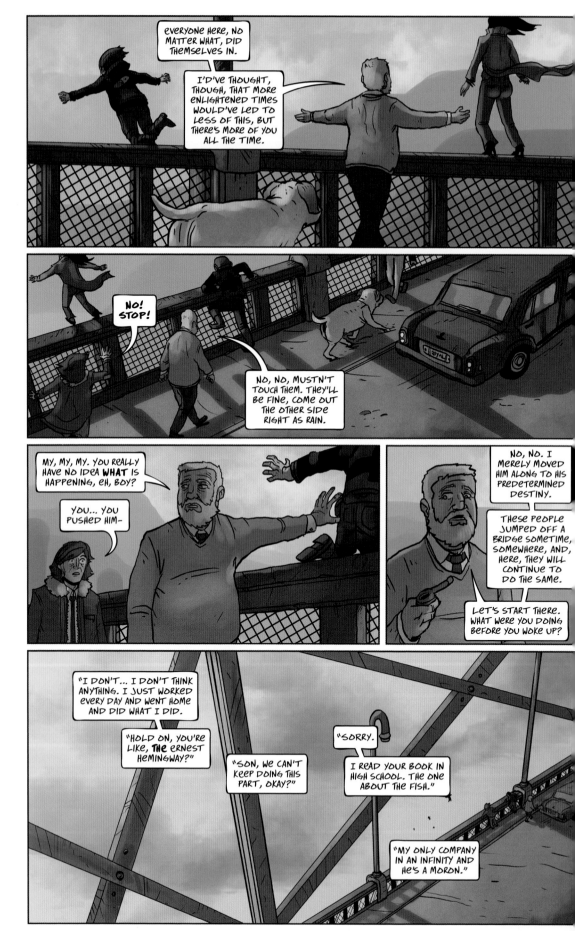

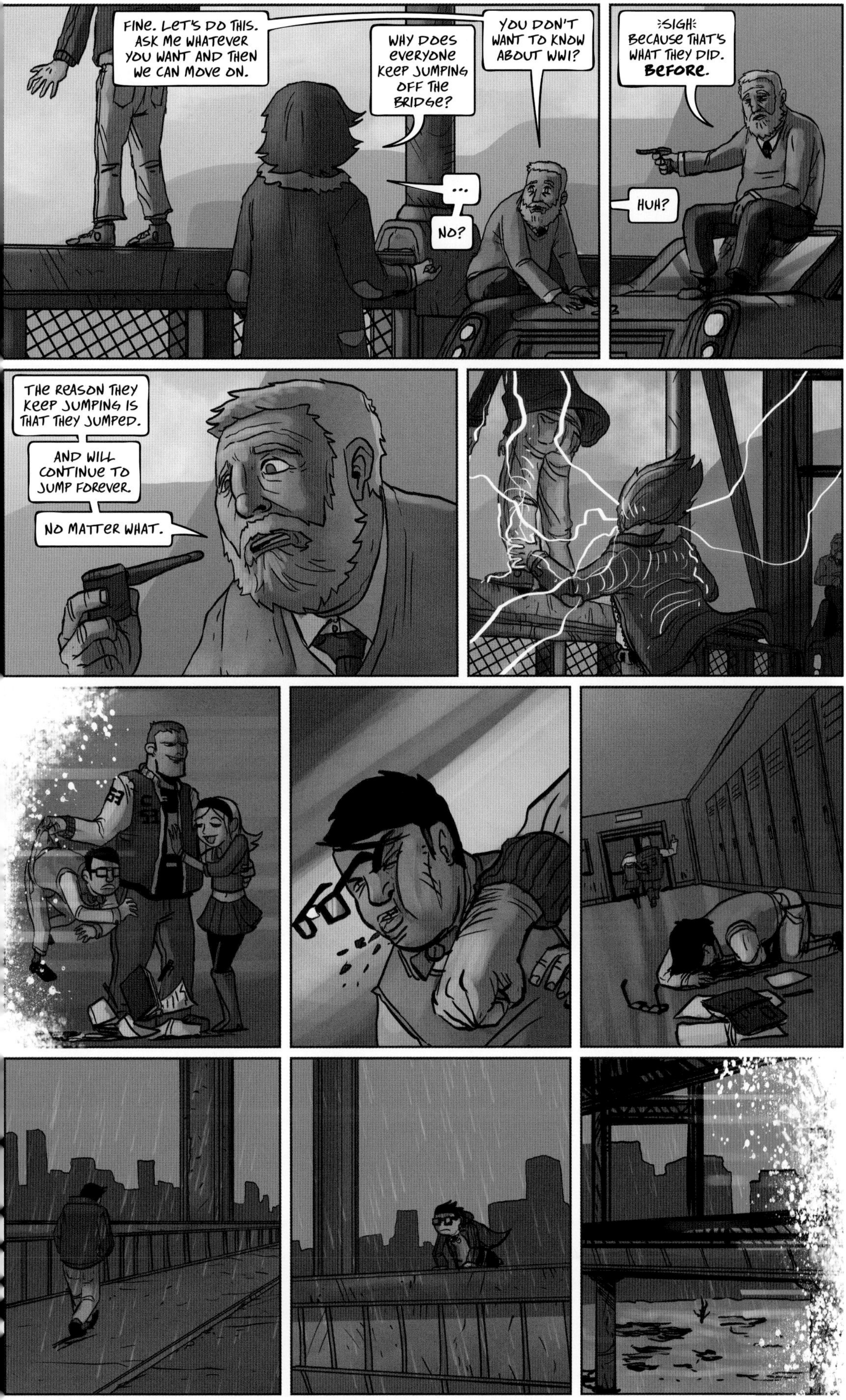
FINE. LET'S DO THIS. ASK ME WHATEVER YOU WANT AND THEN WE CAN MOVE ON.
WHY DOES EVERYONE KEEP JUMPING OFF THE BRIDGE?
YOU DON'T WANT TO KNOW ABOUT WWI?
...
NO?
:SIGH: BECAUSE THAT'S WHAT THEY DID. **BEFORE**.
HUH?
THE REASON THEY KEEP JUMPING IS THAT THEY JUMPED.
AND WILL CONTINUE TO JUMP FOREVER.
NO MATTER WHAT.

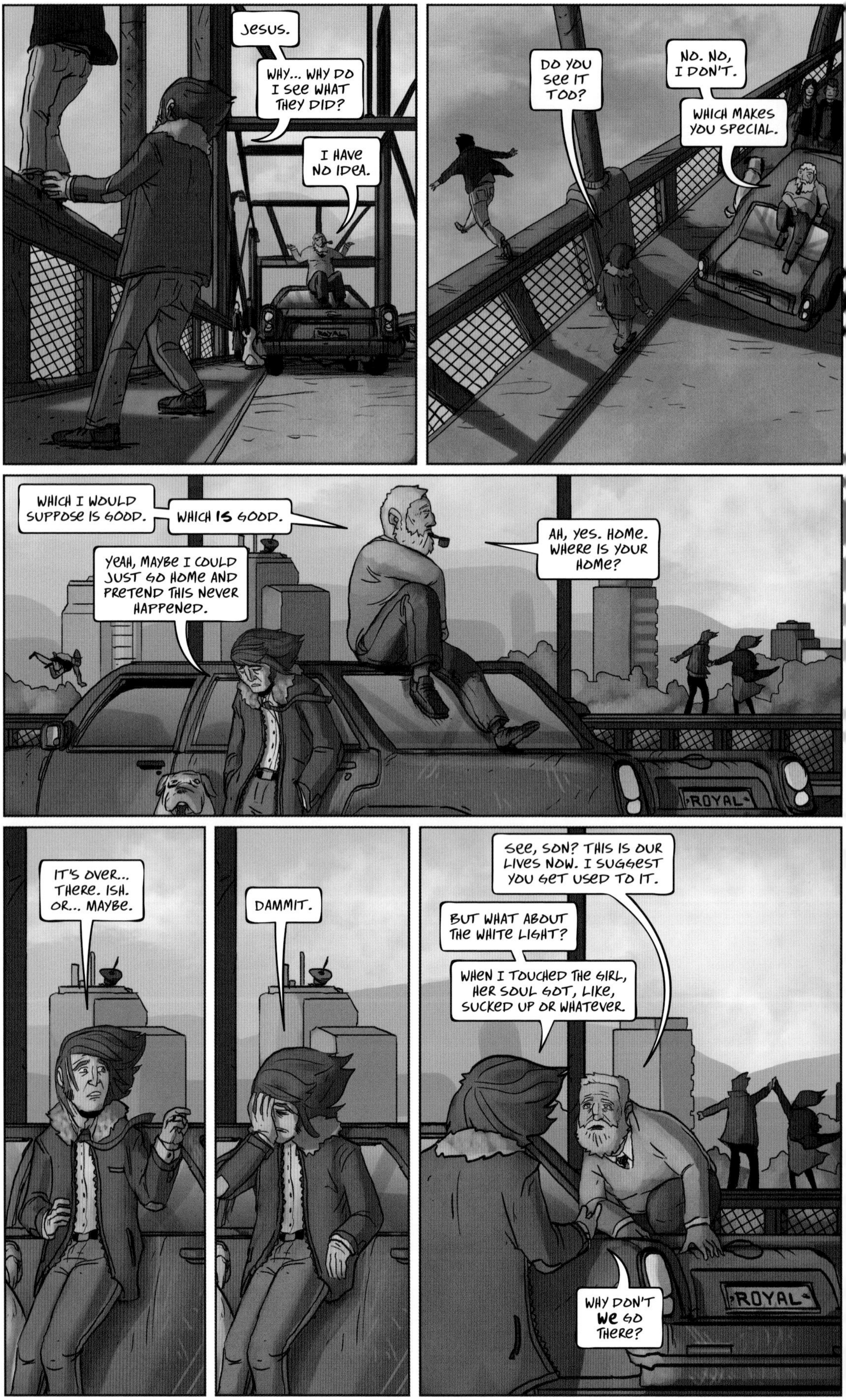
JESUS.
WHY... WHY DO I SEE WHAT THEY DID?
I HAVE NO IDEA.
DO YOU SEE IT TOO?
NO. NO, I DON'T.
WHICH MAKES YOU SPECIAL.
WHICH I WOULD SUPPOSE IS GOOD.
WHICH IS GOOD.
YEAH, MAYBE I COULD JUST GO HOME AND PRETEND THIS NEVER HAPPENED.
AH, YES. HOME. WHERE IS YOUR HOME?
IT'S OVER... THERE. ISH. OR... MAYBE.
DAMMIT.
SEE, SON? THIS IS OUR LIVES NOW. I SUGGEST YOU GET USED TO IT.
BUT WHAT ABOUT THE WHITE LIGHT?
WHEN I TOUCHED THE GIRL, HER SOUL GOT, LIKE, SUCKED UP OR WHATEVER.
WHY DON'T WE GO THERE?

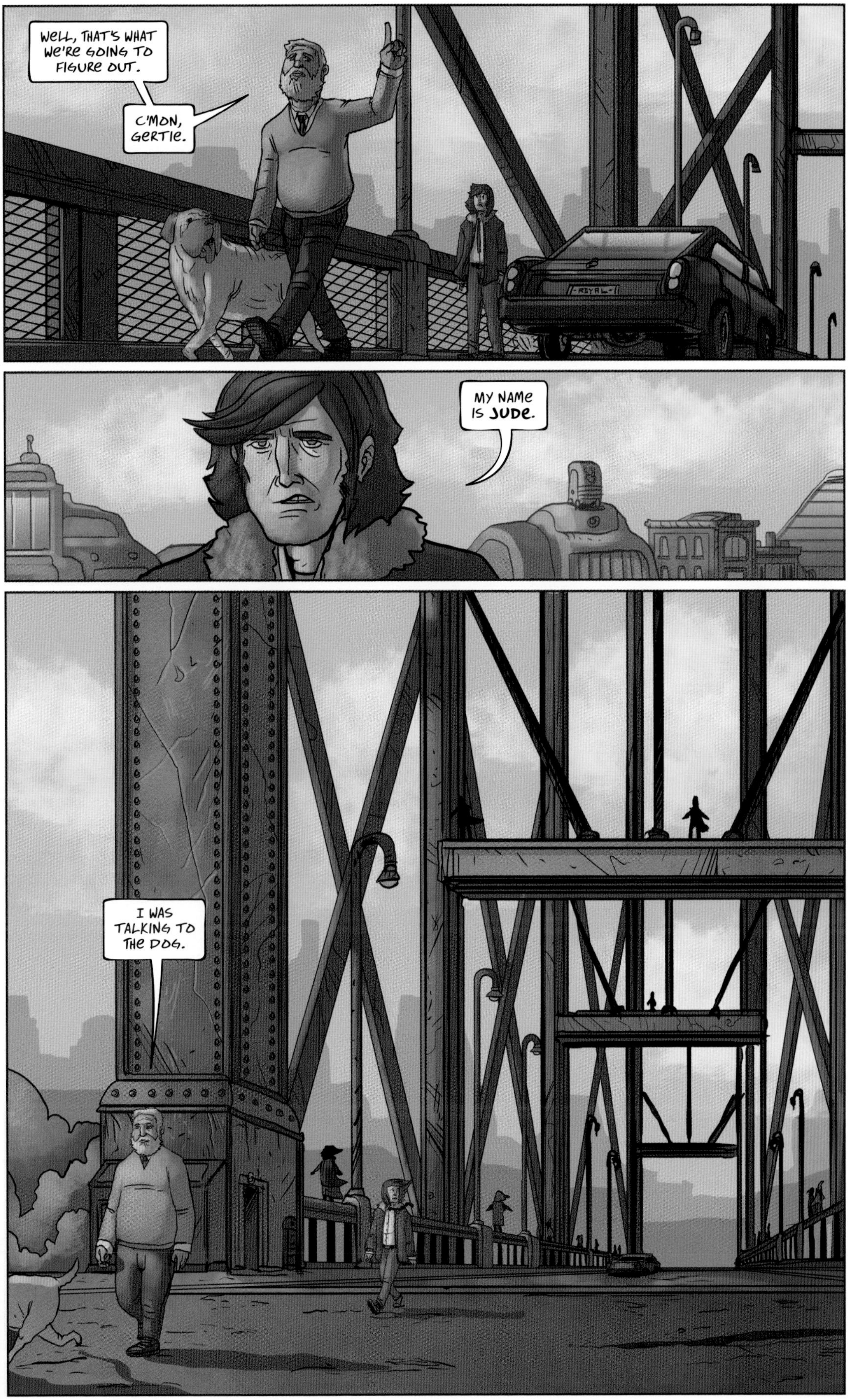
WELL, THAT'S WHAT WE'RE GOING TO FIGURE OUT.
C'MON, GERTIE.
MY NAME IS JUDE.
I WAS TALKING TO THE DOG.

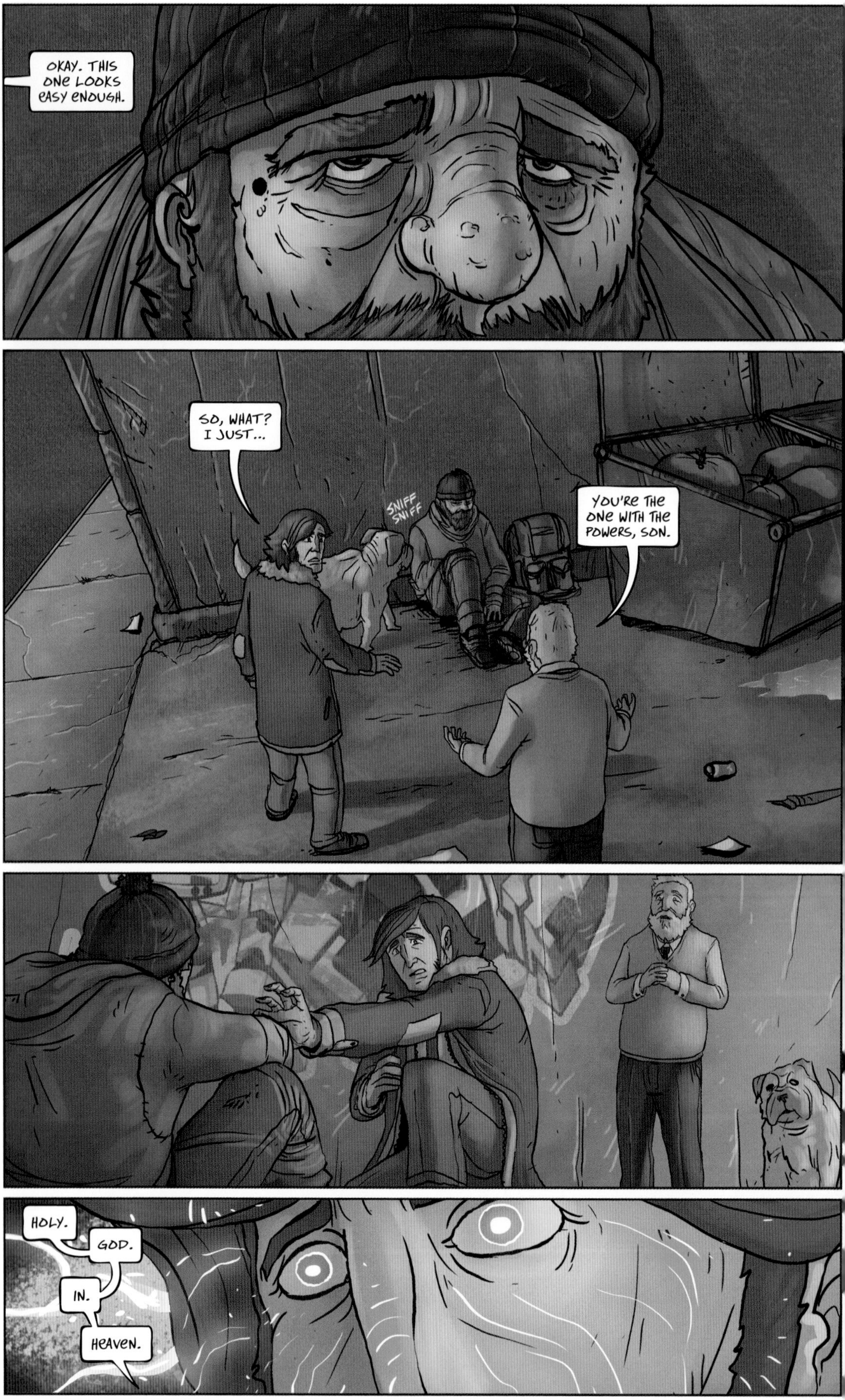
OKAY. THIS ONE LOOKS EASY ENOUGH.
SO, WHAT? I JUST...
SNIFF SNIFF
YOU'RE THE ONE WITH THE POWERS, SON.
HOLY.
GOD.
IN.
HEAVEN.

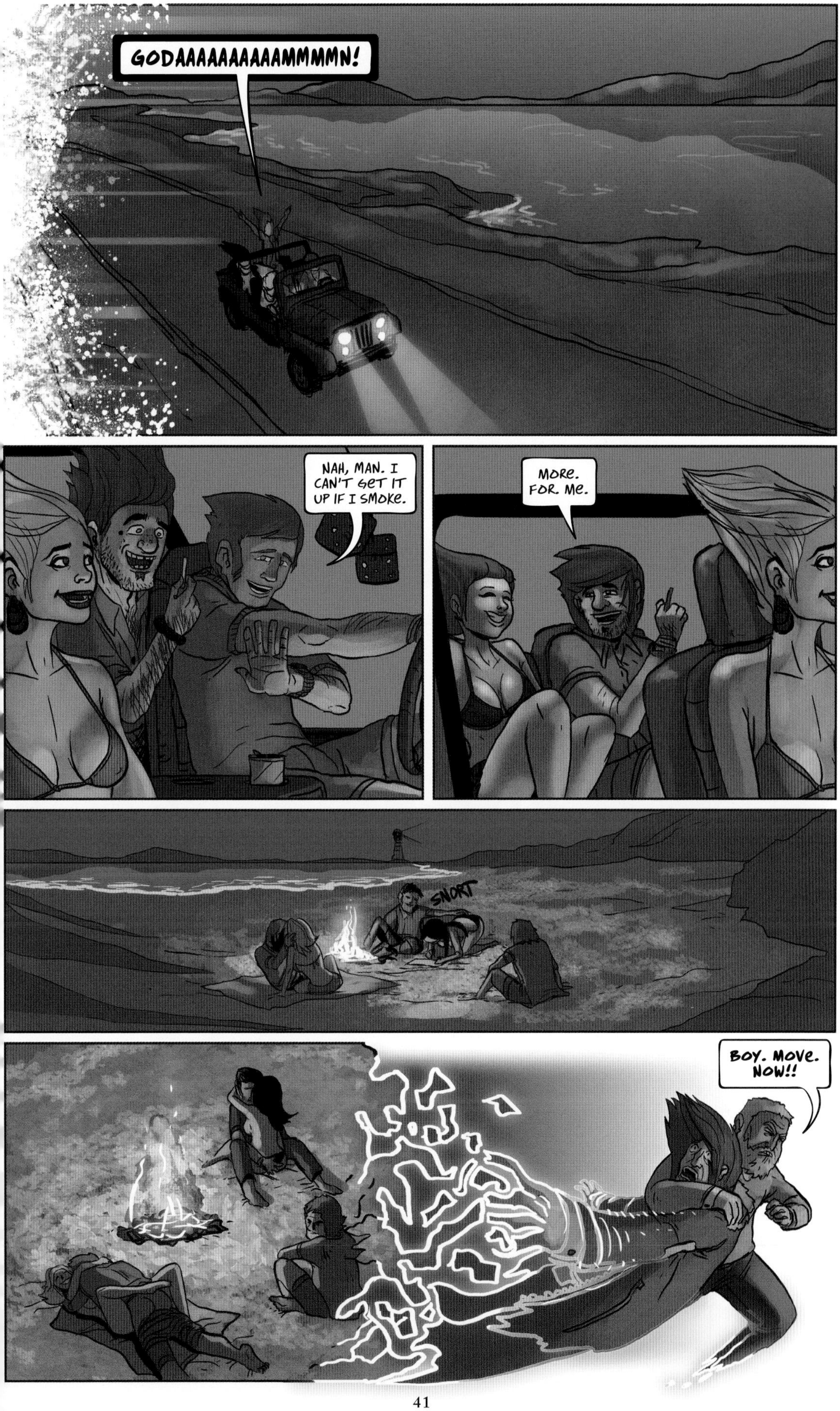
GODAAAAAAAAAAMMMMN!
NAH, MAN. I CAN'T GET IT UP IF I SMOKE.
MORE. FOR. ME.
SNORT
BOY. MOVE. NOW!!

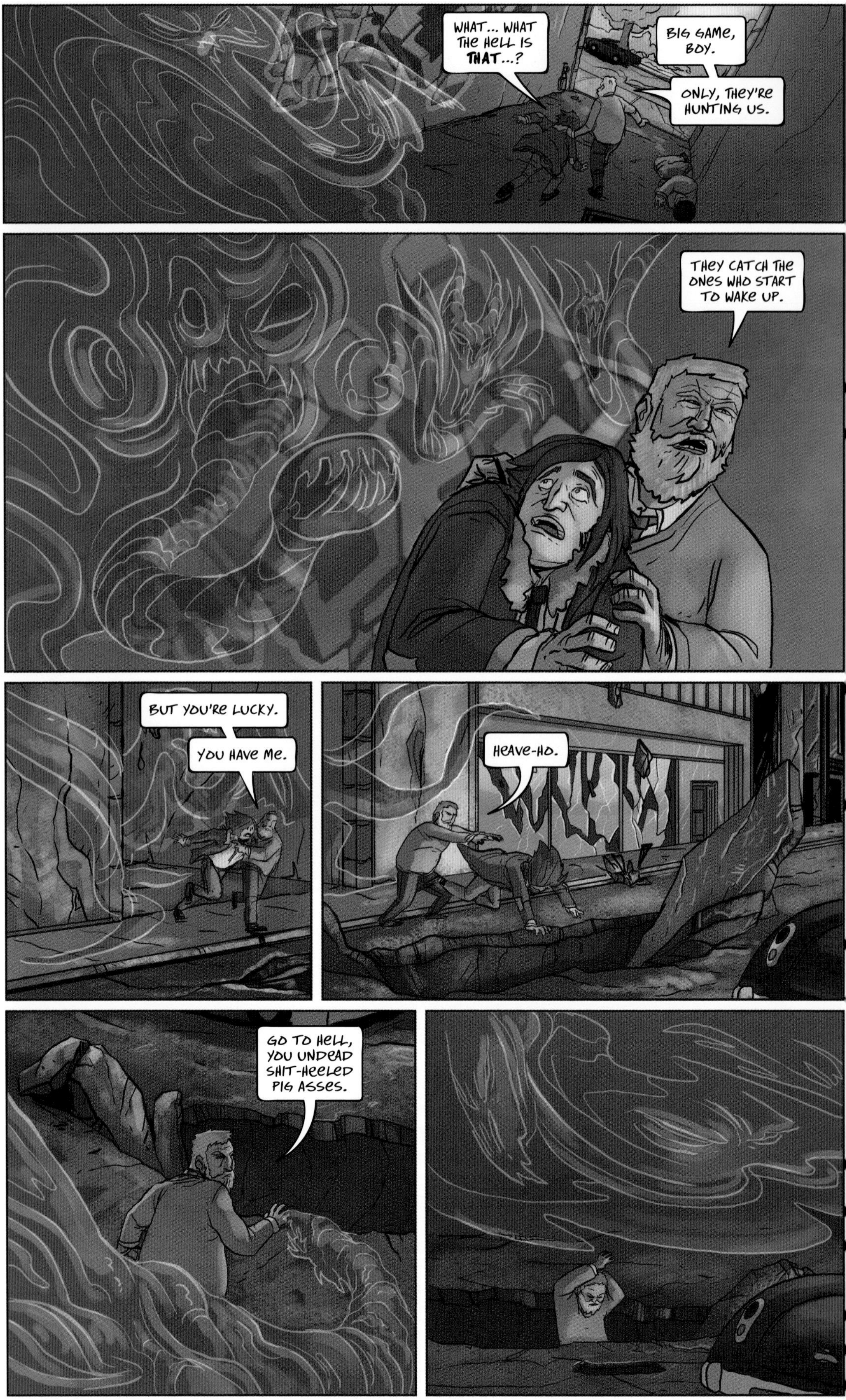
WHAT... WHAT THE HELL IS THAT...?
BIG GAME, BOY.
ONLY, THEY'RE HUNTING US.
THEY CATCH THE ONES WHO START TO WAKE UP.
BUT YOU'RE LUCKY.
YOU HAVE ME.
HEAVE-HO.
GO TO HELL, YOU UNDEAD SHIT-HEELED PIG ASSES.

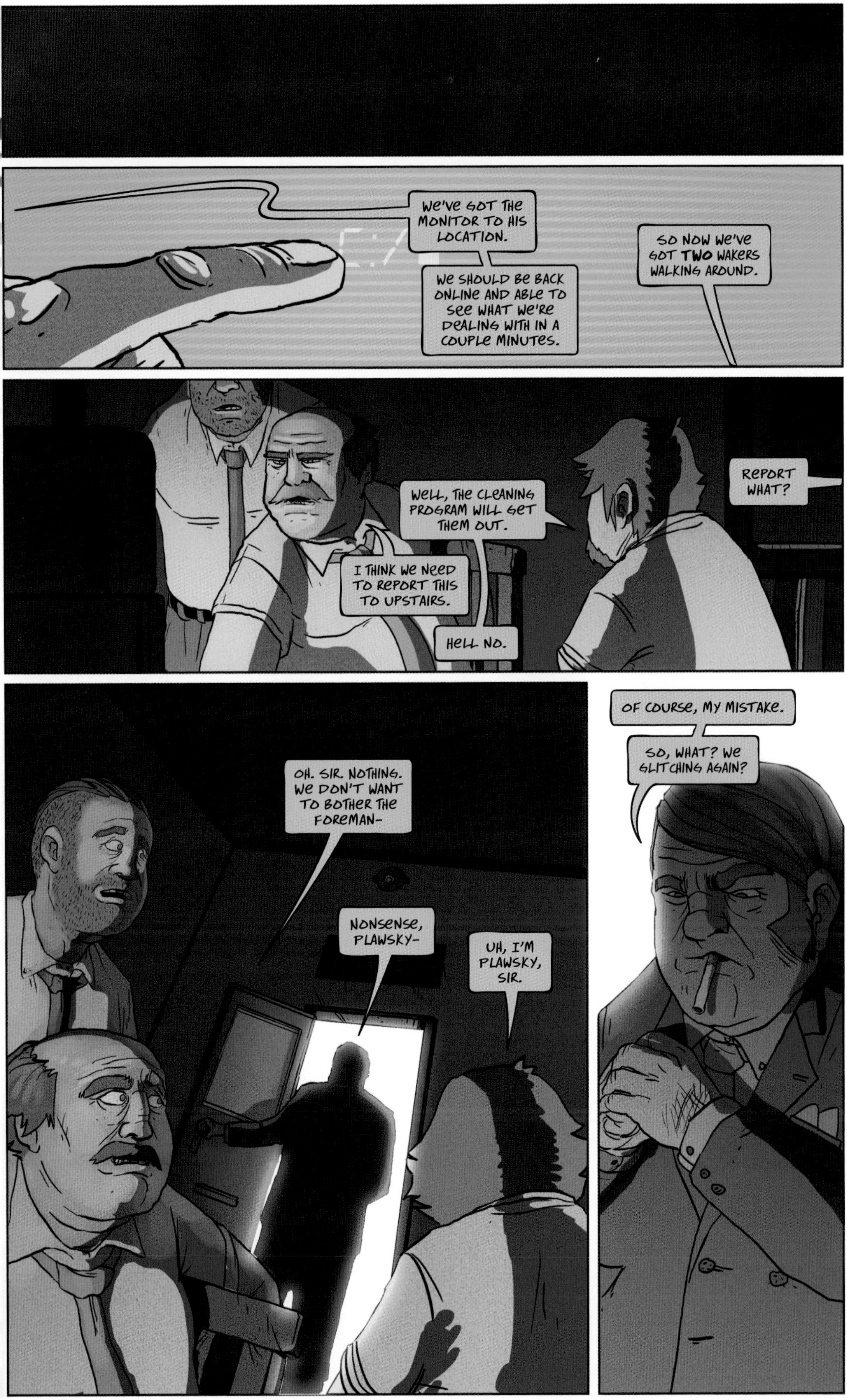
WE'VE GOT THE MONITOR TO HIS LOCATION.
WE SHOULD BE BACK ONLINE AND ABLE TO SEE WHAT WE'RE DEALING WITH IN A COUPLE MINUTES.
SO NOW WE'VE GOT **TWO** WAKERS WALKING AROUND.
WELL, THE CLEANING PROGRAM WILL GET THEM OUT.
REPORT WHAT?
I THINK WE NEED TO REPORT THIS TO UPSTAIRS.
HELL NO.
OH. SIR. NOTHING. WE DON'T WANT TO BOTHER THE FOREMAN-
NONSENSE, PLAWSKY-
UH, I'M PLAWSKY, SIR.
OF COURSE, MY MISTAKE.
SO, WHAT? WE GLITCHING AGAIN?

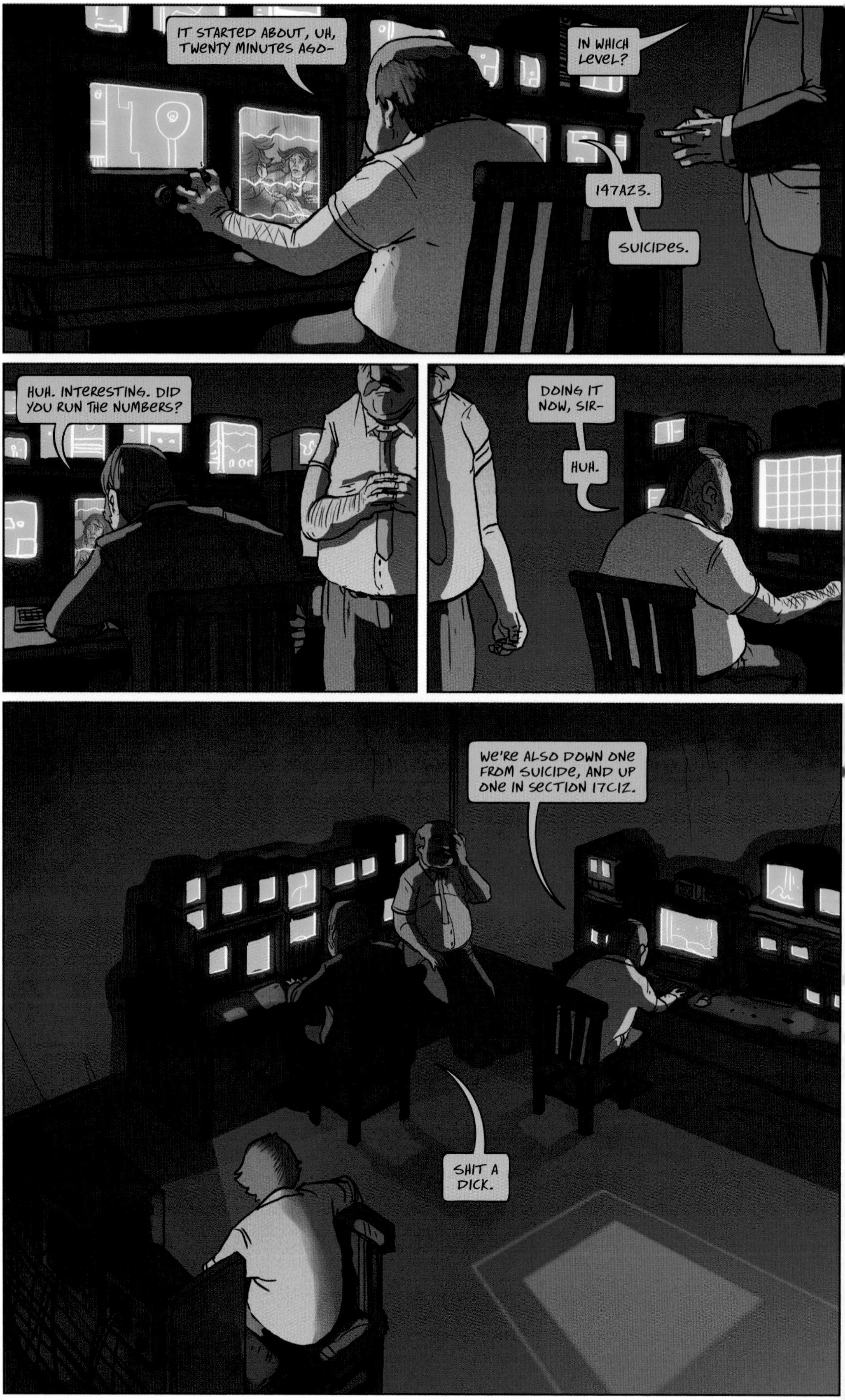
IT STARTED ABOUT, UH, TWENTY MINUTES AGO-
IN WHICH LEVEL?
147A23.
SUICIDES.
HUH. INTERESTING. DID YOU RUN THE NUMBERS?
DOING IT NOW, SIR-
HUH.
WE'RE ALSO DOWN ONE FROM SUICIDE, AND UP ONE IN SECTION 17C12.
SHIT A DICK.

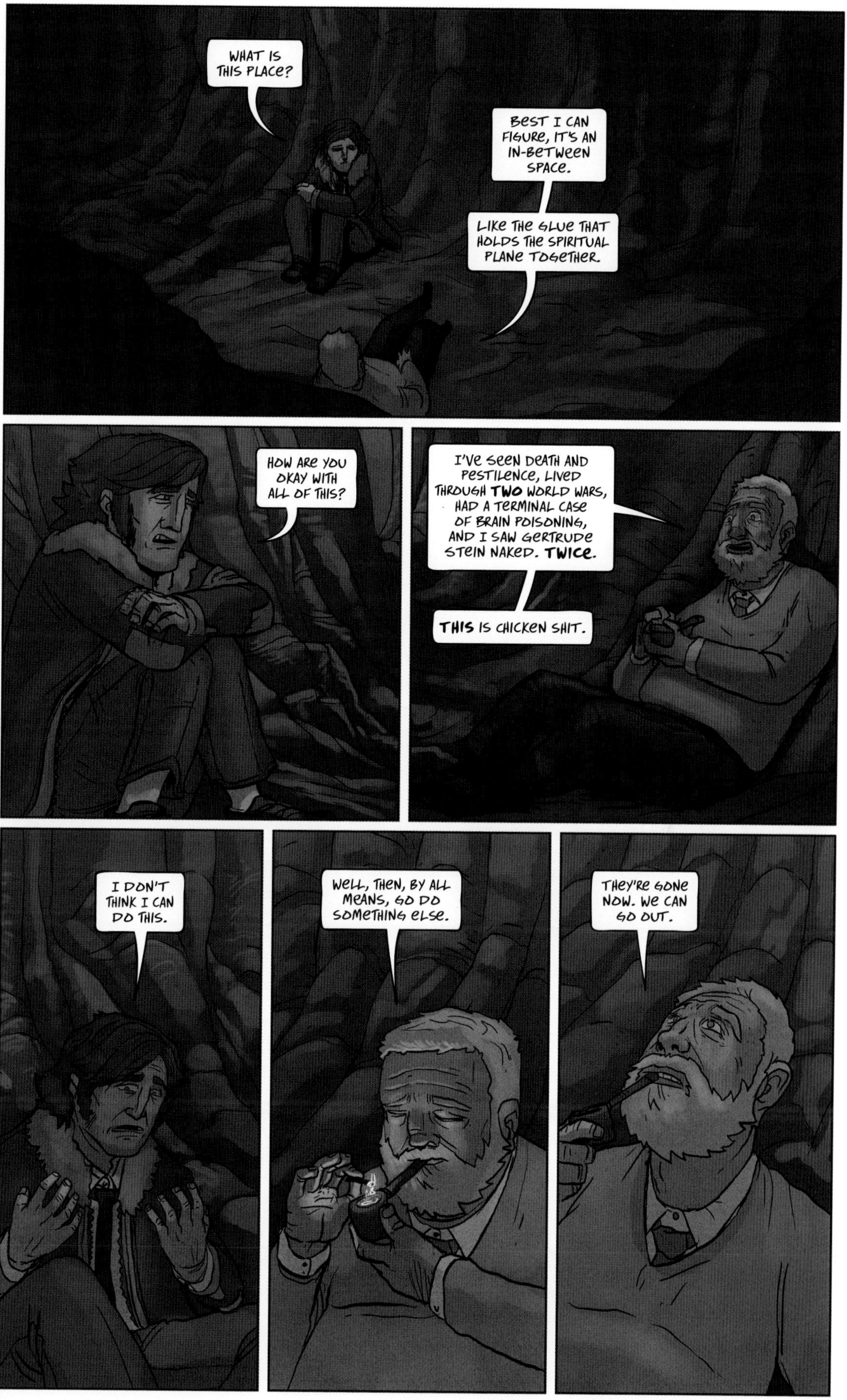
WHAT IS THIS PLACE?
BEST I CAN FIGURE, IT'S AN IN-BETWEEN SPACE.
LIKE THE GLUE THAT HOLDS THE SPIRITUAL PLANE TOGETHER.
HOW ARE YOU OKAY WITH ALL OF THIS?
I'VE SEEN DEATH AND PESTILENCE, LIVED THROUGH TWO WORLD WARS, HAD A TERMINAL CASE OF BRAIN POISONING, AND I SAW GERTRUDE STEIN NAKED. TWICE.
THIS IS CHICKEN SHIT.
I DON'T THINK I CAN DO THIS.
WELL, THEN, BY ALL MEANS, GO DO SOMETHING ELSE.
THEY'RE GONE NOW. WE CAN GO OUT.

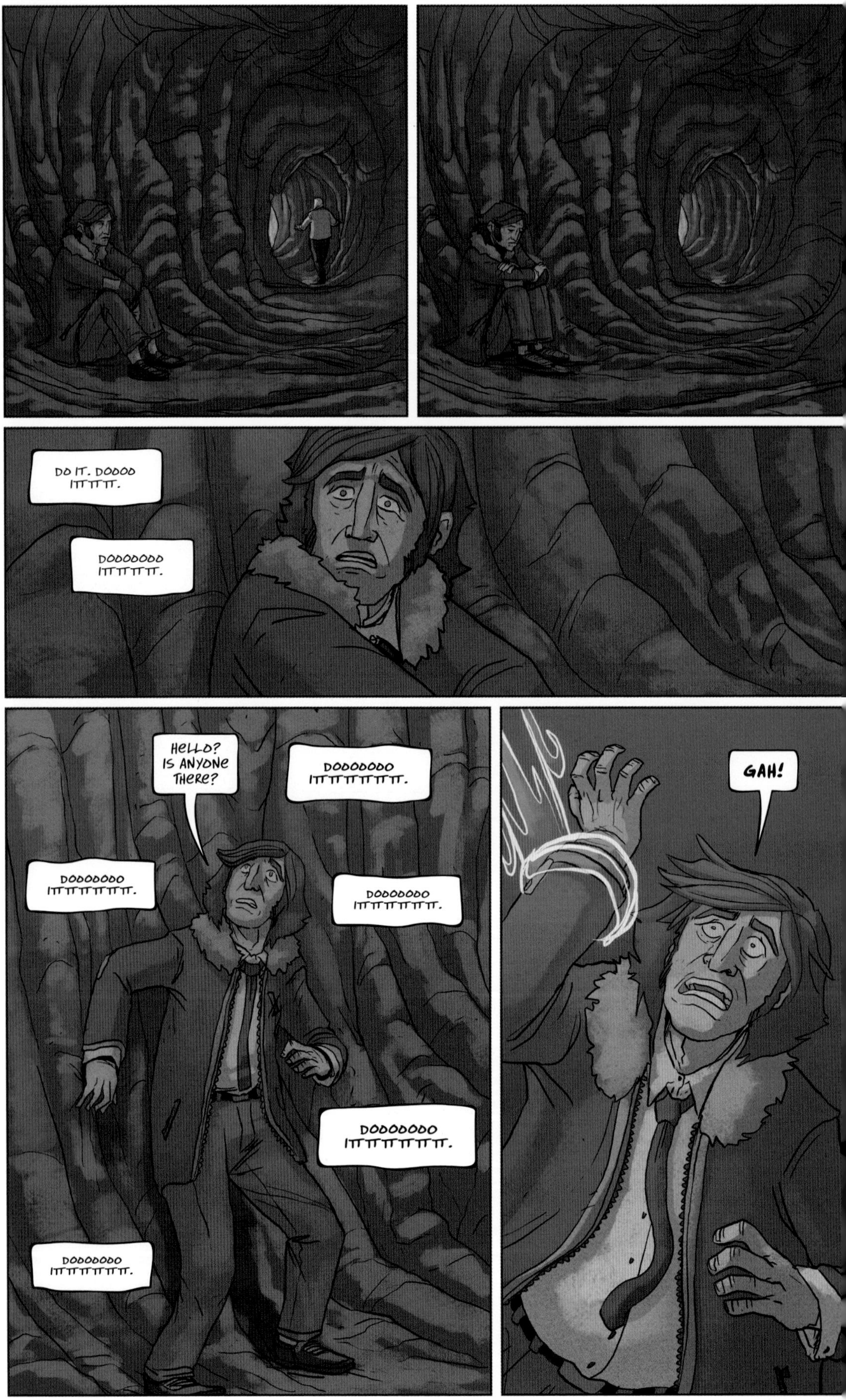
DO IT. DOOOO ITTTTT.
DOOOOOOO ITTTTTT.
HELLO? IS ANYONE THERE?
DOOOOOOO ITTTTTTTTT.
DOOOOOOO ITTTTTTTTT.
DOOOOOOO ITTTTTTTTT.
DOOOOOOO ITTTTTTTTT.
DOOOOOOO ITTTTTTTTT.
GAH!

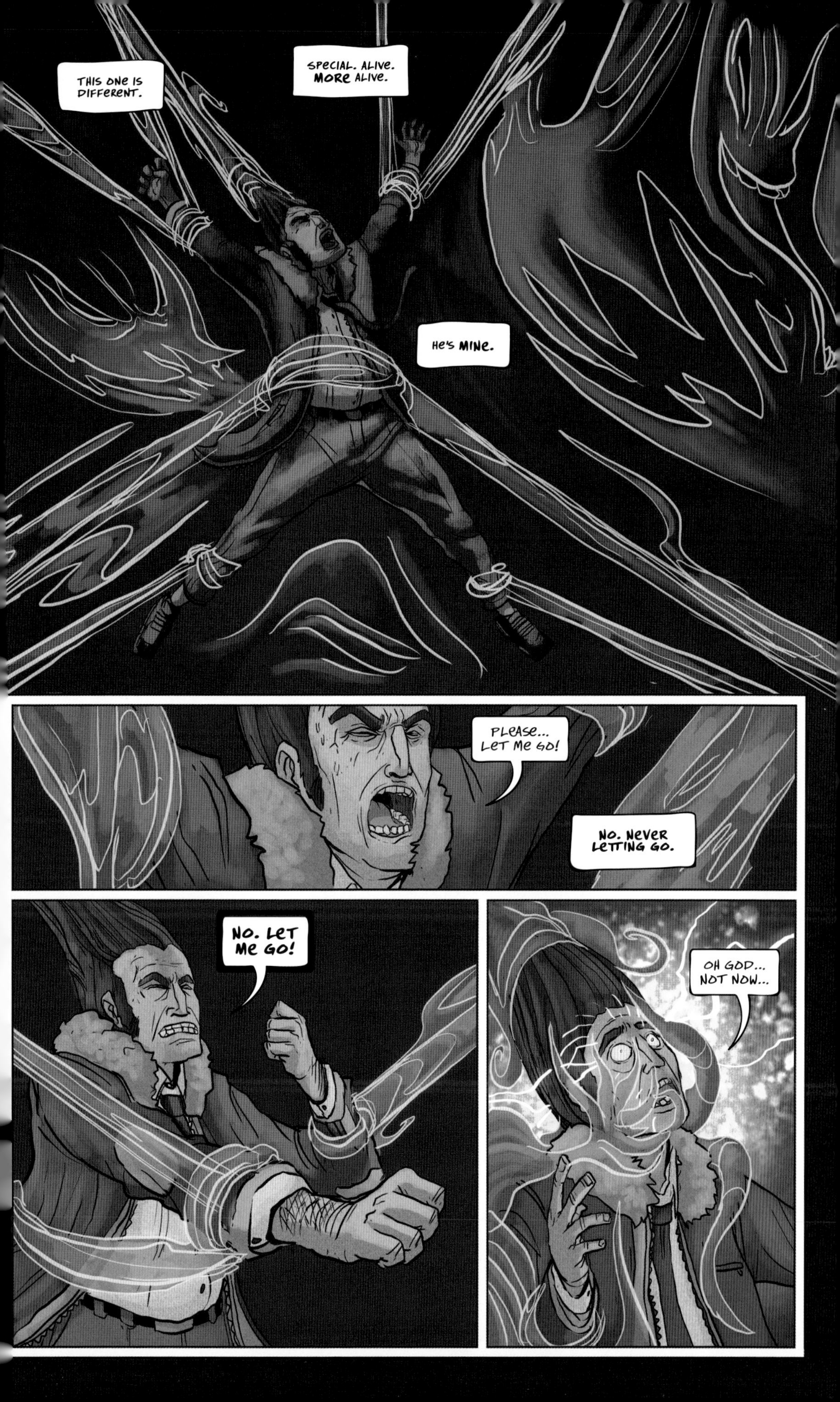
THIS ONE IS DIFFERENT.
SPECIAL. ALIVE. MORE ALIVE.
HE'S MINE.
PLEASE... LET ME GO!
NO. NEVER LETTING GO.
NO. LET ME GO!
OH GOD... NOT NOW...

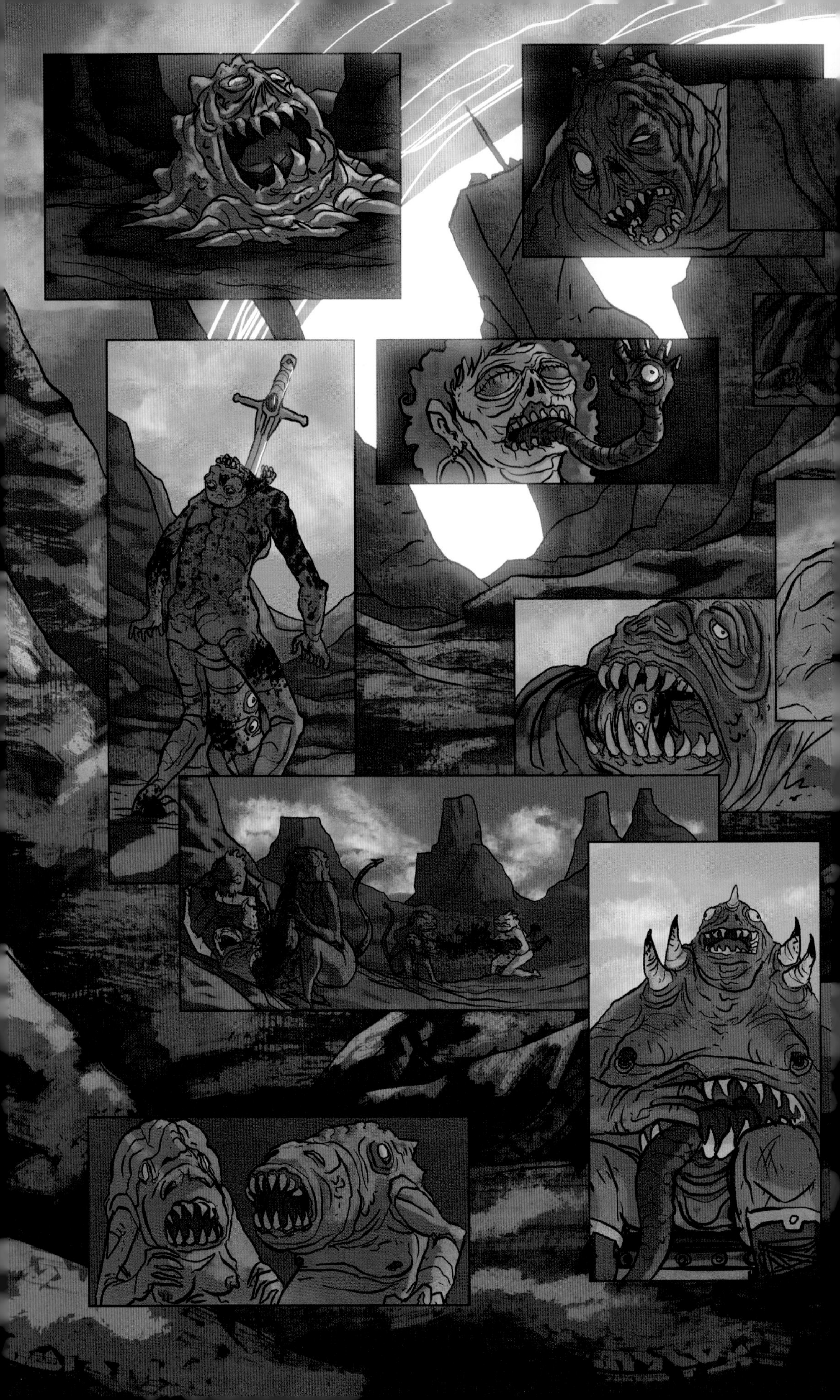

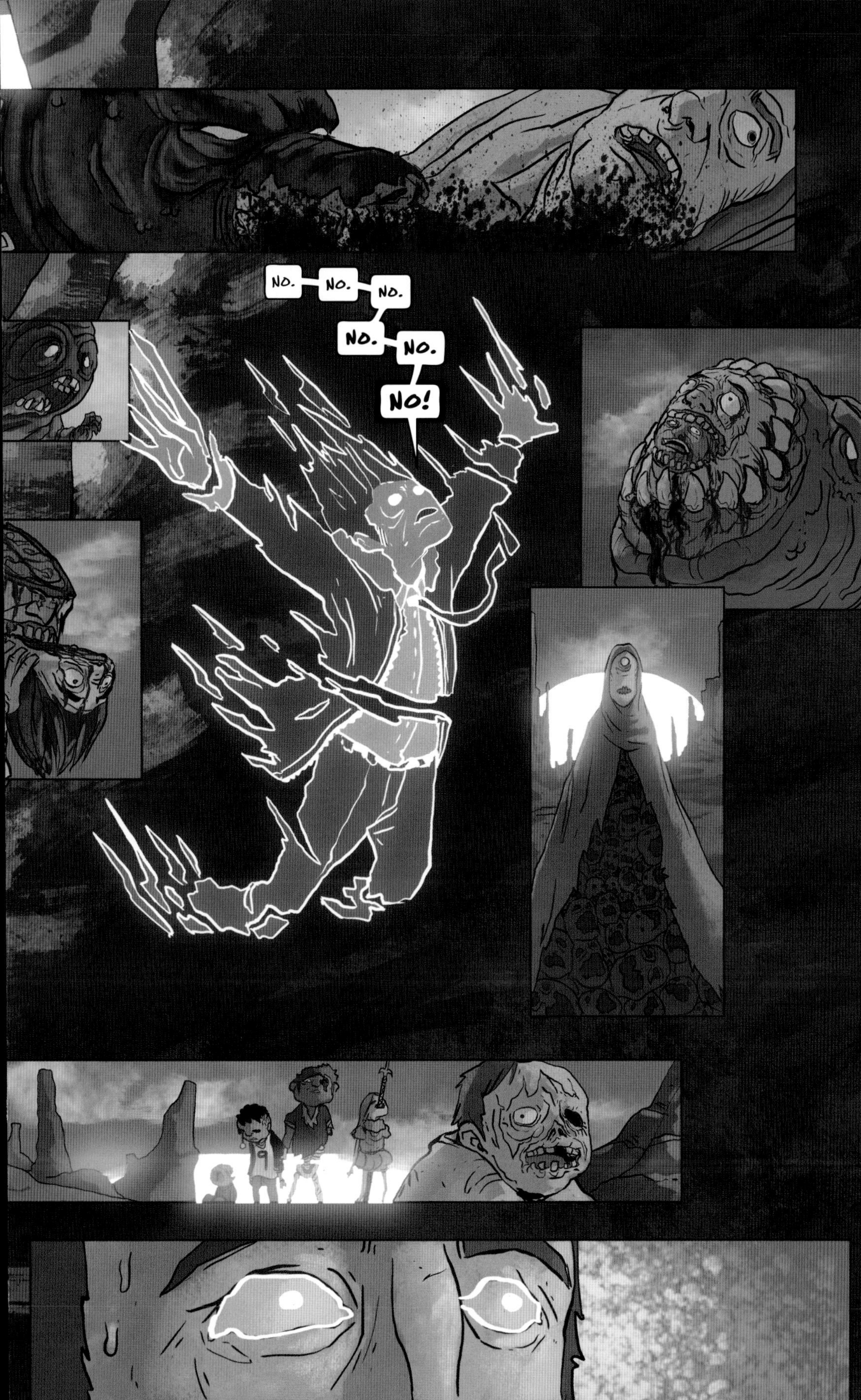
NO.
NO.
NO.
NO.
NO.
NO!

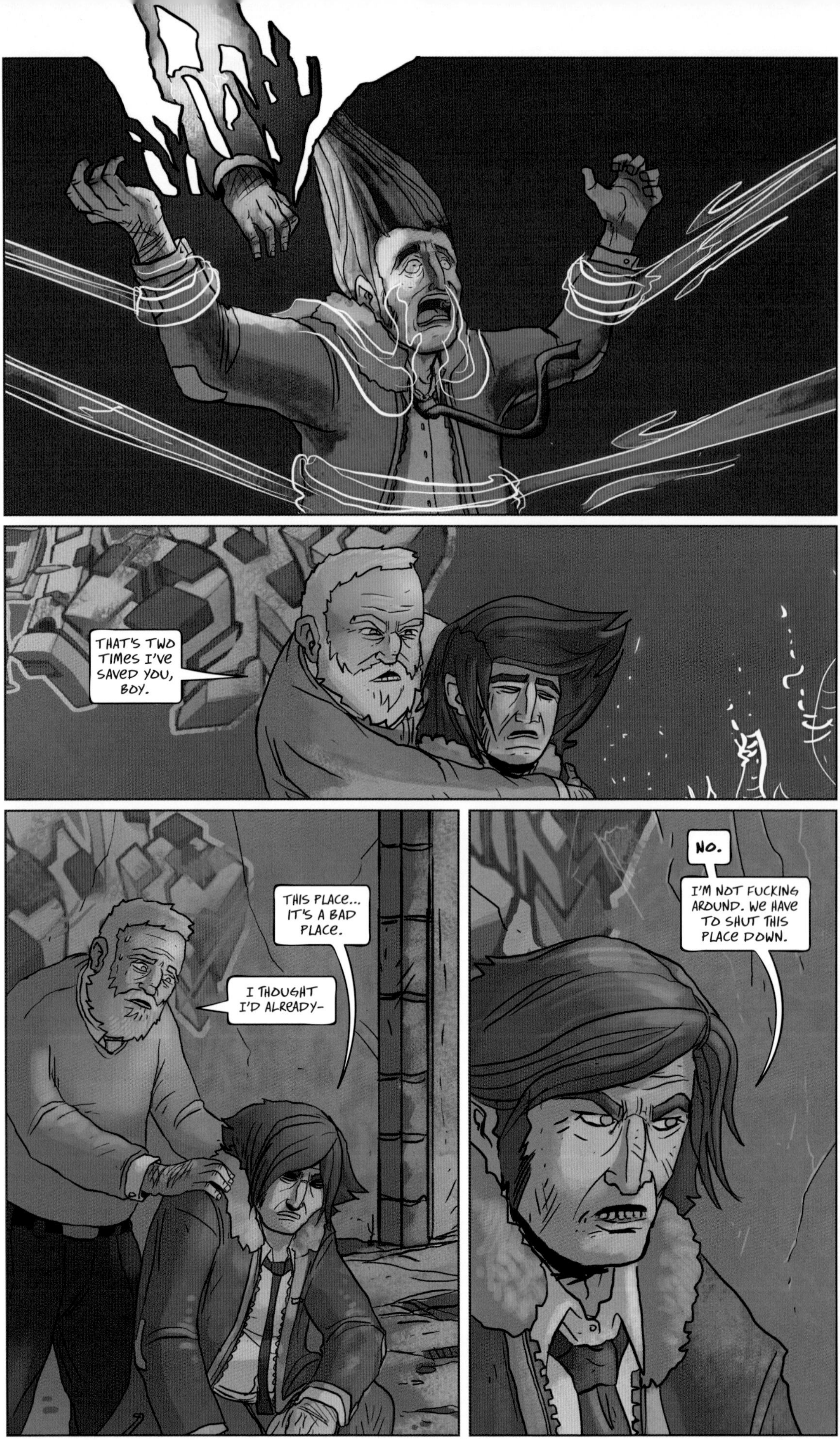
THAT'S TWO TIMES I'VE SAVED YOU, BOY.
THIS PLACE... IT'S A BAD PLACE.
I THOUGHT I'D ALREADY-
NO.
I'M NOT FUCKING AROUND. WE HAVE TO SHUT THIS PLACE DOWN.

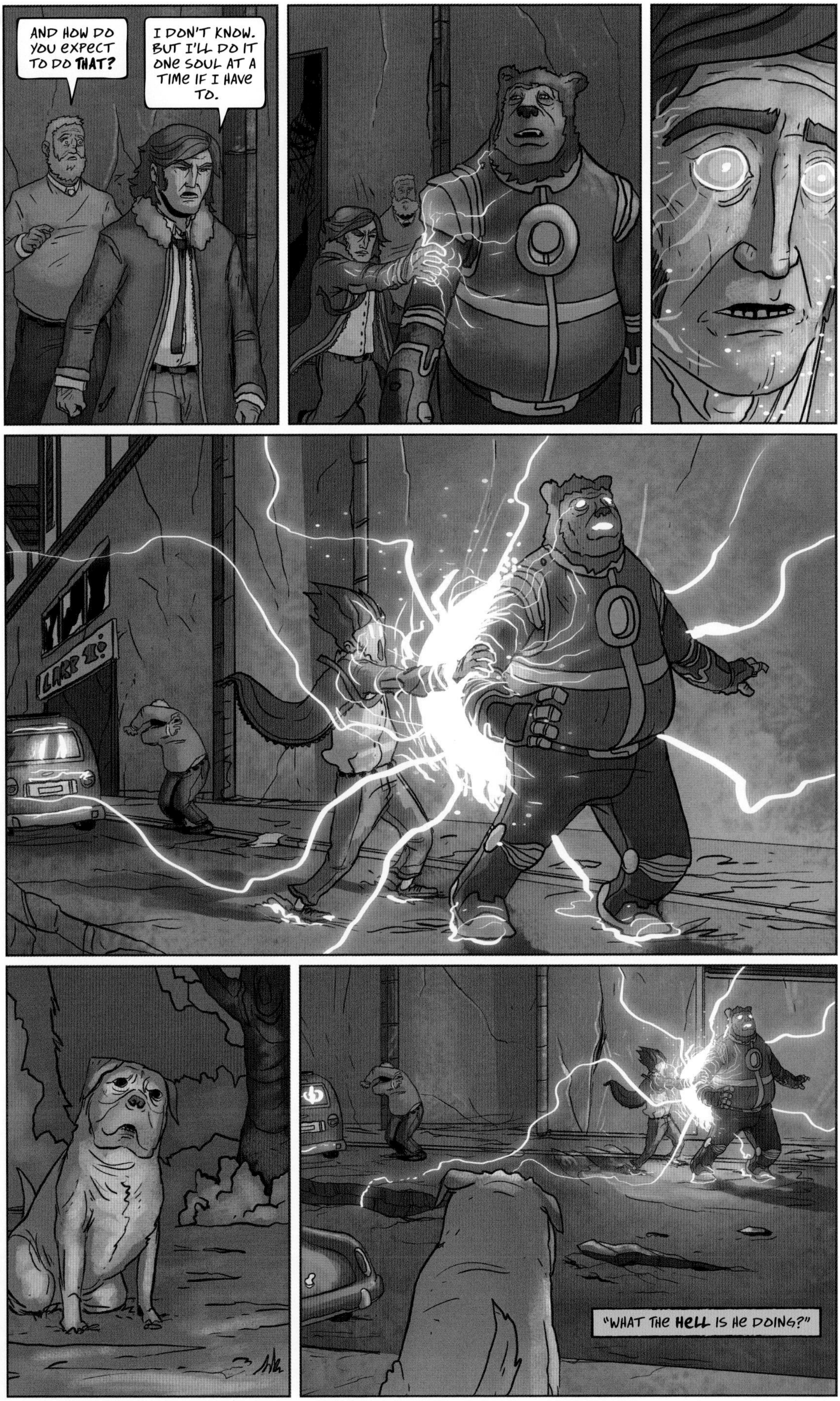
AND HOW DO YOU EXPECT TO DO THAT?
I DON'T KNOW. BUT I'LL DO IT ONE SOUL AT A TIME IF I HAVE TO.
"WHAT THE HELL IS HE DOING?"

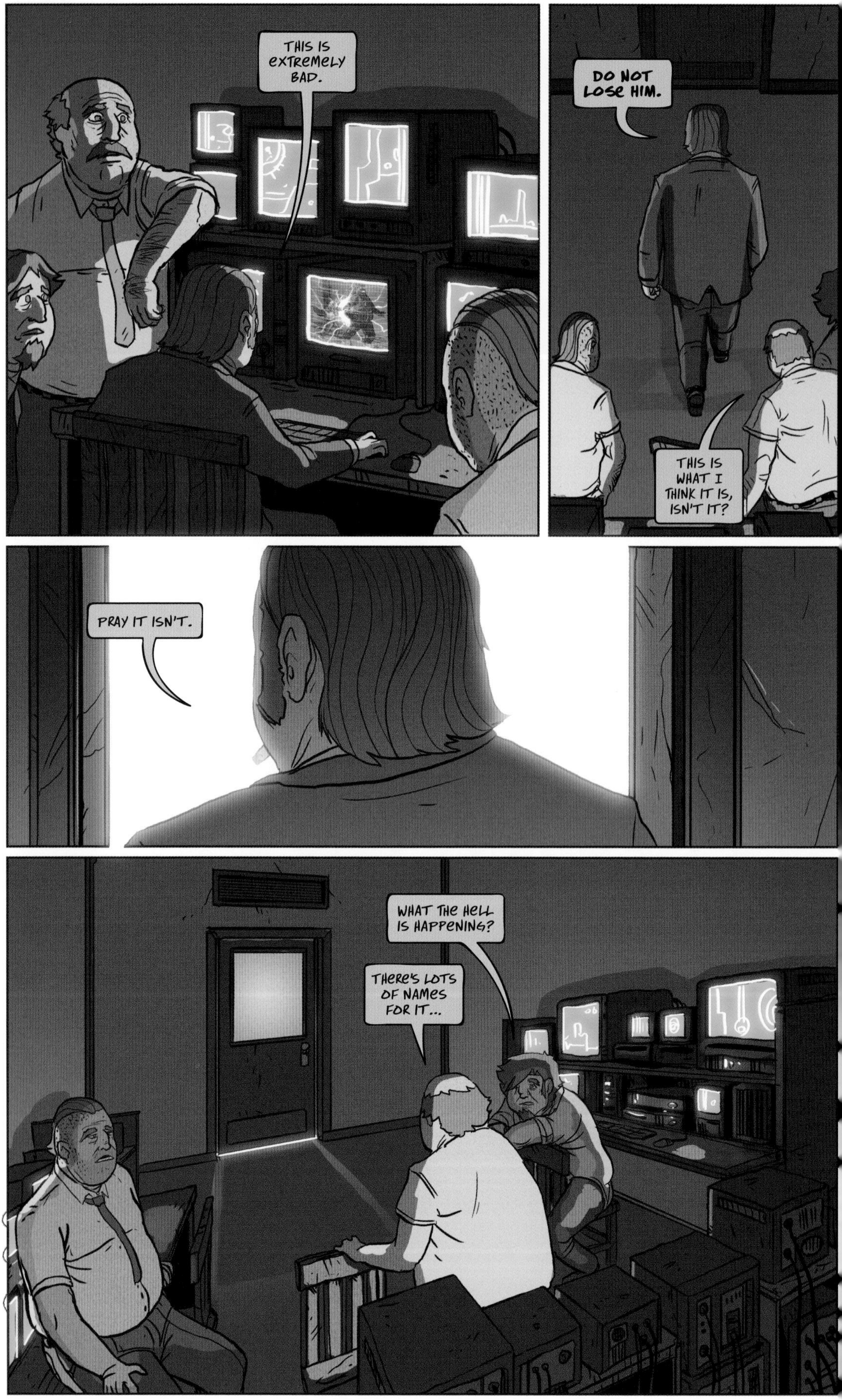
THIS IS EXTREMELY BAD.
DO NOT LOSE HIM.
THIS IS WHAT I THINK IT IS, ISN'T IT?
PRAY IT ISN'T.
WHAT THE HELL IS HAPPENING?
THERE'S LOTS OF NAMES FOR IT...

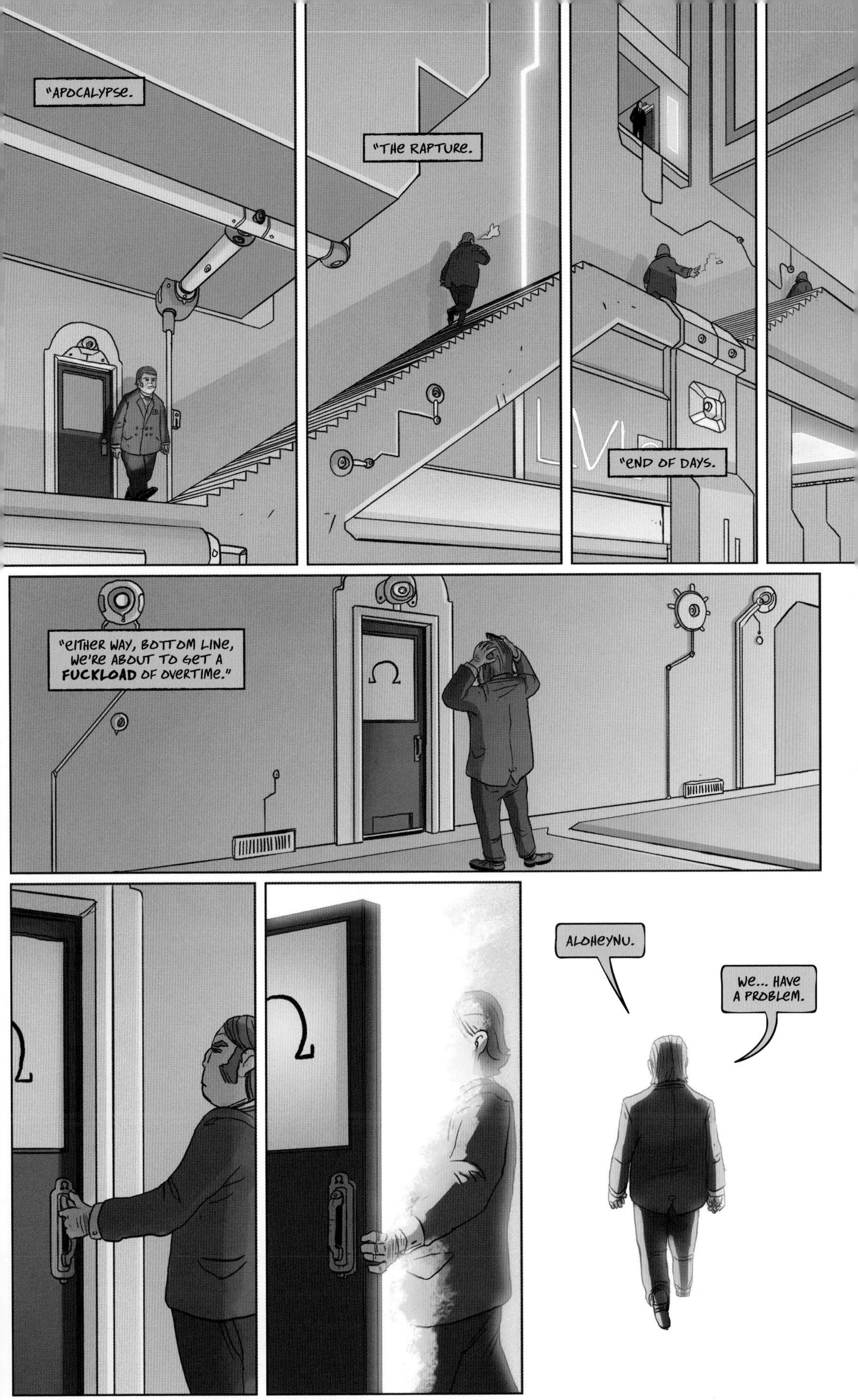
"APOCALYPSE.
"THE RAPTURE.
"END OF DAYS.
"EITHER WAY, BOTTOM LINE, WE'RE ABOUT TO GET A FUCKLOAD OF OVERTIME."
ALOHEYNU.
WE... HAVE A PROBLEM.

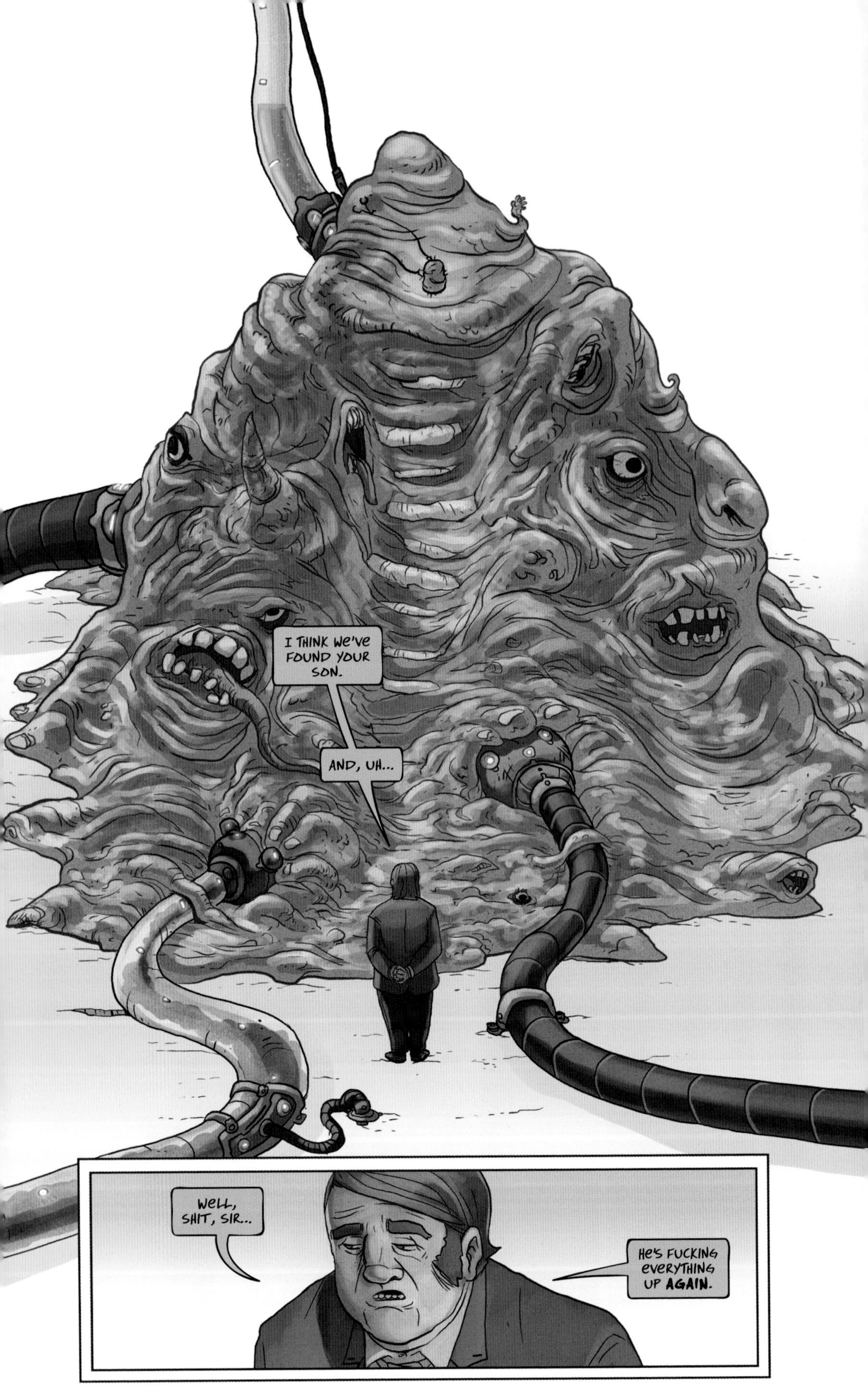

I THINK WE'VE FOUND YOUR SON.
AND, UH...
WELL, SHIT, SIR...
HE'S FUCKING EVERYTHING UP **AGAIN**.

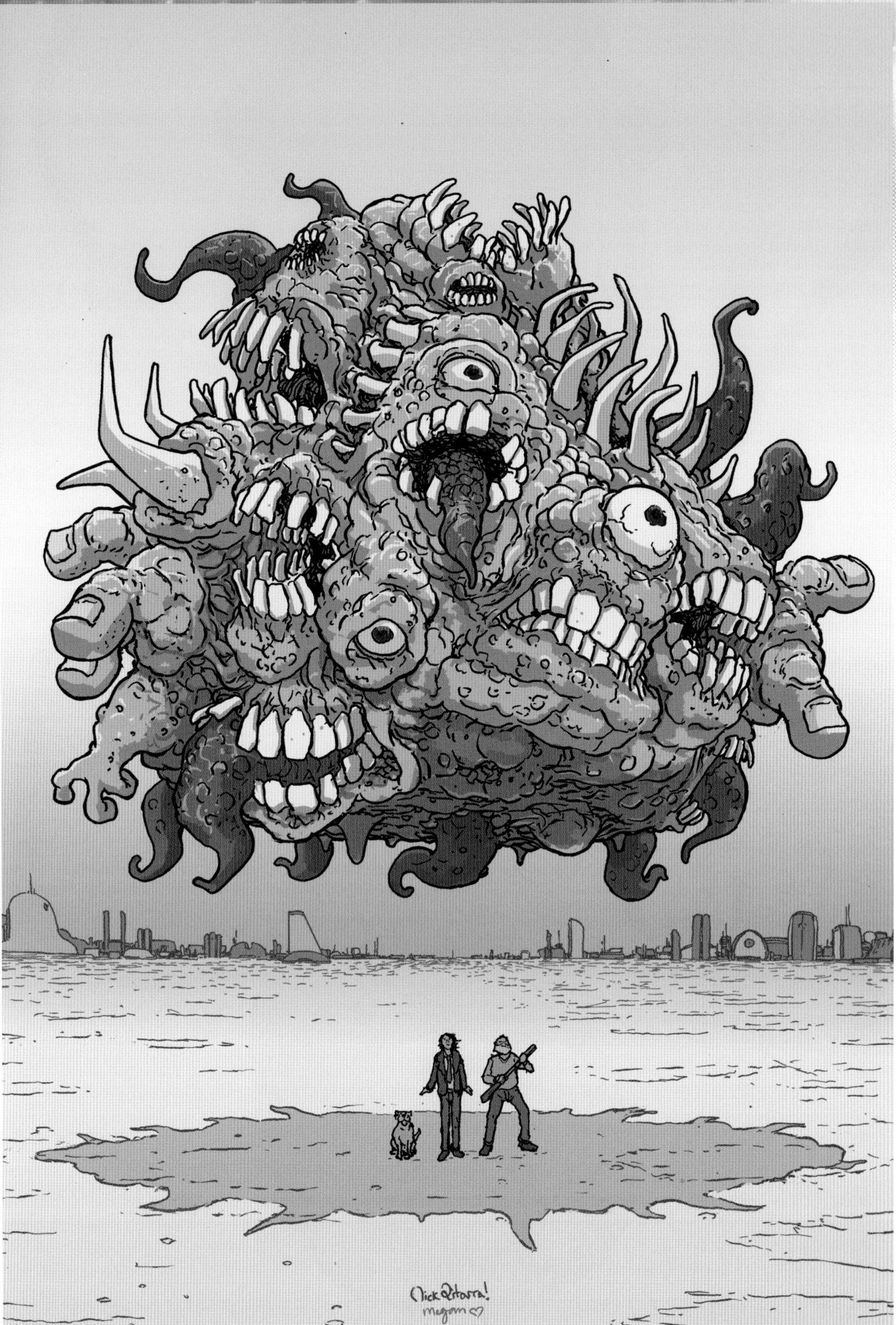
Nick Pitarra!
megan

Chapter Three

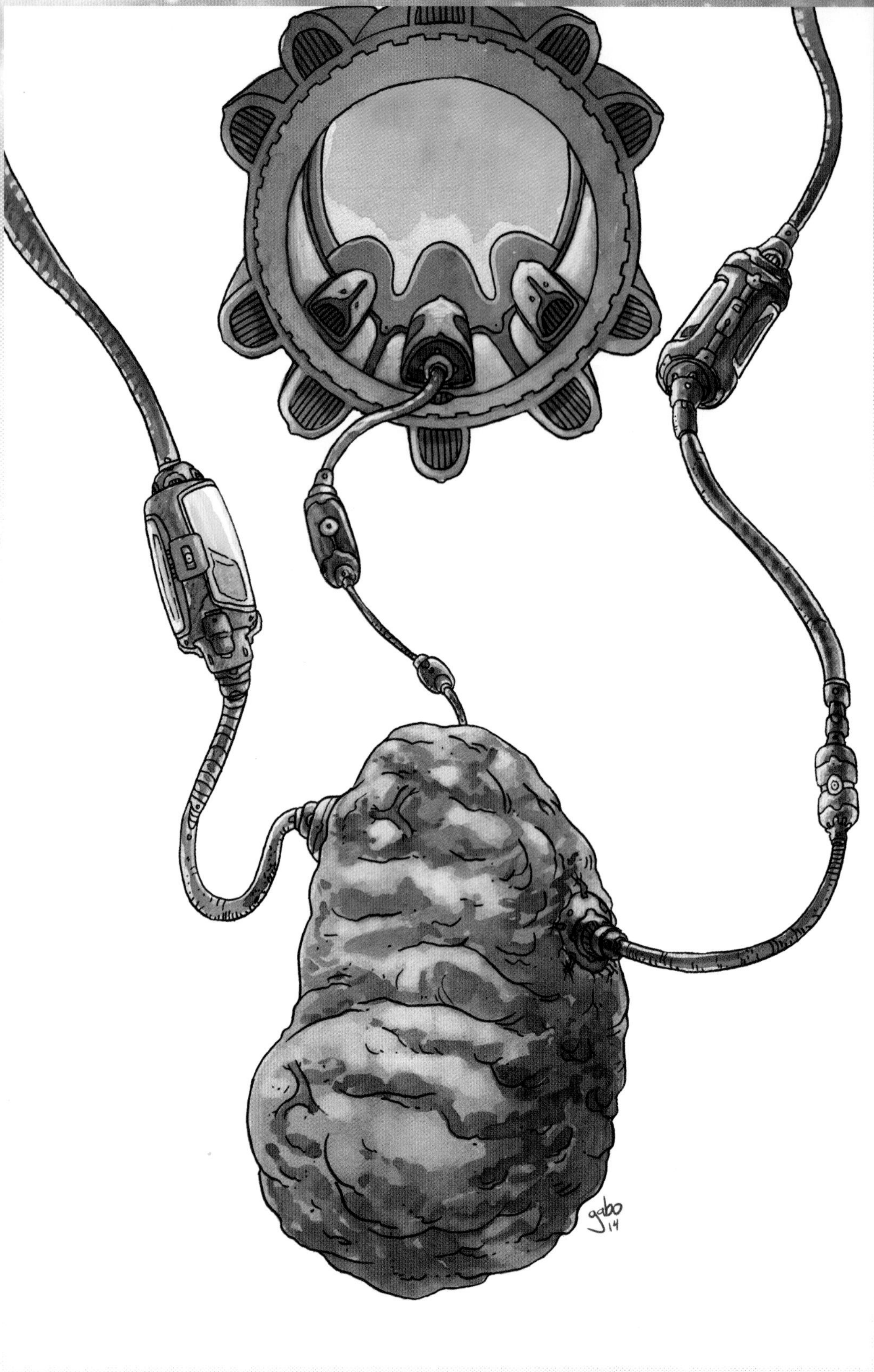
gabo
14

THE LIFE AFTER

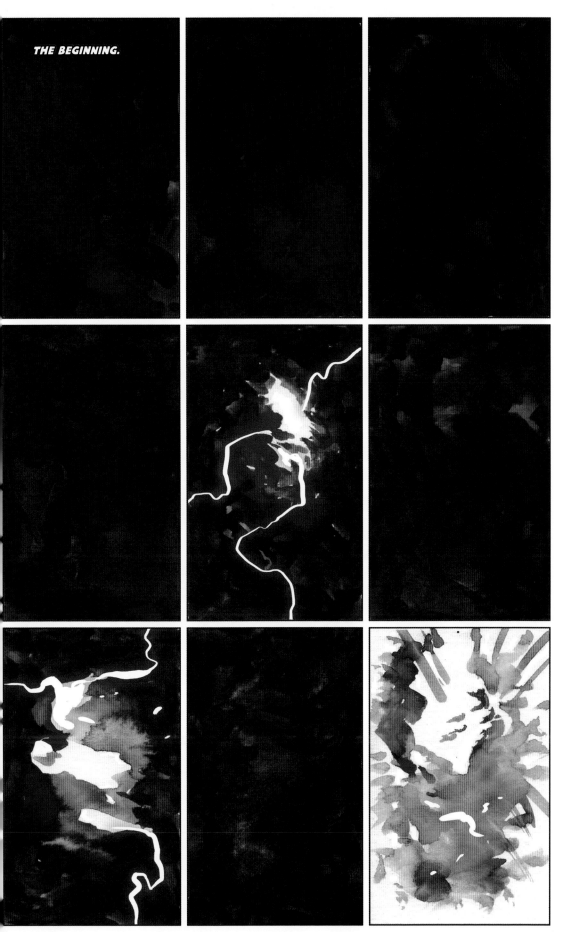

THE BEGINNING.

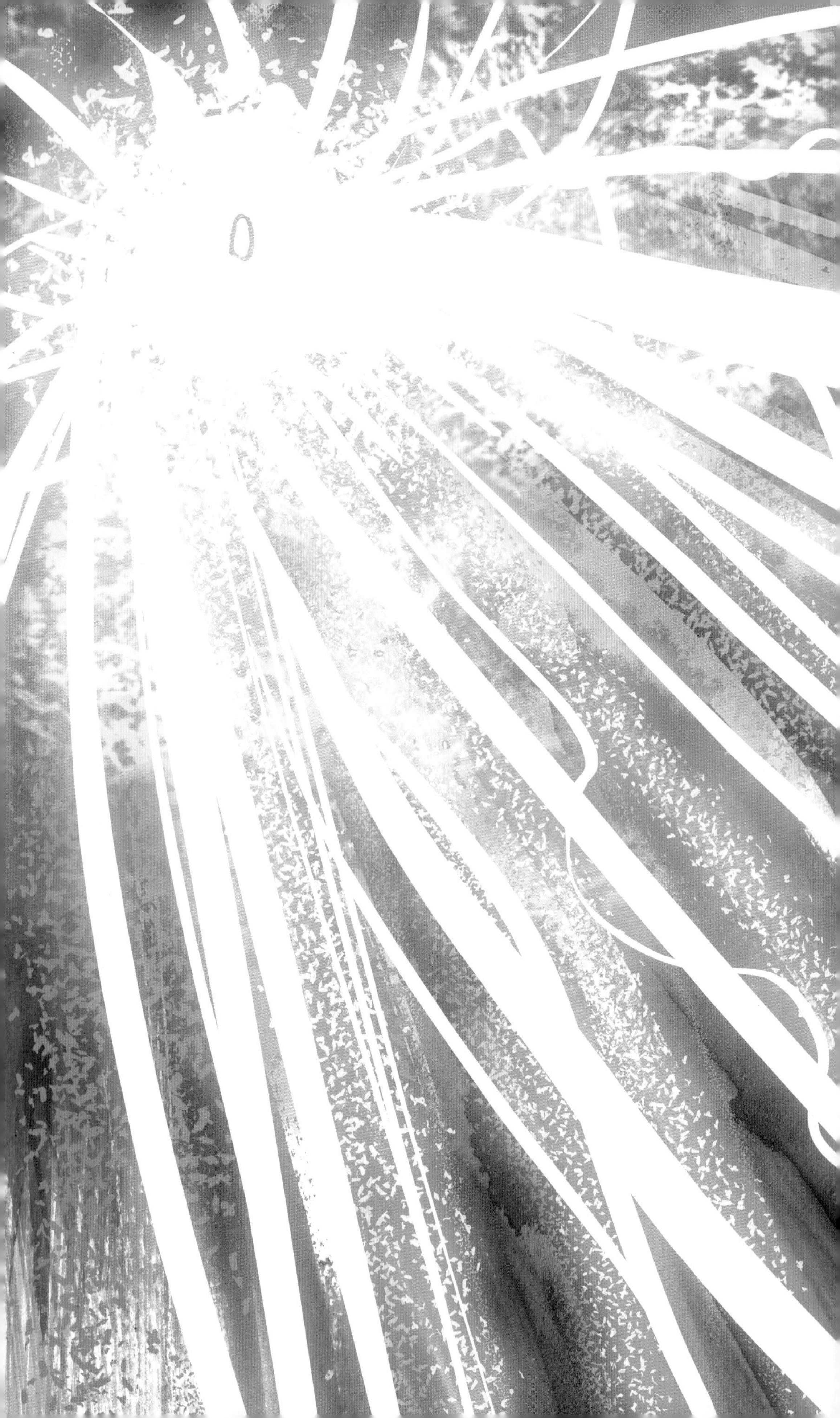

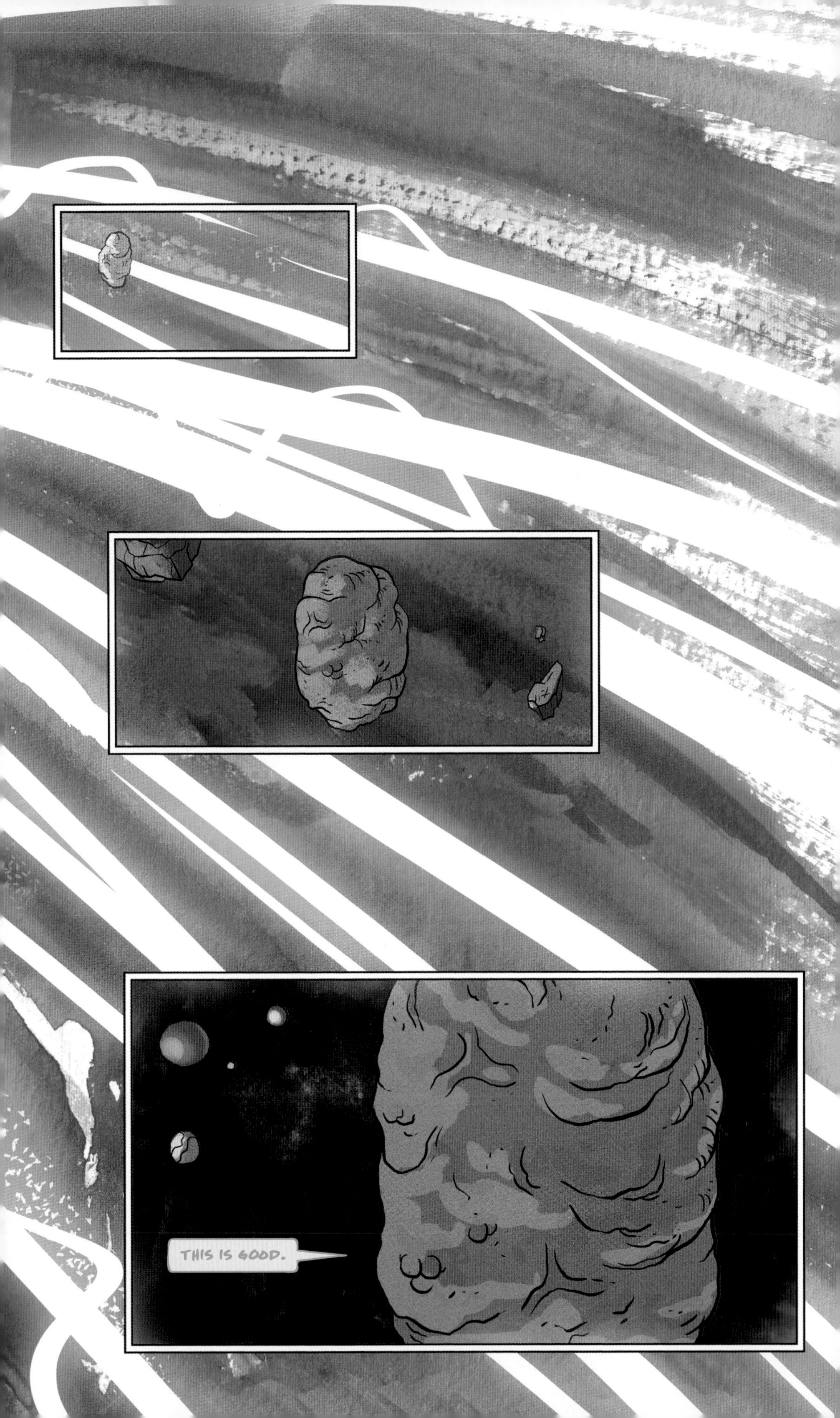
THIS IS GOOD.

HELLLLLLOOOO, NURSE.

MIRYAM "MARY" CHRIST

SO, YOU COME HERE OFTEN OR...?

NO, I'M FROM GALILEE... MY BETROTHED—

SHHH... LET'S NOT TALK ABOUT HIM—

33 YEARS LATER...

THE NEXT TWO THOUSAND YEARS.

OY VEY. THIS AGAIN.

SOMEONE NEEDS A SMITING.

60

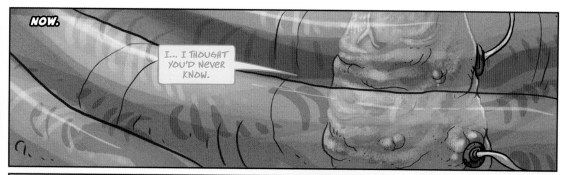

I... I THOUGHT YOU'D NEVER KNOW.

YOU... WORK IN MYSTERIOUS WAYS, SIR.

YEAH. ≥SIGH≤ I THOUGHT—

LAST TIME, IT DIDN'T GO GREAT. I HAD A KID, HE CAME TO SAVE THE WORLD, PEOPLE HATED HIM, MURDERED HIM...

YADA YADA YADA.

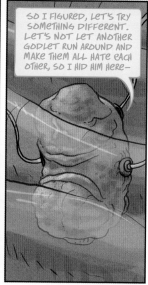

SO I FIGURED, LET'S TRY SOMETHING DIFFERENT. LET'S NOT LET ANOTHER GODLET RUN AROUND AND MAKE THEM ALL HATE EACH OTHER, SO I HID HIM HERE—

WHAT DO YOU WANT US TO DO...?

BRING HIM HERE, PLEASE.

NO. WAIT. CAN WE SOMEHOW GET HIM BACK IN LINE? ERASE HIS MEMORY OR SOMETHING—

SIR, WITH YOUR PERMISSION, I'D LIKE TO HANDLE THE SITUATION MYSELF, FOR YOU.

OF COURSE, OF COURSE.

JUST WHATEVER YOU DO, DON'T TELL THE OTHER SECTION LEADERS ABOUT IT. AND NO DEALS.

ESPECIALLY NOT WITH HIM.

ANGELS AND DEVILS AREN'T MY THING, SIR. I'M A BUREAUCRAT.

WE'RE MUCH, MUCH WORSE.

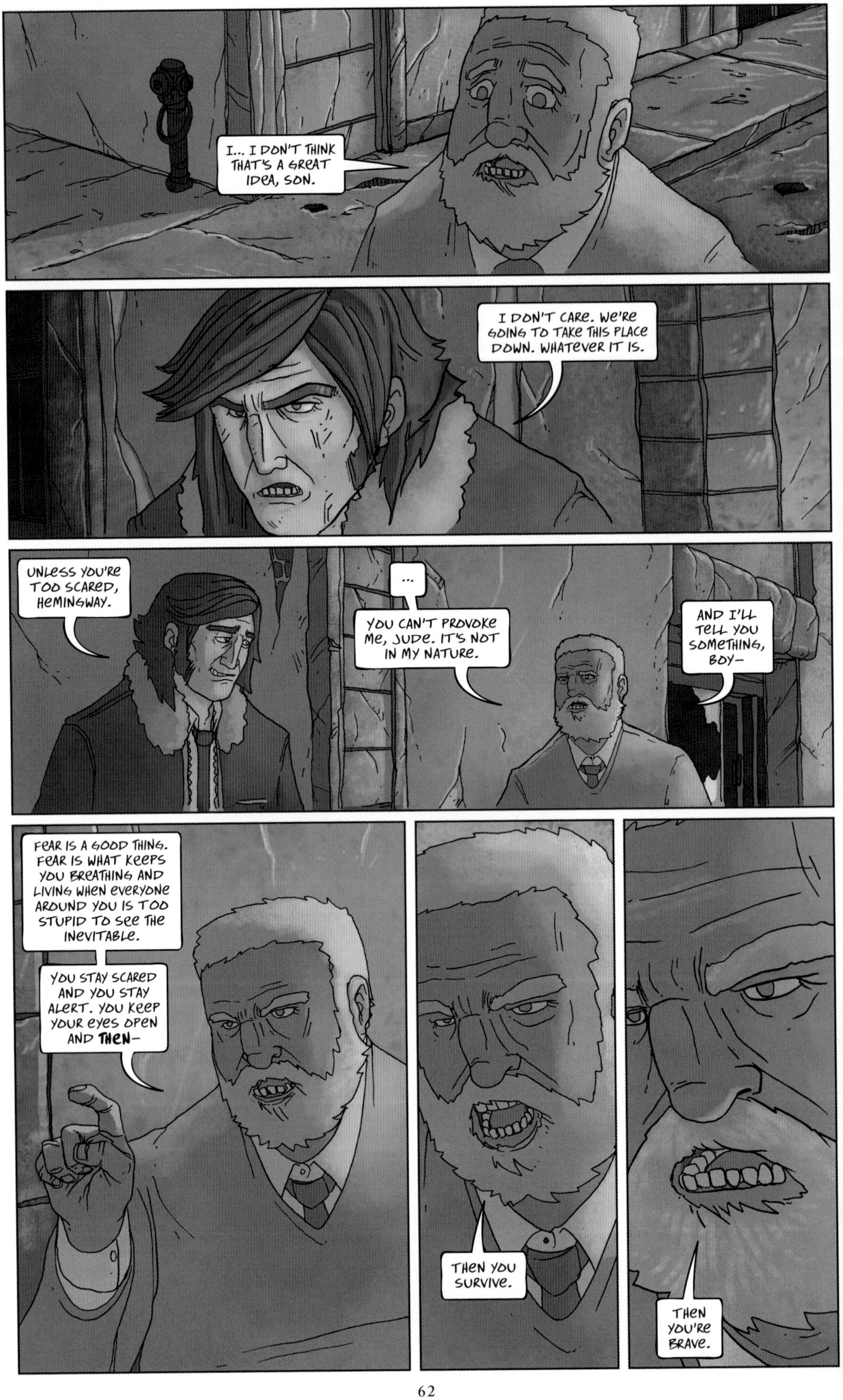
I... I DON'T THINK THAT'S A GREAT IDEA, SON.
I DON'T CARE. WE'RE GOING TO TAKE THIS PLACE DOWN. WHATEVER IT IS.
UNLESS YOU'RE TOO SCARED, HEMINGWAY.
...
YOU CAN'T PROVOKE ME, JUDE. IT'S NOT IN MY NATURE.
AND I'LL TELL YOU SOMETHING, BOY–
FEAR IS A GOOD THING. FEAR IS WHAT KEEPS YOU BREATHING AND LIVING WHEN EVERYONE AROUND YOU IS TOO STUPID TO SEE THE INEVITABLE.
YOU STAY SCARED AND YOU STAY ALERT. YOU KEEP YOUR EYES OPEN AND THEN–
THEN YOU SURVIVE.
THEN YOU'RE BRAVE.

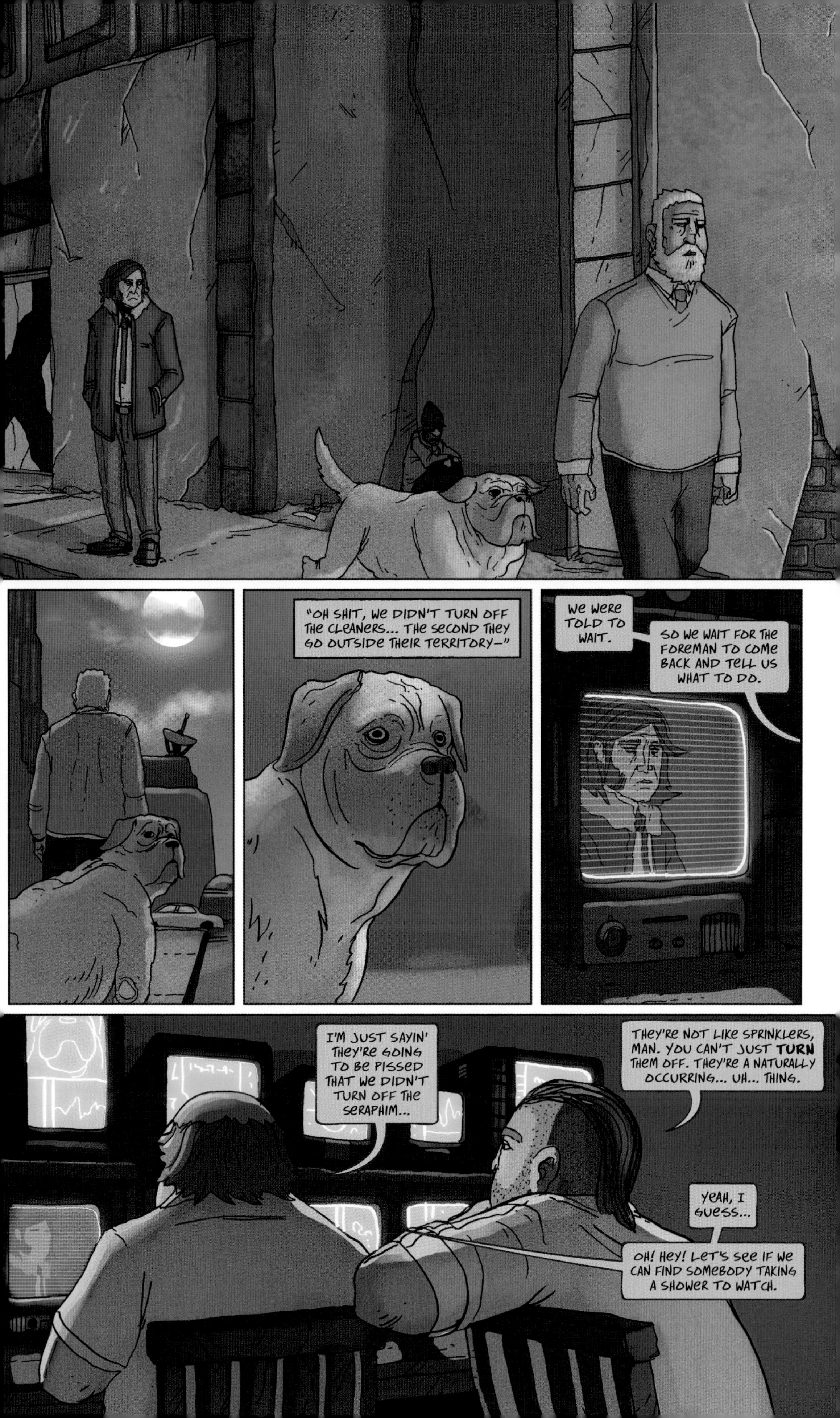
"OH SHIT, WE DIDN'T TURN OFF THE CLEANERS... THE SECOND THEY GO OUTSIDE THEIR TERRITORY—"
WE WERE TOLD TO WAIT.
SO WE WAIT FOR THE FOREMAN TO COME BACK AND TELL US WHAT TO DO.
I'M JUST SAYIN' THEY'RE GOING TO BE PISSED THAT WE DIDN'T TURN OFF THE SERAPHIM...
THEY'RE NOT LIKE SPRINKLERS, MAN. YOU CAN'T JUST TURN THEM OFF. THEY'RE A NATURALLY OCCURRING... UH... THING.
YEAH, I GUESS...
OH! HEY! LET'S SEE IF WE CAN FIND SOMEBODY TAKING A SHOWER TO WATCH.

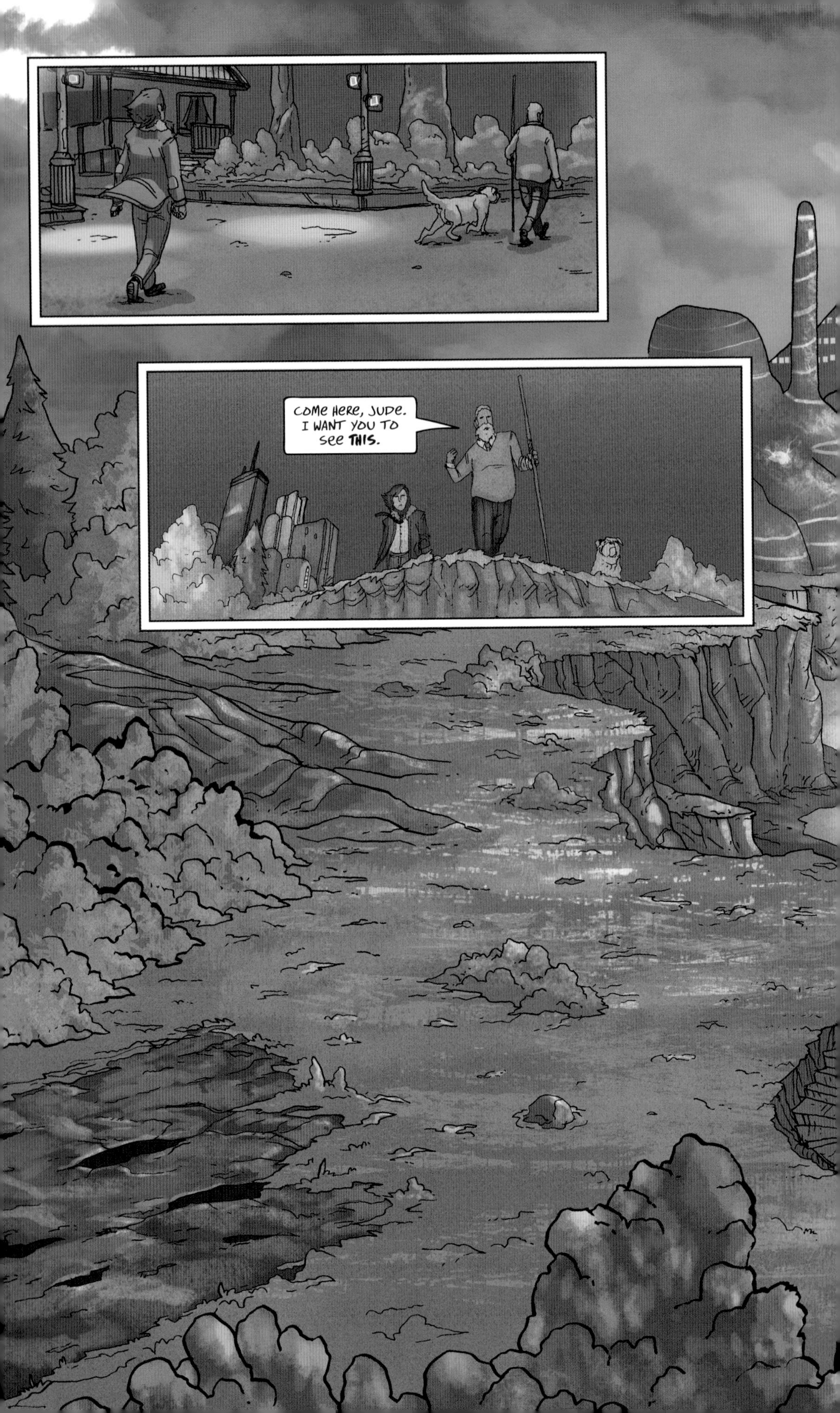
COME HERE, JUDE. I WANT YOU TO SEE THIS.

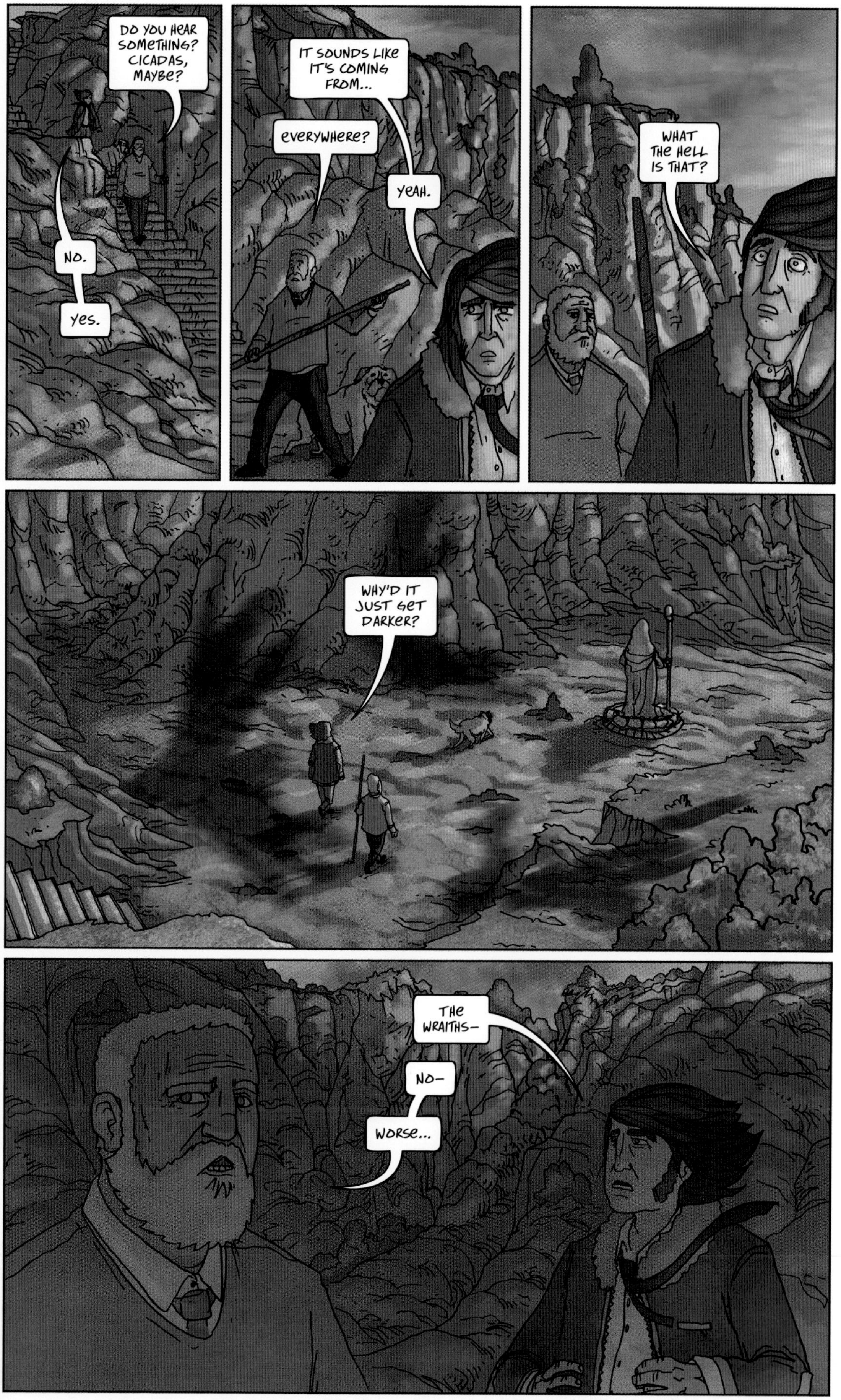
DO YOU HEAR SOMETHING? CICADAS, MAYBE?
NO.
YES.
IT SOUNDS LIKE IT'S COMING FROM...
EVERYWHERE?
YEAH.
WHAT THE HELL IS THAT?
WHY'D IT JUST GET DARKER?
THE WRAITHS—
NO—
WORSE...

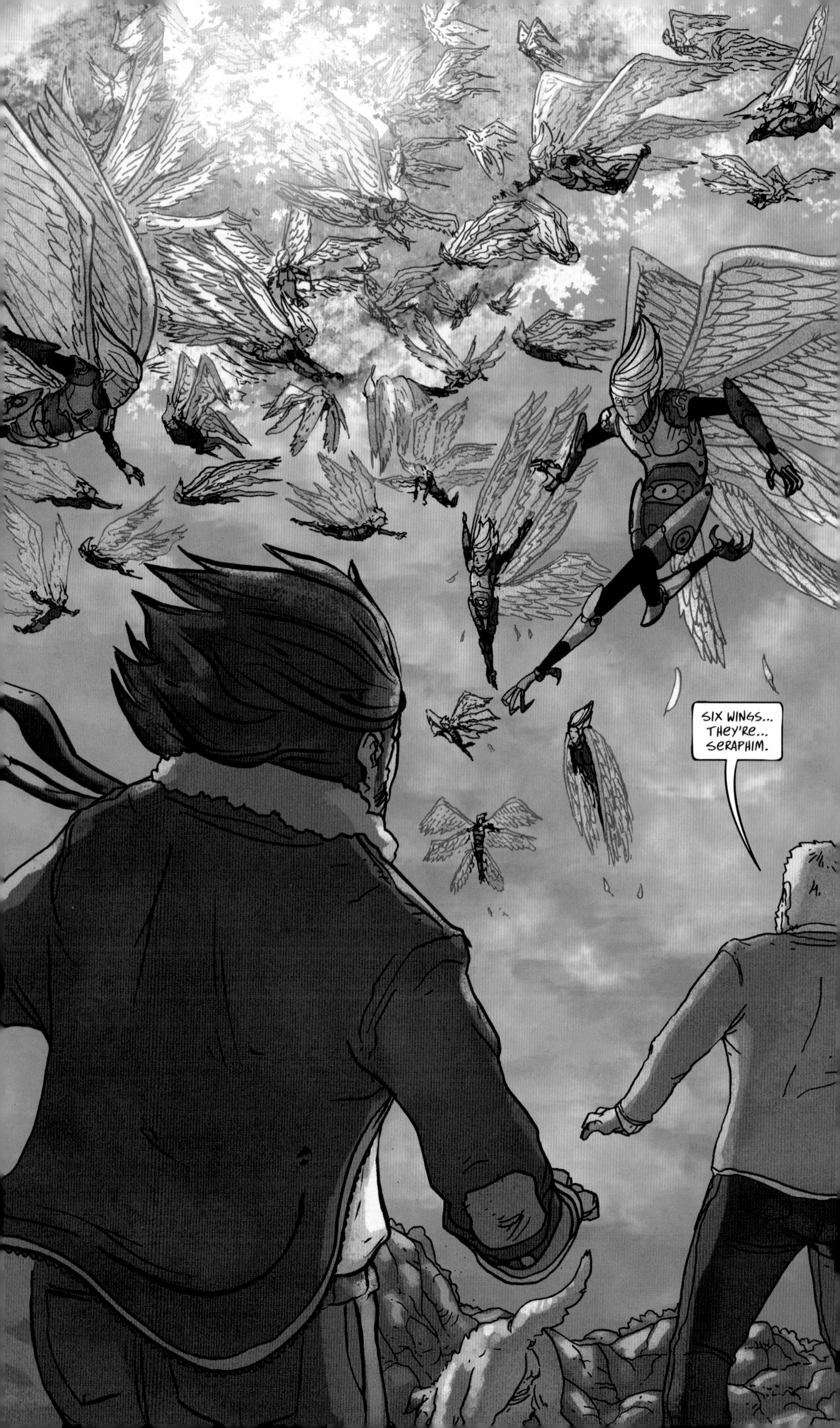
SIX WINGS... THEY'RE... SERAPHIM.

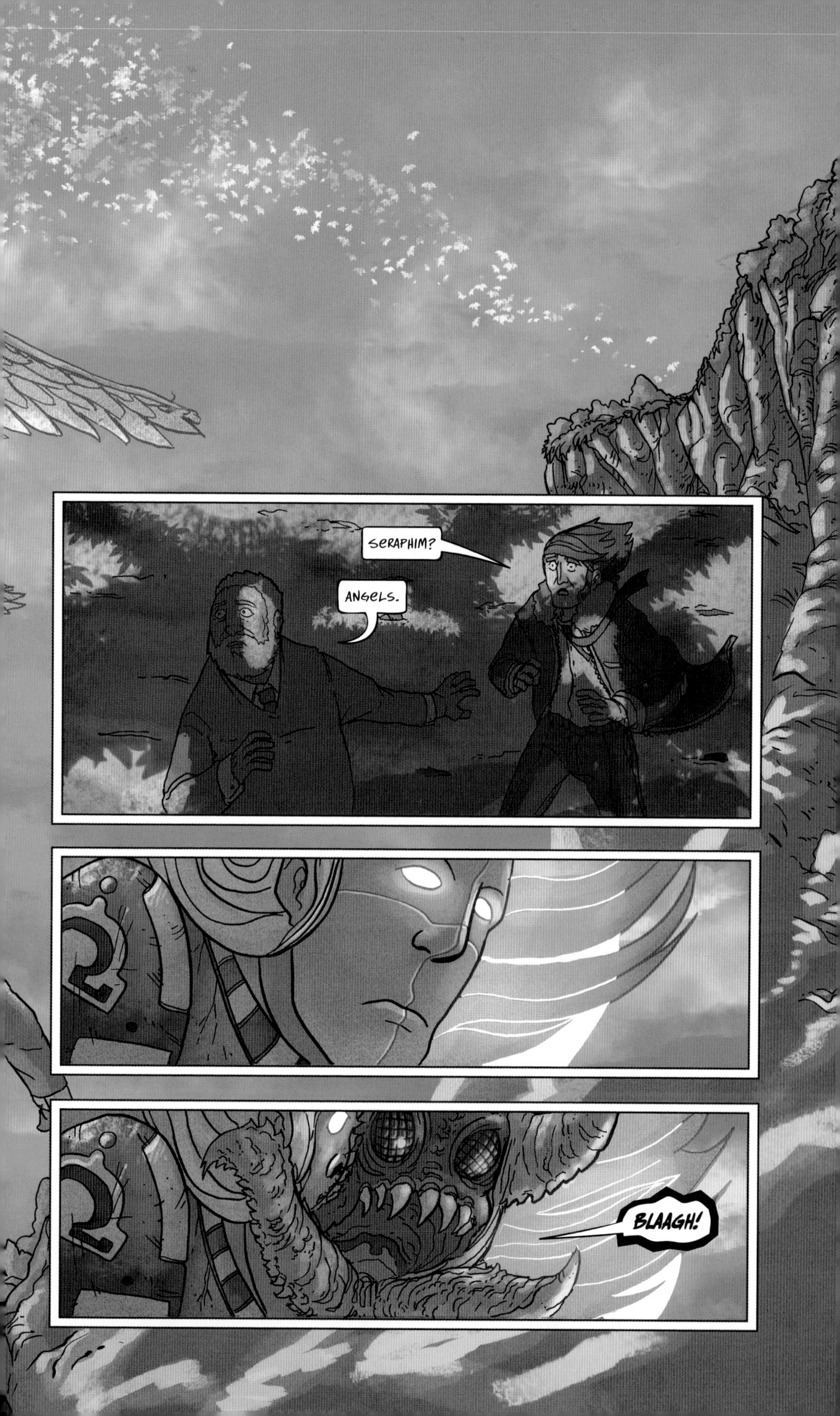
SERAPHIM?
ANGELS.
BLAAGH!

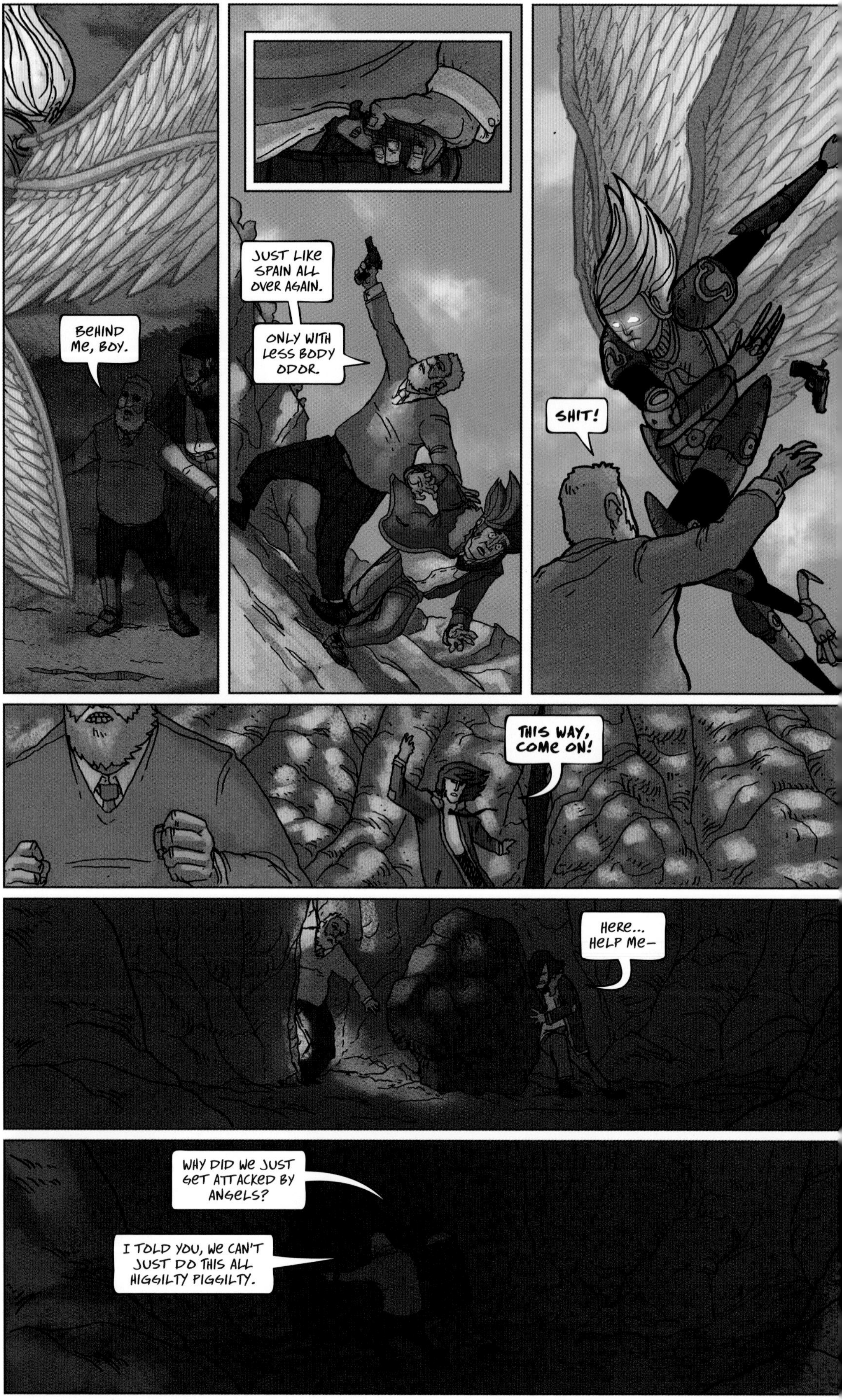

BEHIND ME, BOY.
JUST LIKE SPAIN ALL OVER AGAIN.
ONLY WITH LESS BODY ODOR.
SHIT!
THIS WAY, COME ON!
HERE... HELP ME—
WHY DID WE JUST GET ATTACKED BY ANGELS?
I TOLD YOU, WE CAN'T JUST DO THIS ALL HIGGILTY PIGGILTY.

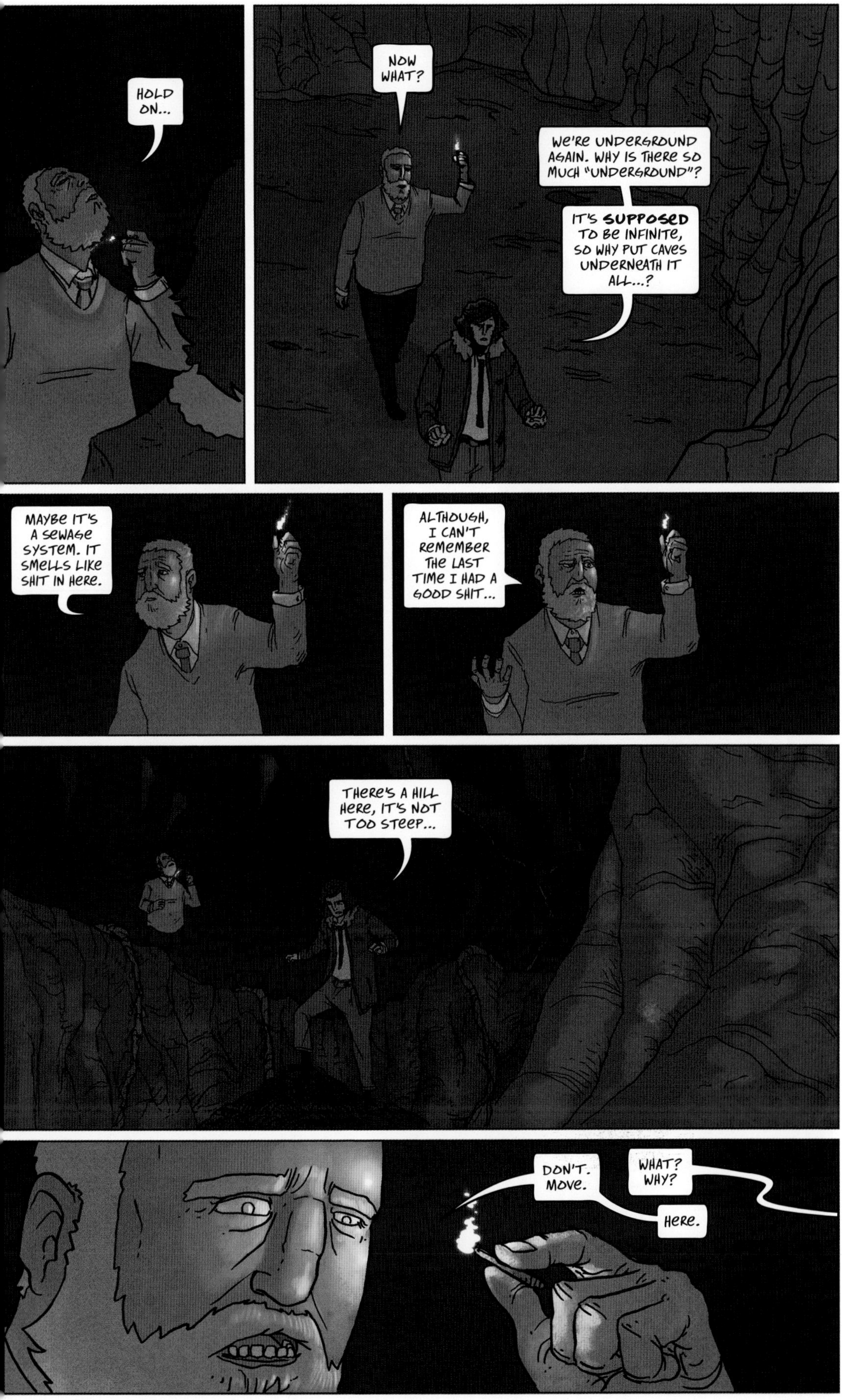
HOLD ON...
NOW WHAT?
WE'RE UNDERGROUND AGAIN. WHY IS THERE SO MUCH "UNDERGROUND"?
IT'S **SUPPOSED** TO BE INFINITE, SO WHY PUT CAVES UNDERNEATH IT ALL...?
MAYBE IT'S A SEWAGE SYSTEM. IT SMELLS LIKE SHIT IN HERE.
ALTHOUGH, I CAN'T REMEMBER THE LAST TIME I HAD A GOOD SHIT...
THERE'S A HILL HERE, IT'S NOT TOO STEEP...
DON'T. MOVE.
WHAT? WHY?
HERE.

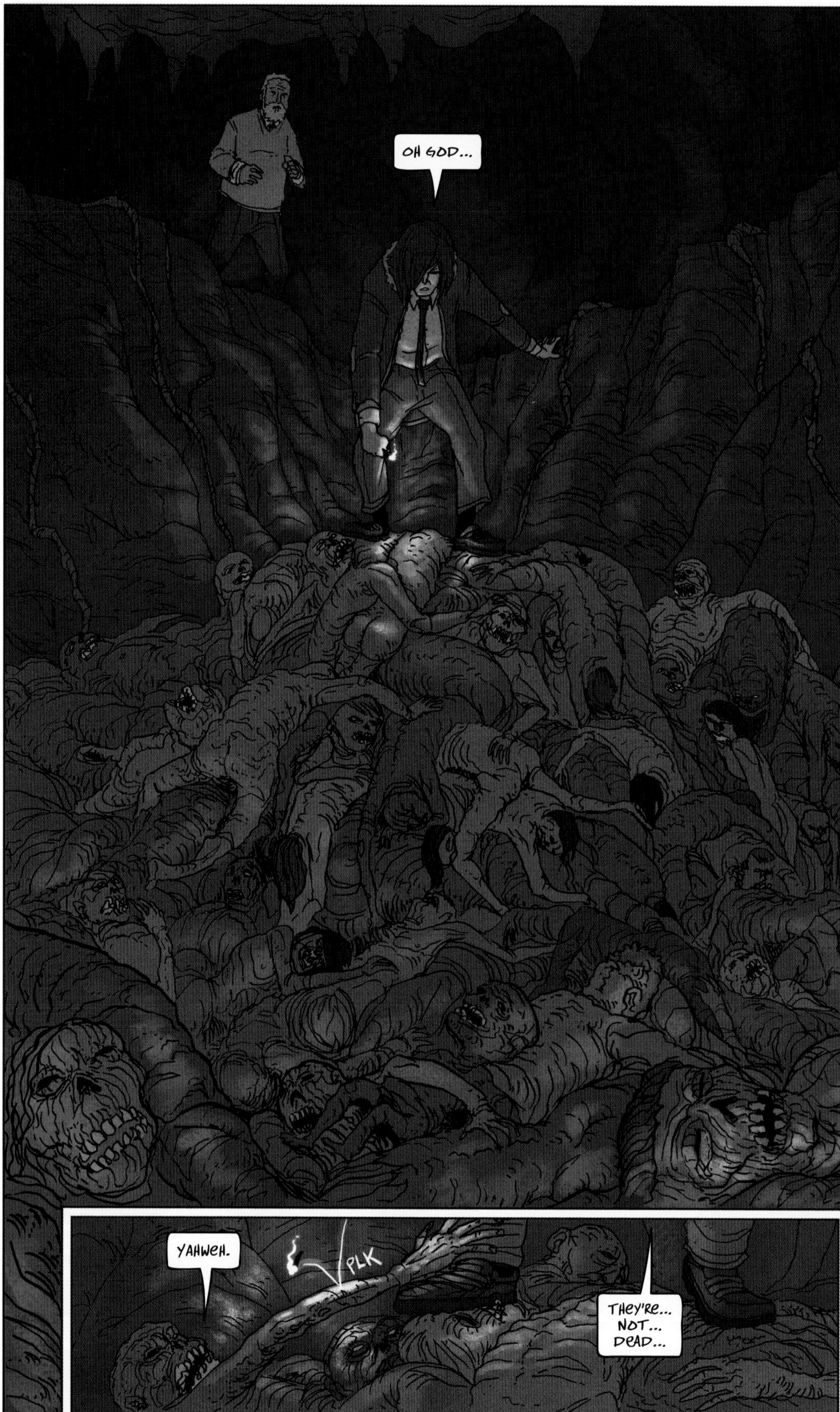
OH GOD...
YAHWEH.
PLK
THEY'RE... NOT... DEAD...

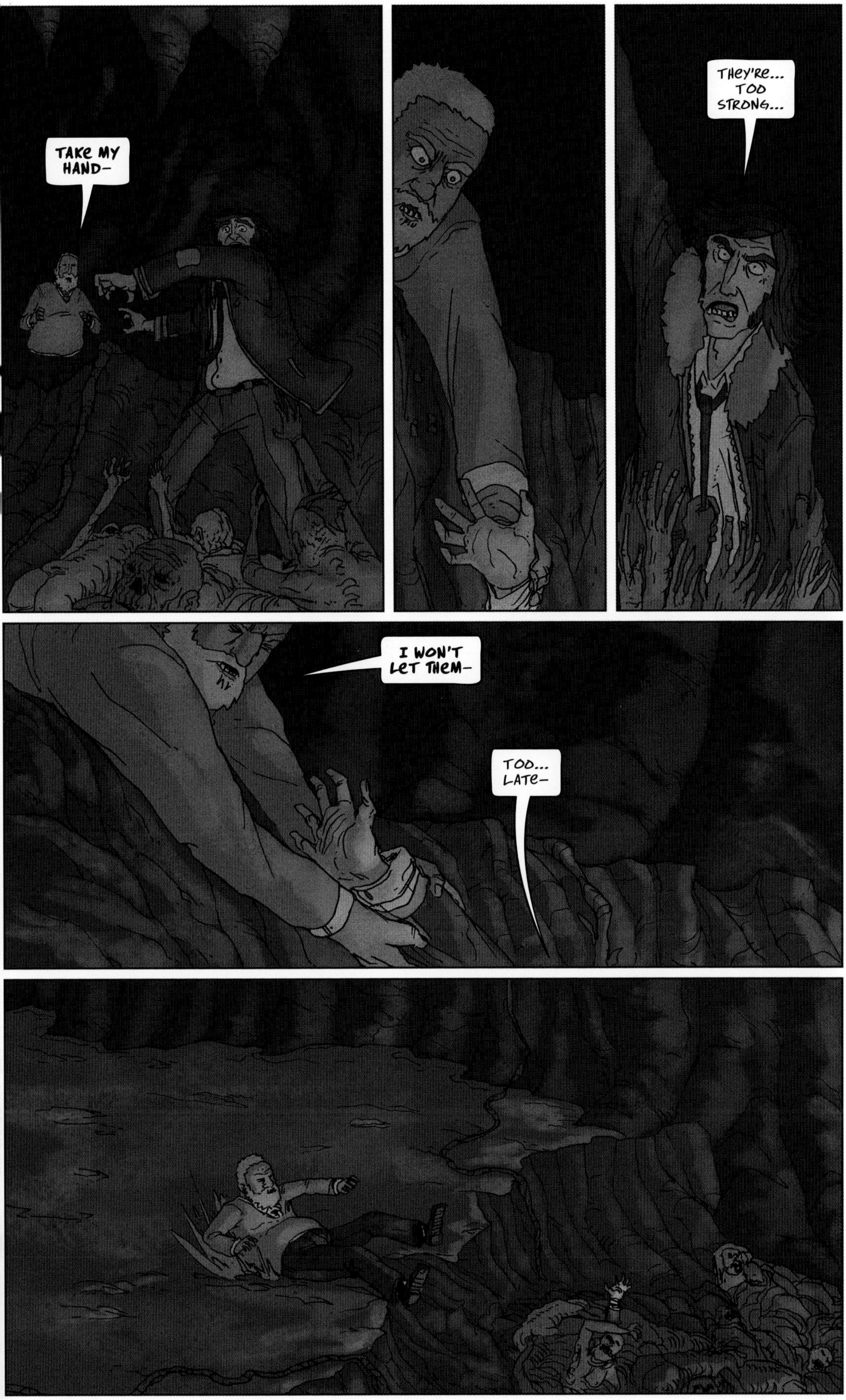
TAKE MY HAND-
THEY'RE... TOO STRONG...
I WON'T LET THEM-
TOO... LATE-

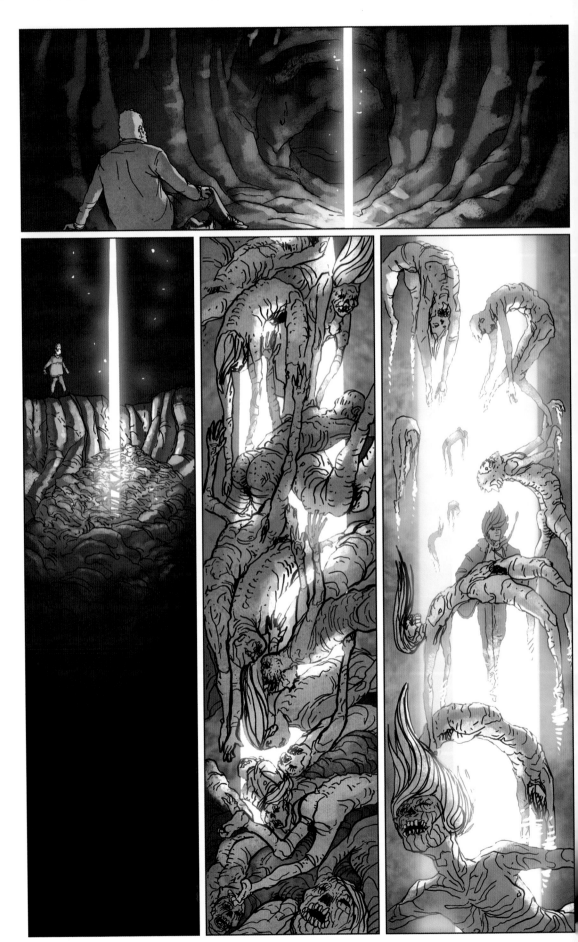

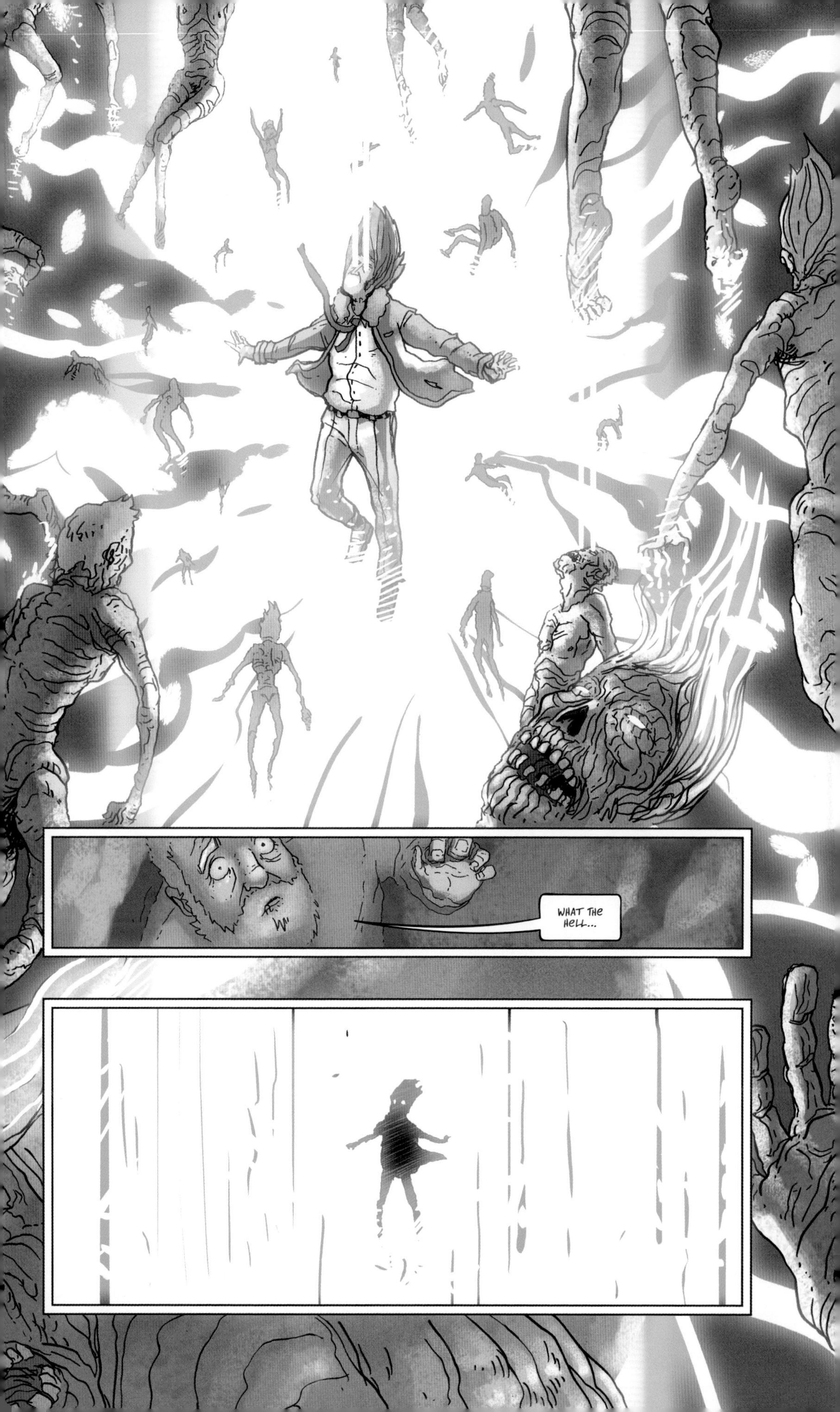
WHAT THE HELL...

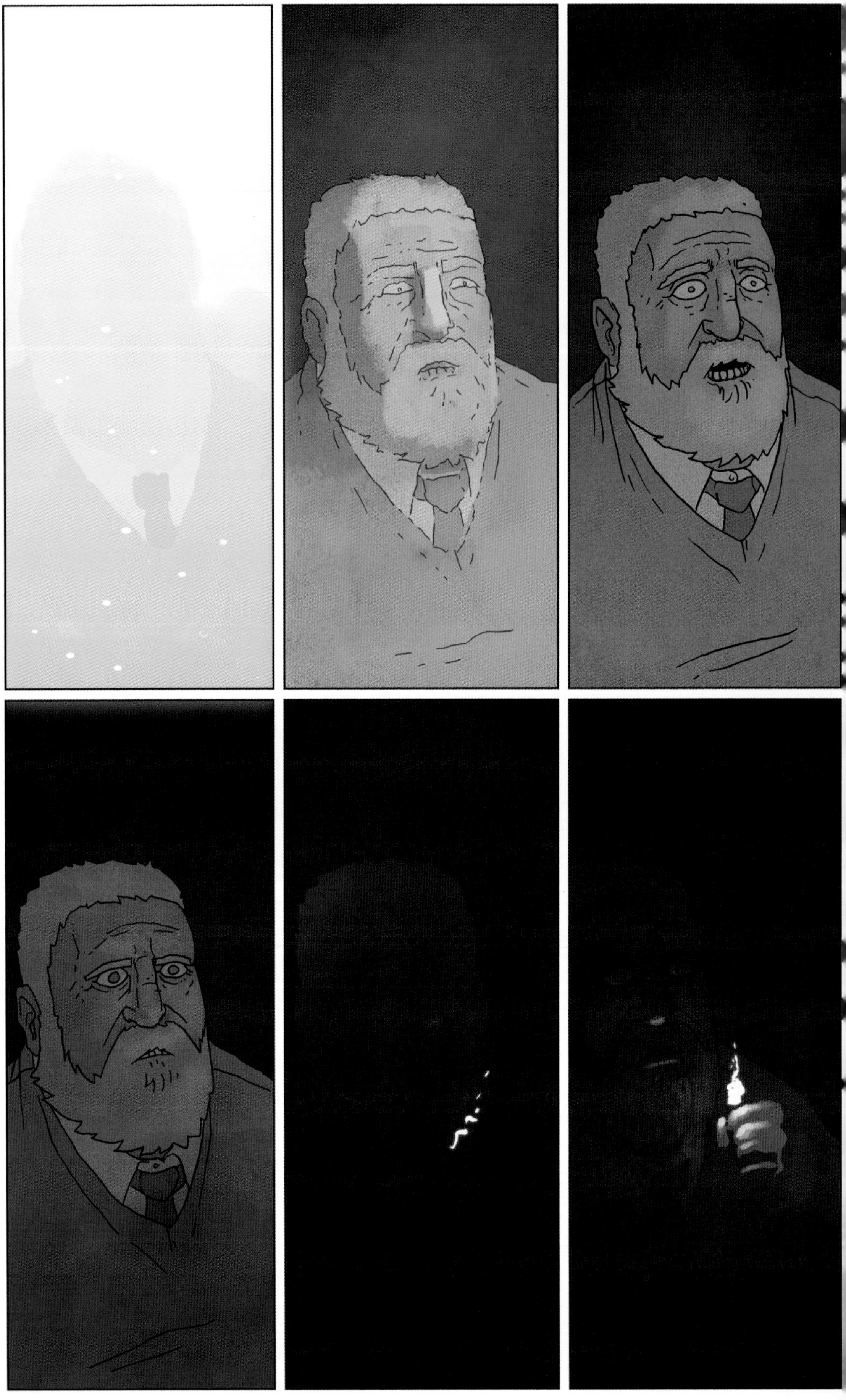

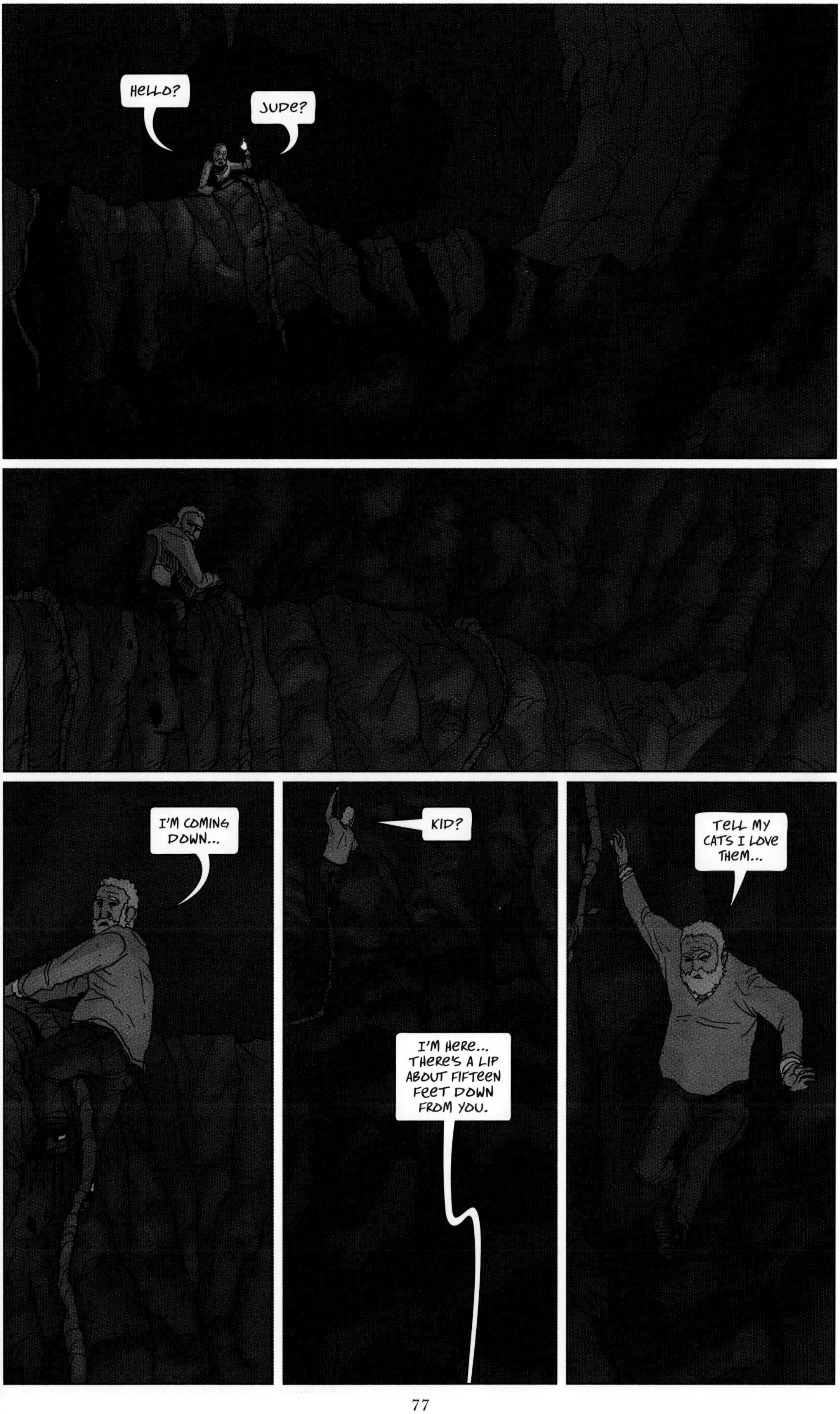
HELLO?
JUDE?
I'M COMING DOWN...
KID?
I'M HERE... THERE'S A LIP ABOUT FIFTEEN FEET DOWN FROM YOU.
TELL MY CATS I LOVE THEM...

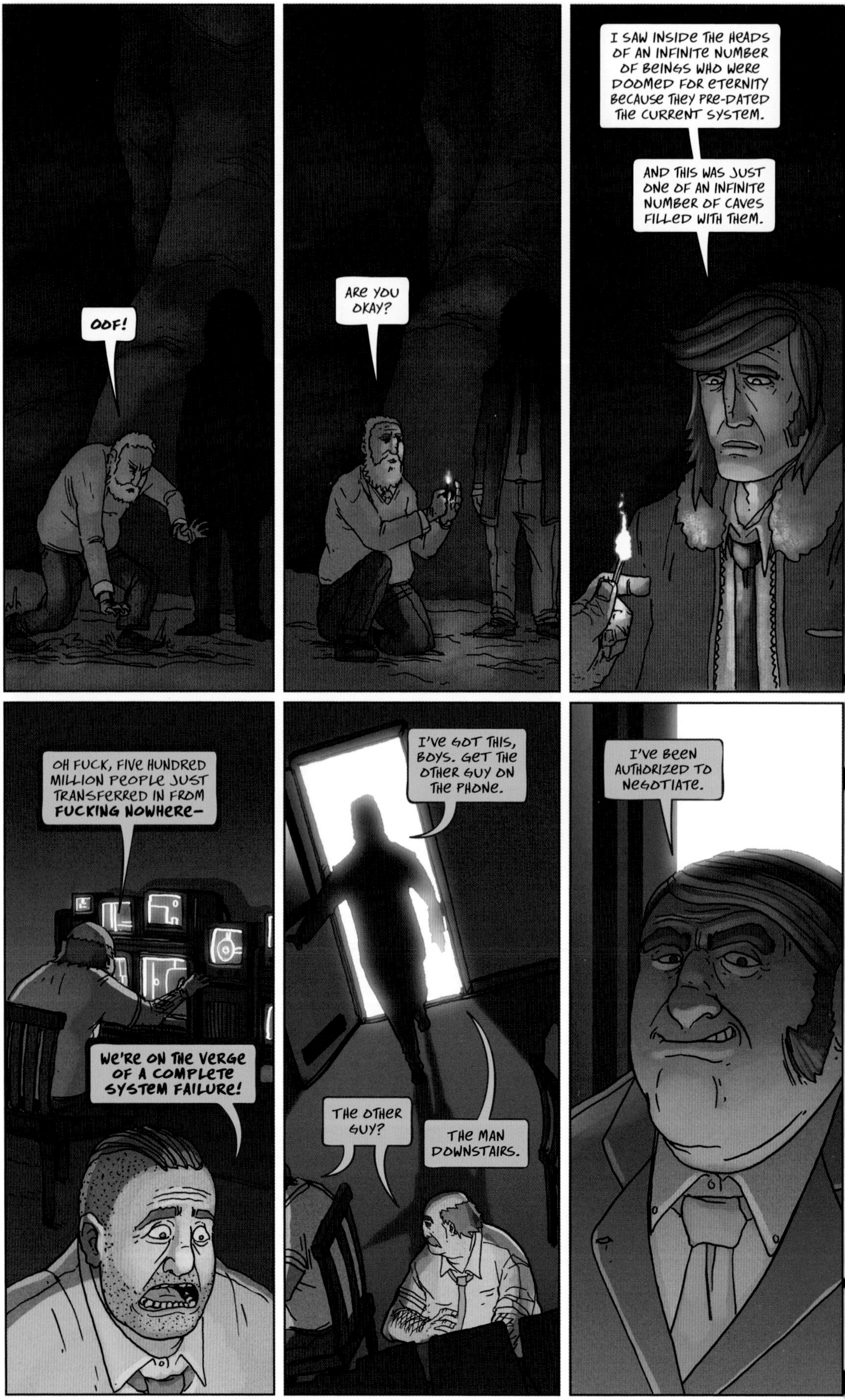
OOF!
ARE YOU OKAY?
I SAW INSIDE THE HEADS OF AN INFINITE NUMBER OF BEINGS WHO WERE DOOMED FOR ETERNITY BECAUSE THEY PRE-DATED THE CURRENT SYSTEM.
AND THIS WAS JUST ONE OF AN INFINITE NUMBER OF CAVES FILLED WITH THEM.
OH FUCK, FIVE HUNDRED MILLION PEOPLE JUST TRANSFERRED IN FROM FUCKING NOWHERE—
WE'RE ON THE VERGE OF A COMPLETE SYSTEM FAILURE!
I'VE GOT THIS, BOYS. GET THE OTHER GUY ON THE PHONE.
THE OTHER GUY?
THE MAN DOWNSTAIRS.
I'VE BEEN AUTHORIZED TO NEGOTIATE.

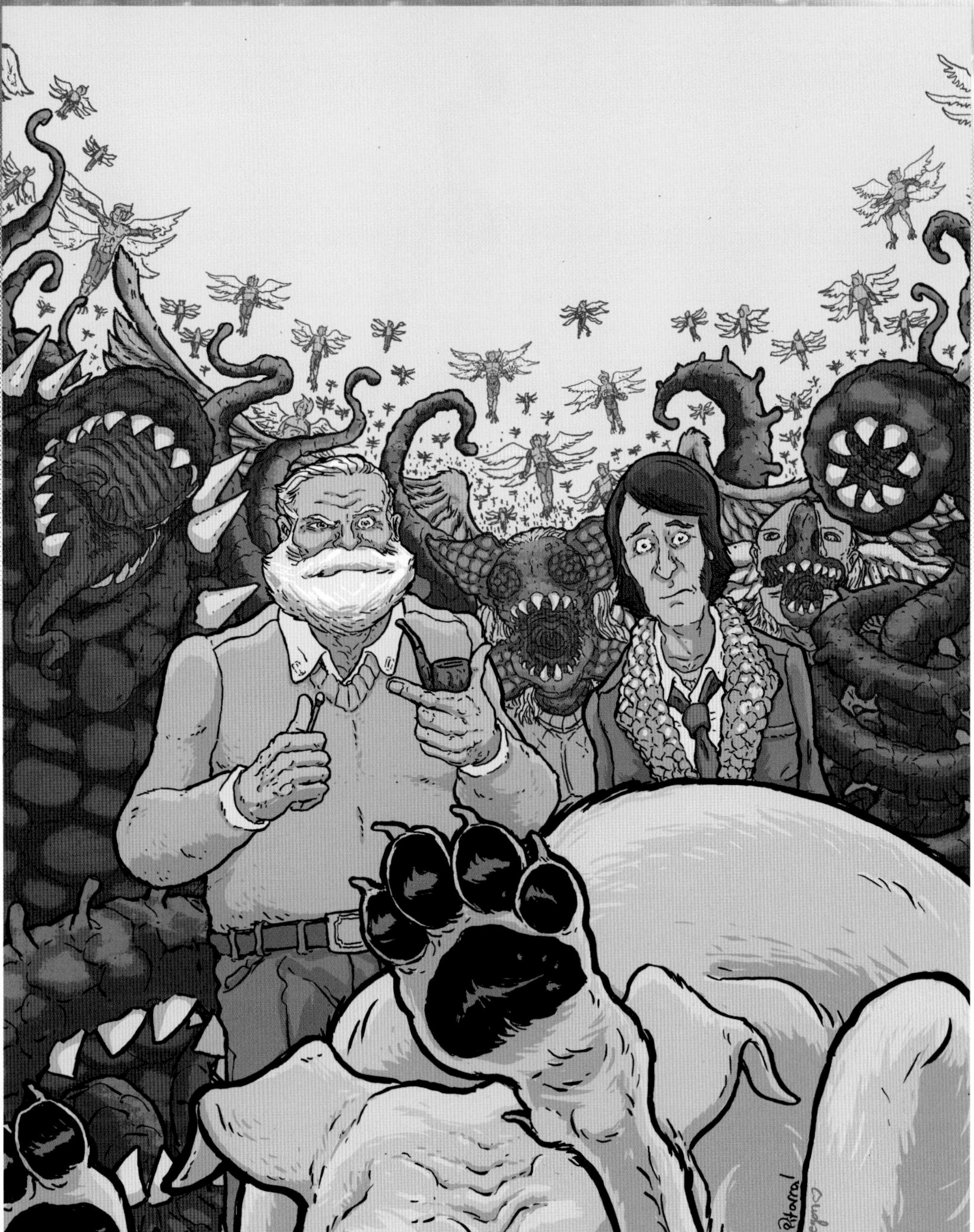

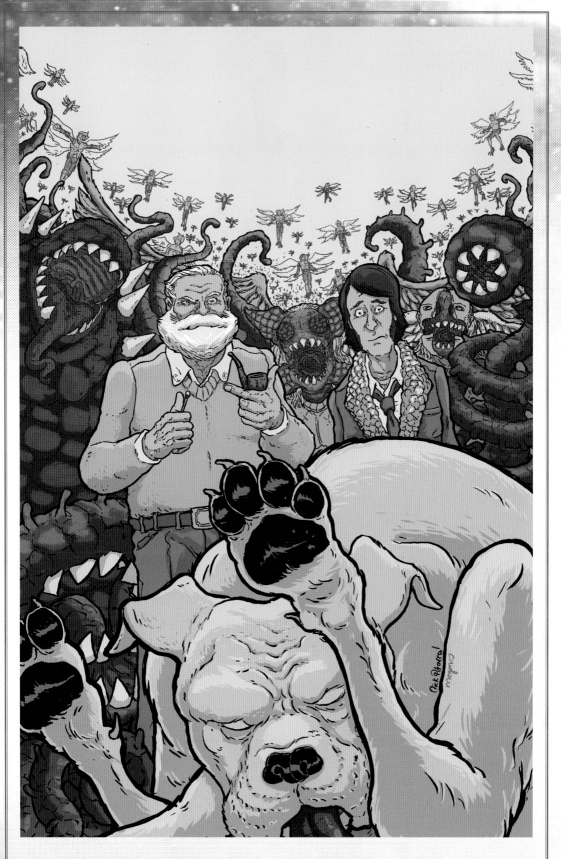

Chapter Four

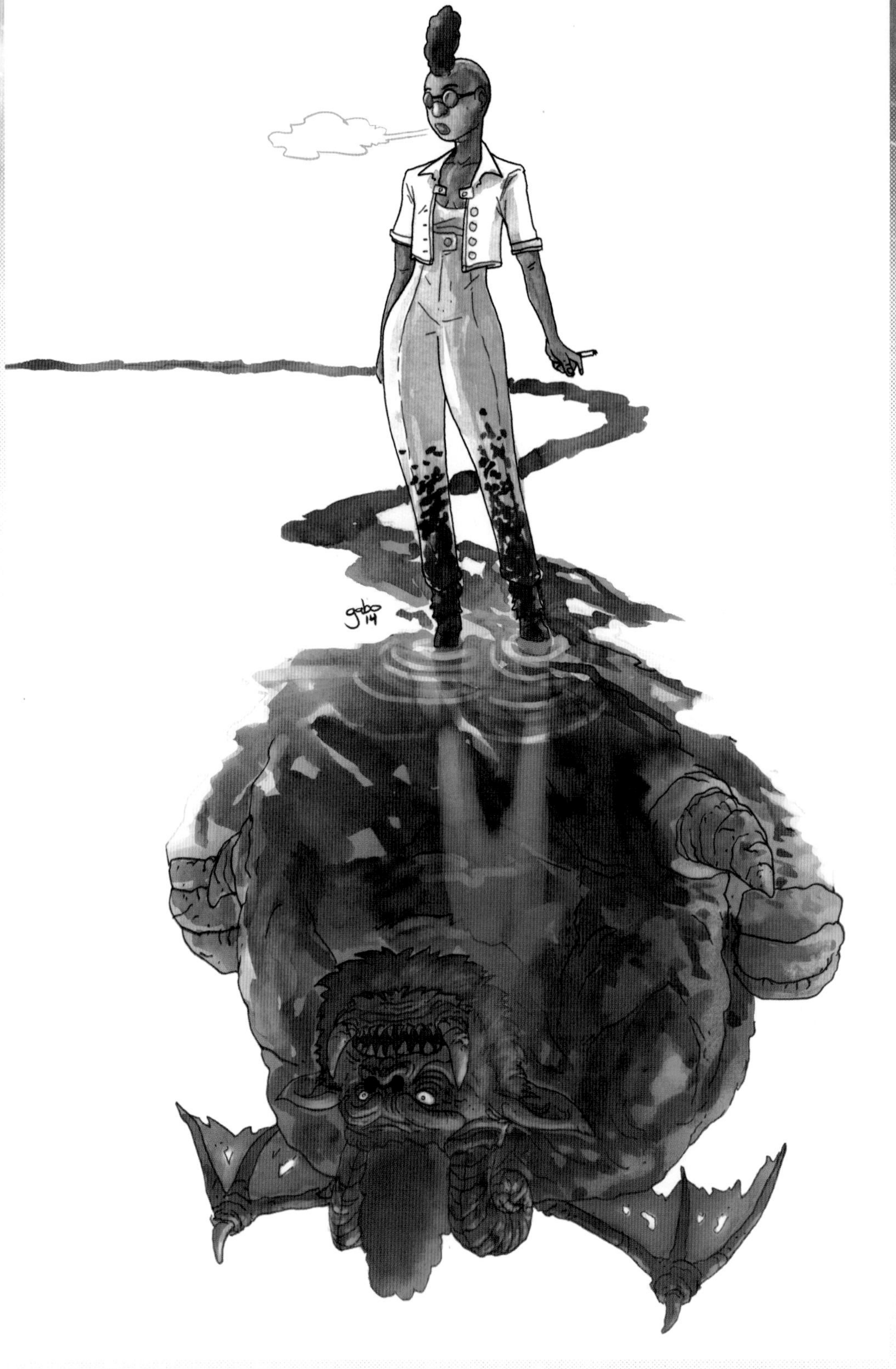
gabo
14

THE LIFE AFTER

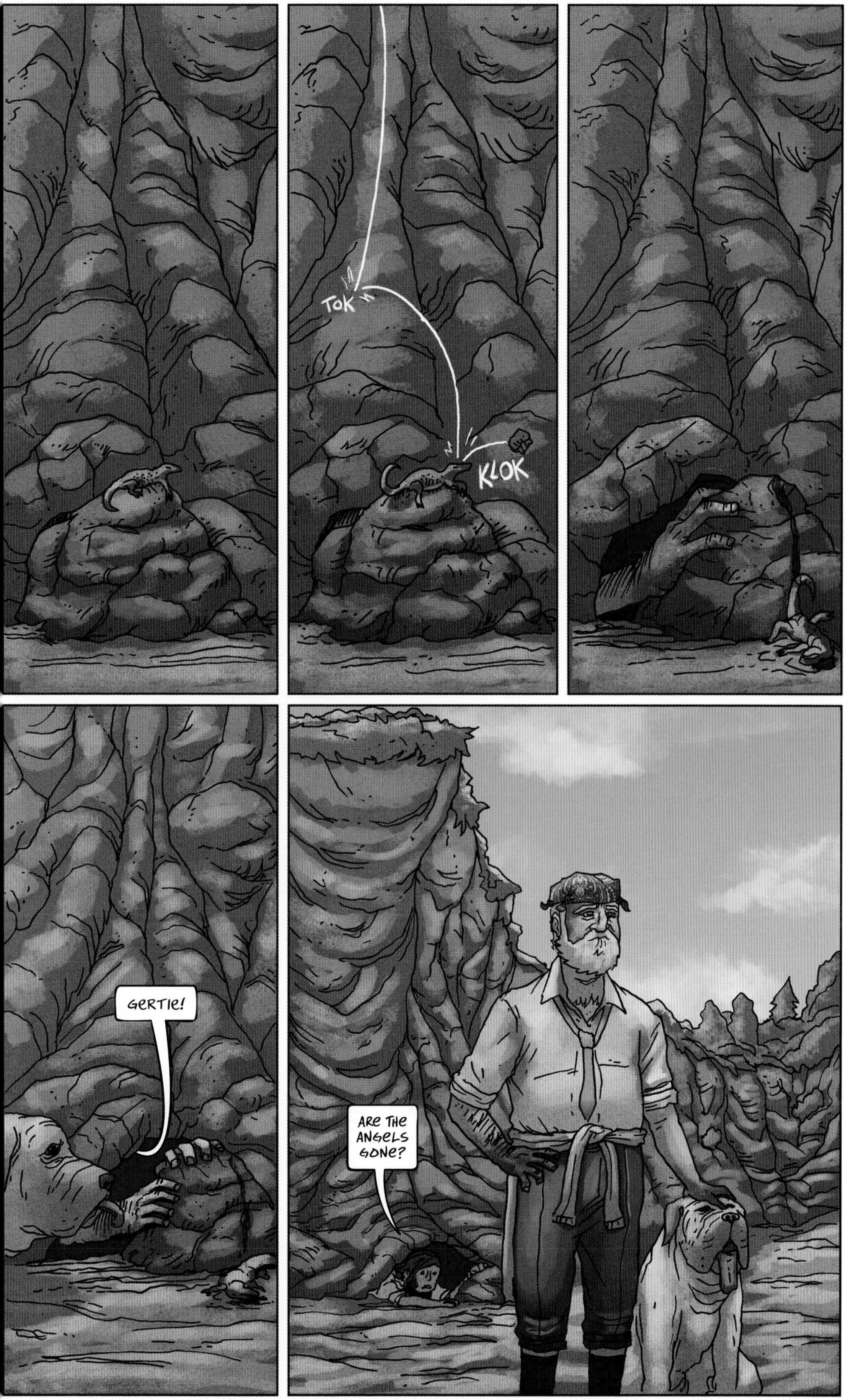
TOK
KLOK
GERTIE!
ARE THE ANGELS GONE?

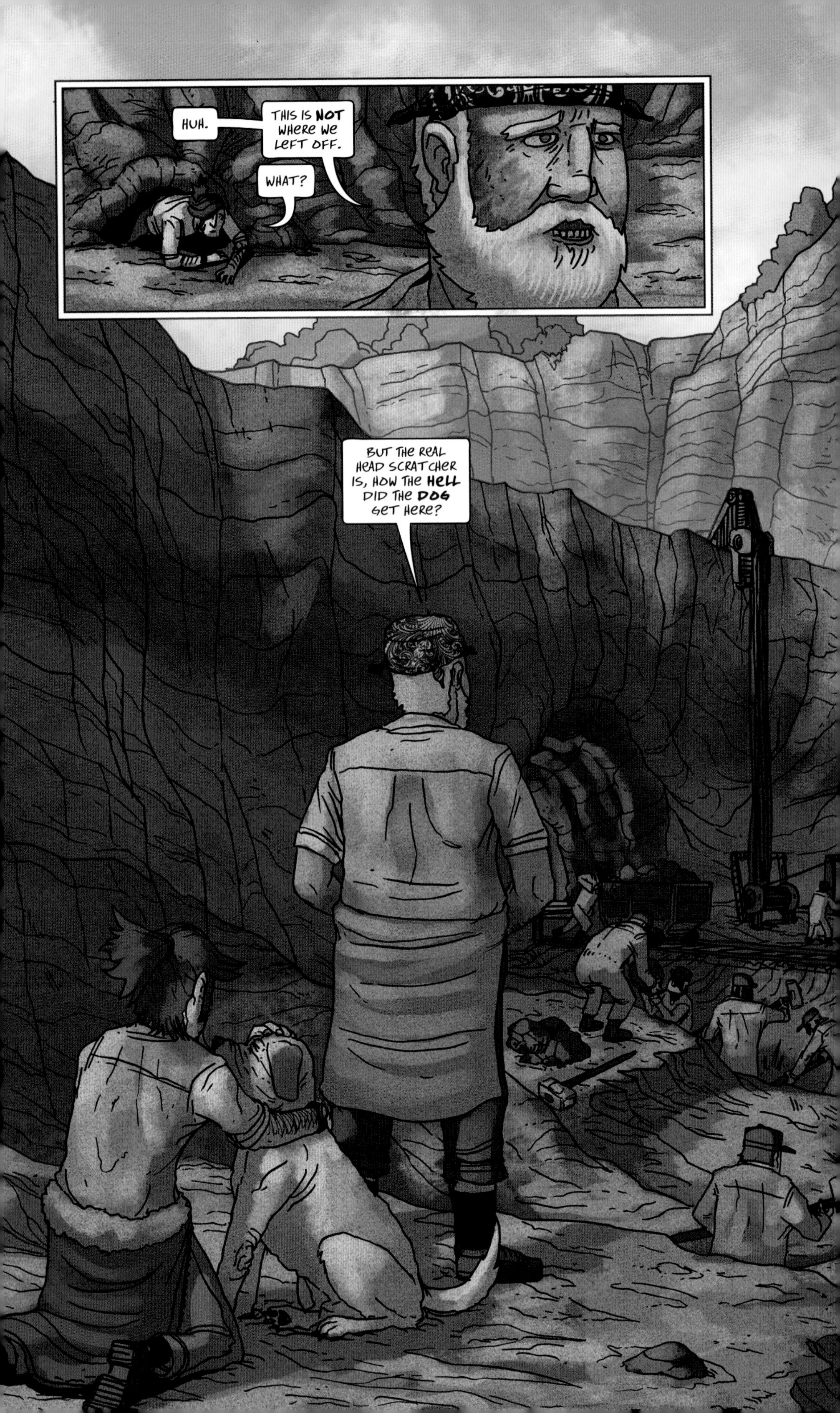
HUH.
THIS IS NOT WHERE WE LEFT OFF.
WHAT?
BUT THE REAL HEAD SCRATCHER IS, HOW THE HELL DID THE DOG GET HERE?

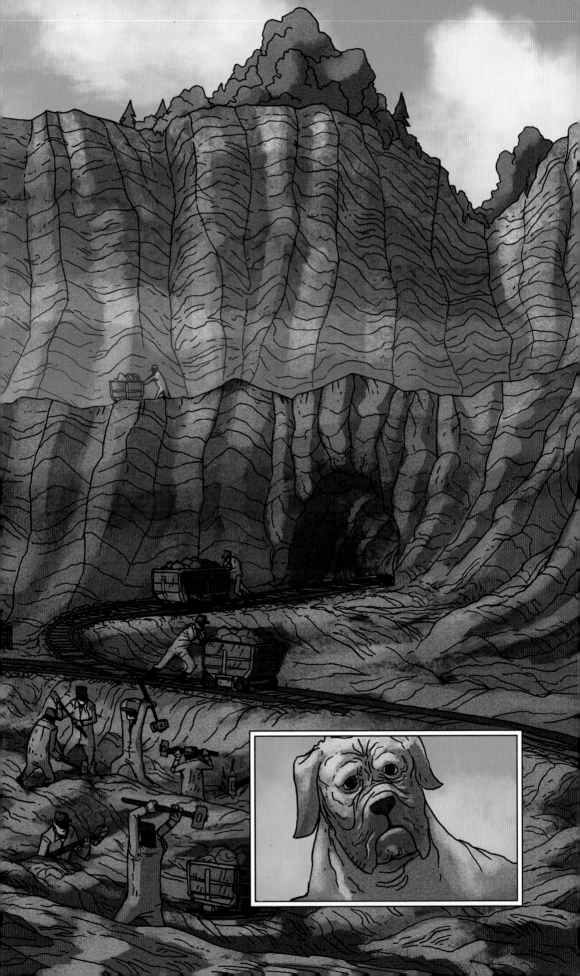

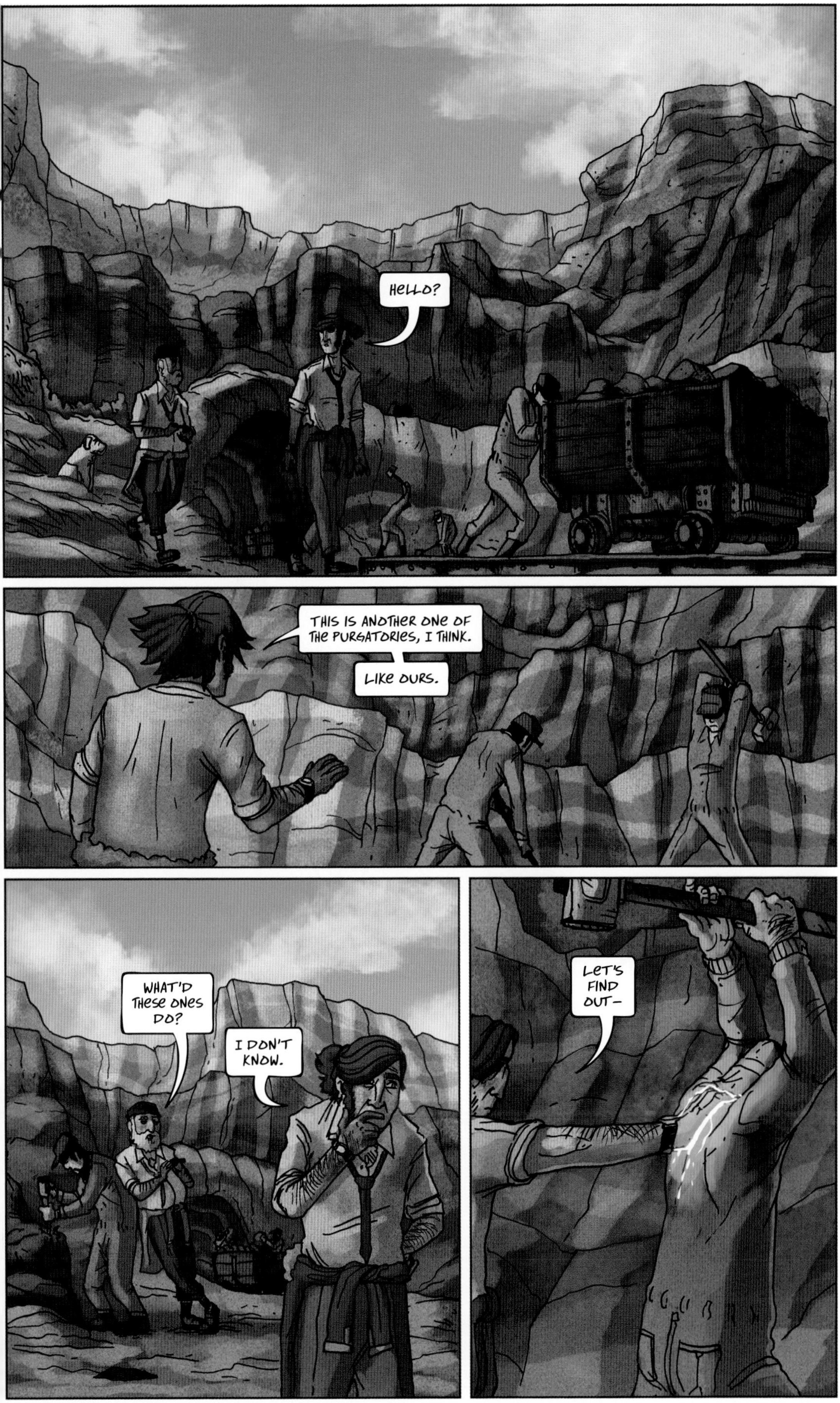
HELLO?
THIS IS ANOTHER ONE OF THE PURGATORIES, I THINK.
LIKE OURS.
WHAT'D THESE ONES DO?
I DON'T KNOW.
LET'S FIND OUT–

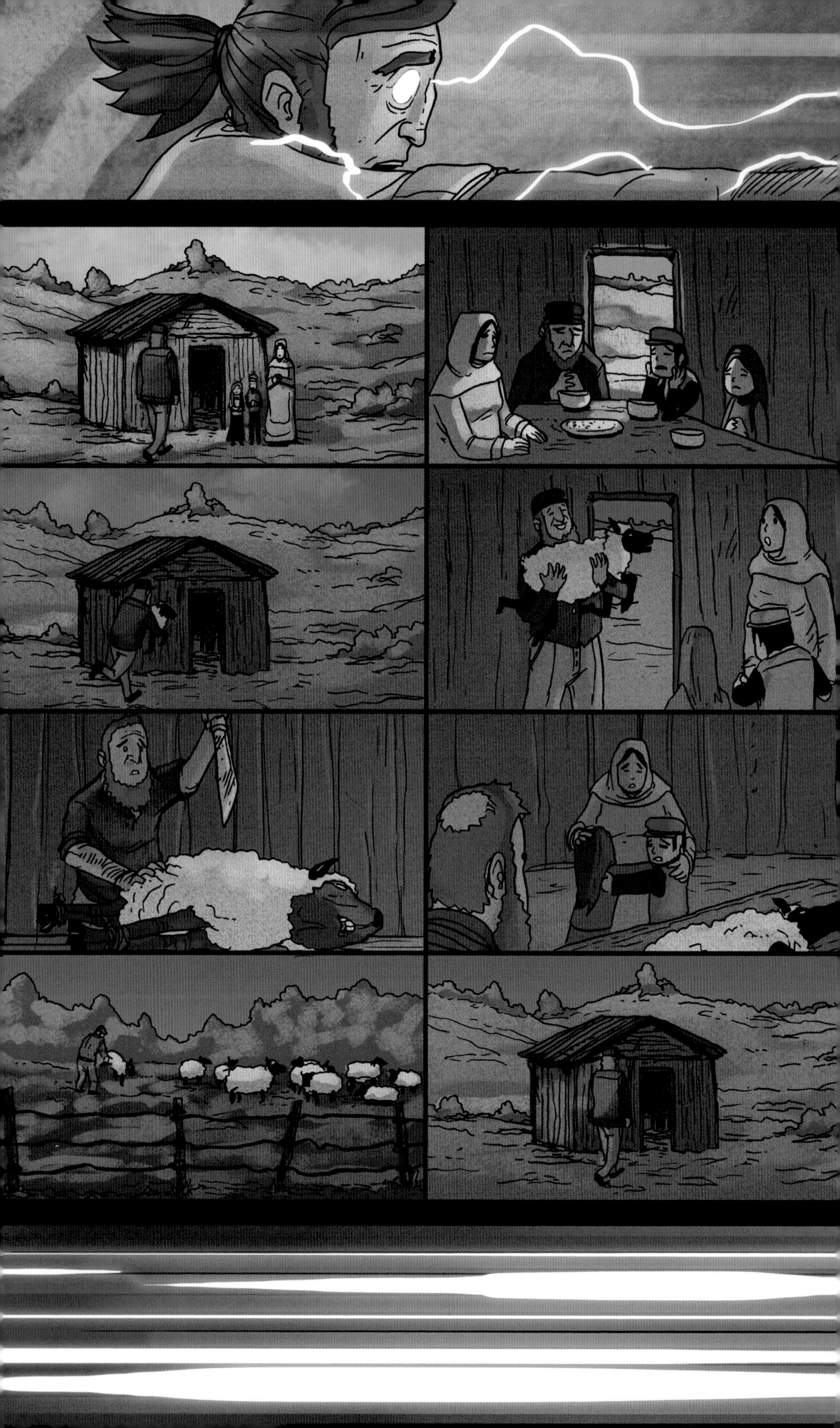

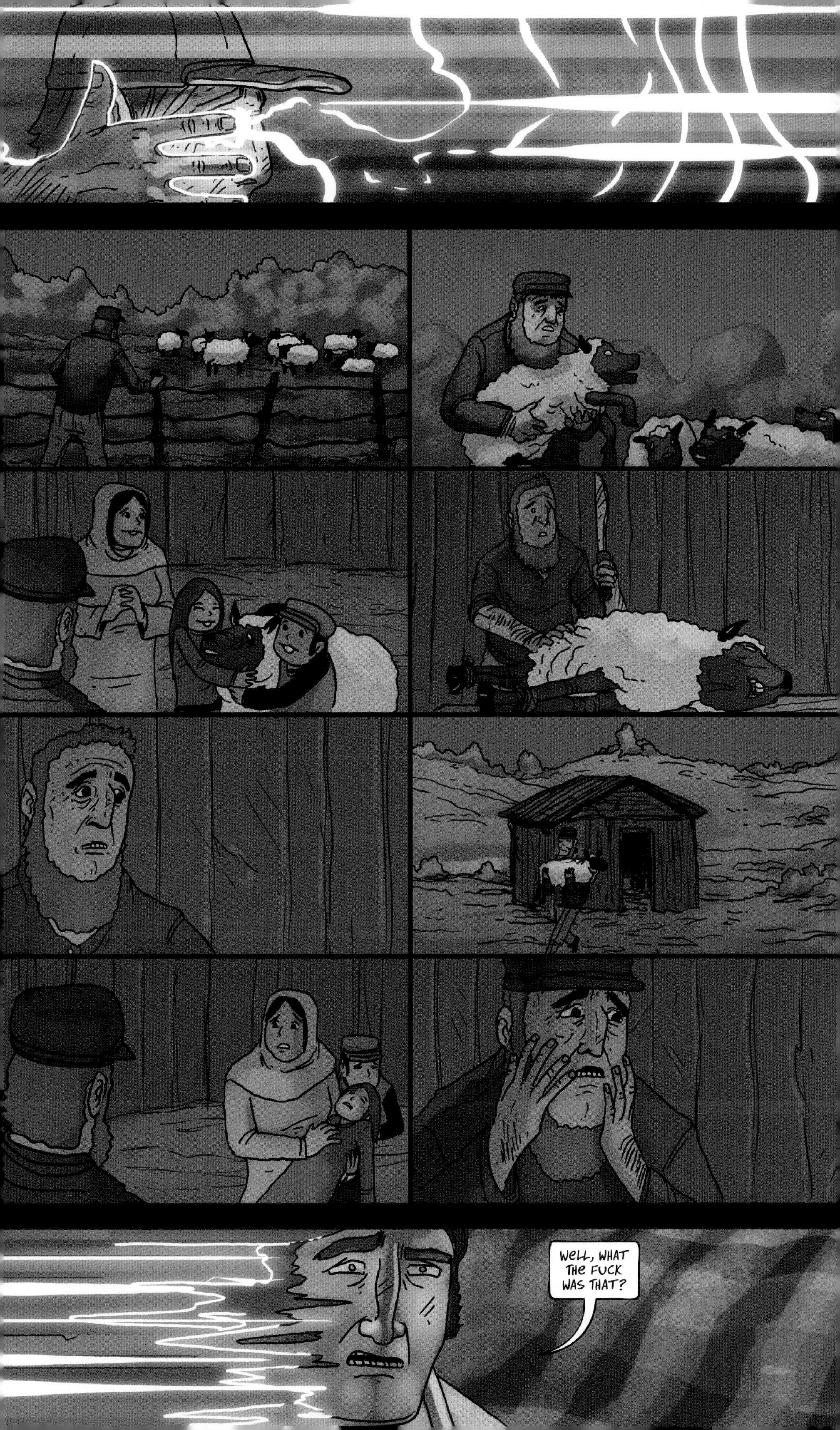
WELL, WHAT THE FUCK WAS THAT?

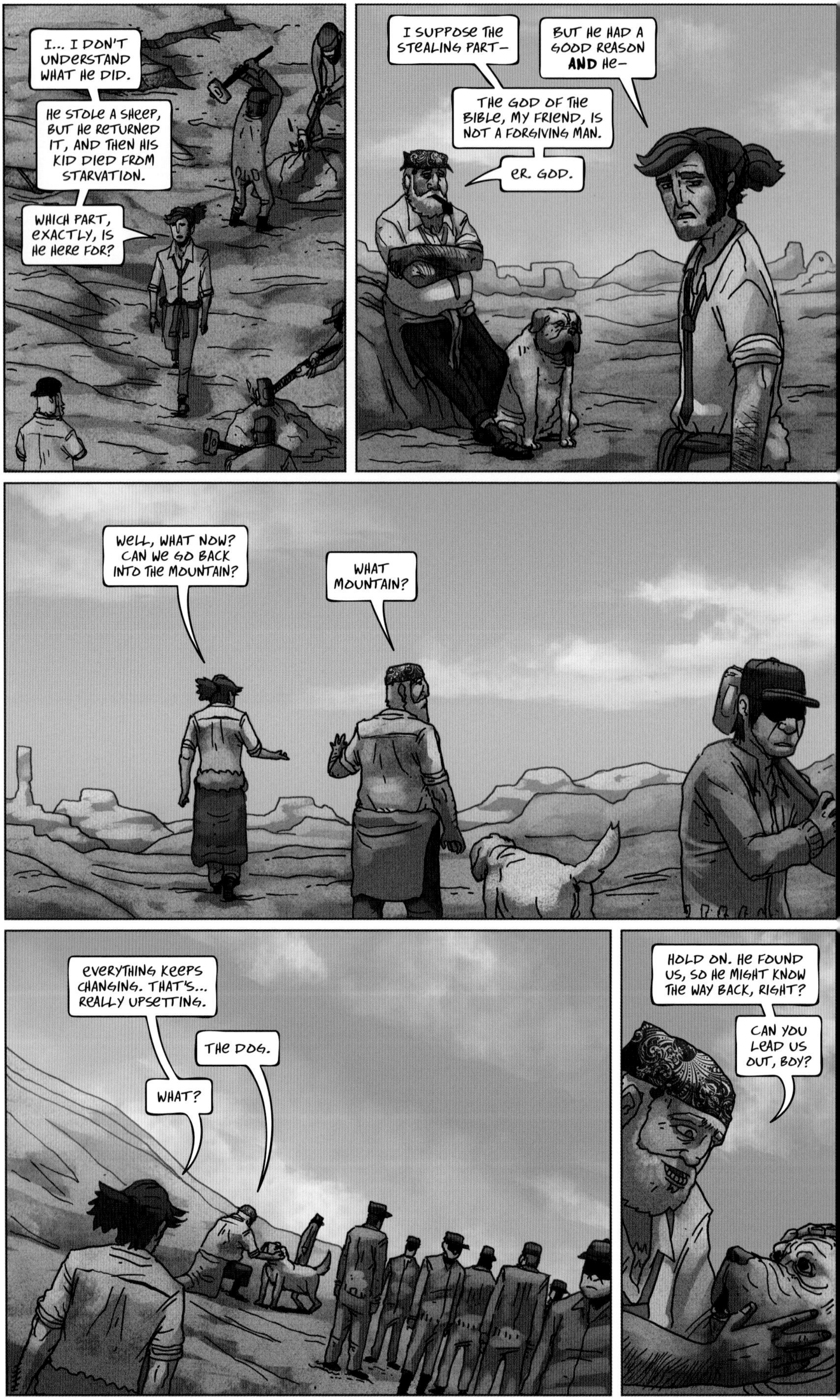
I... I DON'T UNDERSTAND WHAT HE DID.
HE STOLE A SHEEP, BUT HE RETURNED IT, AND THEN HIS KID DIED FROM STARVATION.
WHICH PART, EXACTLY, IS HE HERE FOR?
I SUPPOSE THE STEALING PART—
BUT HE HAD A GOOD REASON **AND** HE—
THE GOD OF THE BIBLE, MY FRIEND, IS NOT A FORGIVING MAN.
ER. GOD.
WELL, WHAT NOW? CAN WE GO BACK INTO THE MOUNTAIN?
WHAT MOUNTAIN?
EVERYTHING KEEPS CHANGING. THAT'S... REALLY UPSETTING.
THE DOG.
WHAT?
HOLD ON. HE FOUND US, SO HE MIGHT KNOW THE WAY BACK, RIGHT?
CAN YOU LEAD US OUT, BOY?

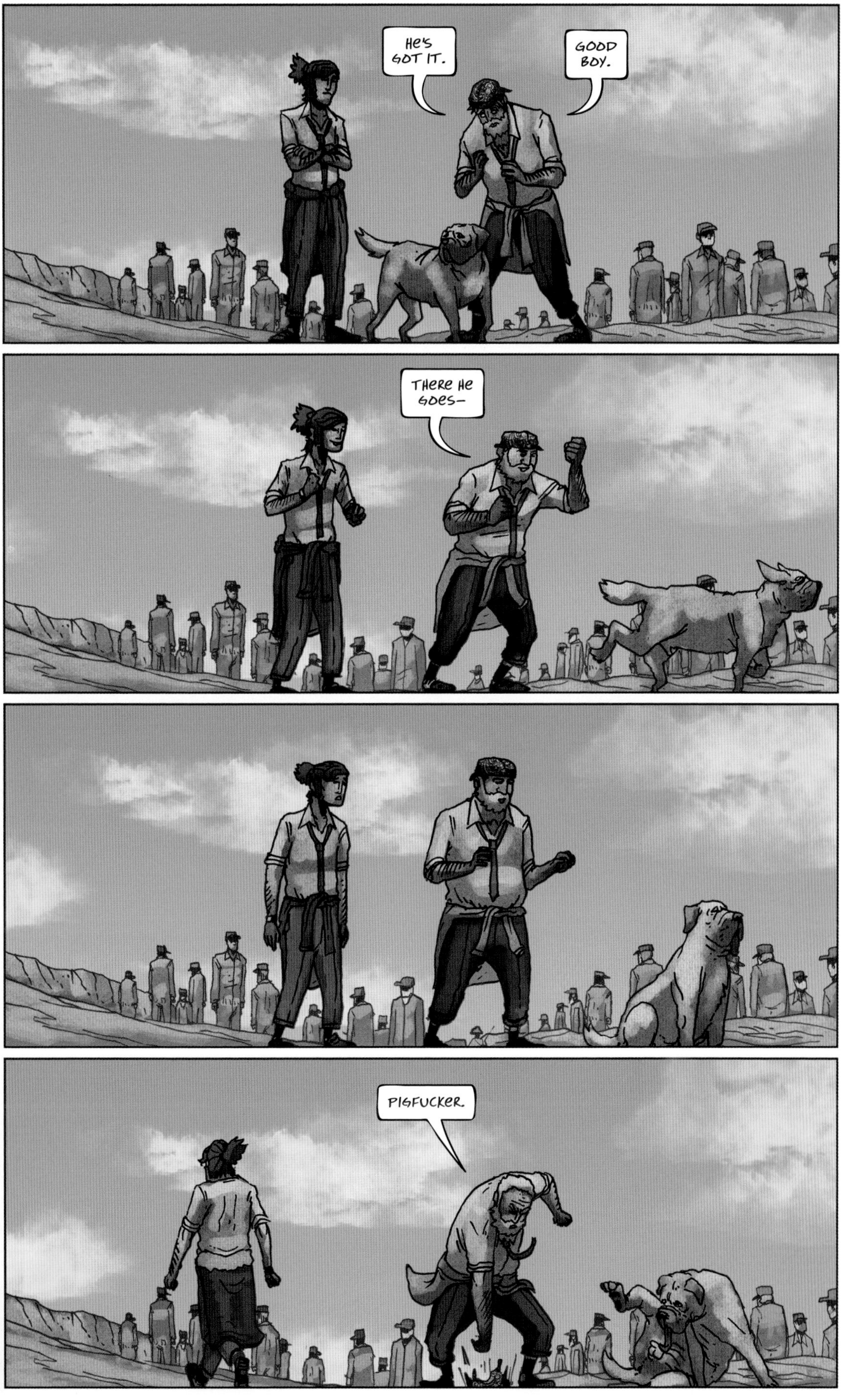
HE'S GOT IT.
GOOD BOY.
THERE HE GOES—
PIGFUCKER.

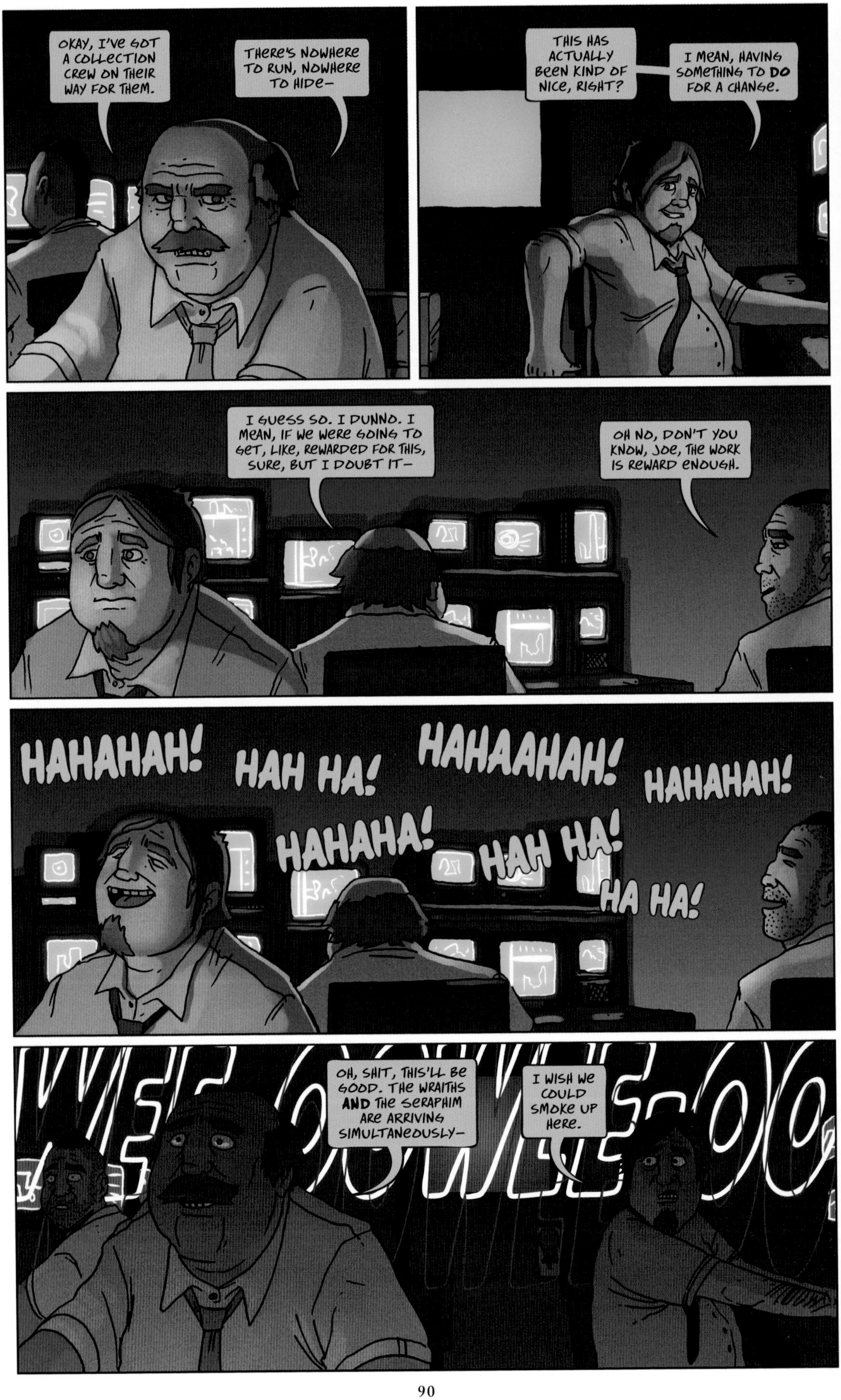
OKAY, I'VE GOT A COLLECTION CREW ON THEIR WAY FOR THEM.
THERE'S NOWHERE TO RUN, NOWHERE TO HIDE—
THIS HAS ACTUALLY BEEN KIND OF NICE, RIGHT?
I MEAN, HAVING SOMETHING TO **DO** FOR A CHANGE.
I GUESS SO. I DUNNO. I MEAN, IF WE WERE GOING TO GET, LIKE, REWARDED FOR THIS, SURE, BUT I DOUBT IT—
OH NO, DON'T YOU KNOW, JOE, THE WORK IS REWARD ENOUGH.
HAHAHAH!
HAH HA!
HAHAAAHAH!
HAHAHAH!
HAHAHA!
HAH HA!
HA HA!
OH, SHIT, THIS'LL BE GOOD. THE WRAITHS **AND** THE SERAPHIM ARE ARRIVING SIMULTANEOUSLY—
I WISH WE COULD SMOKE UP HERE.

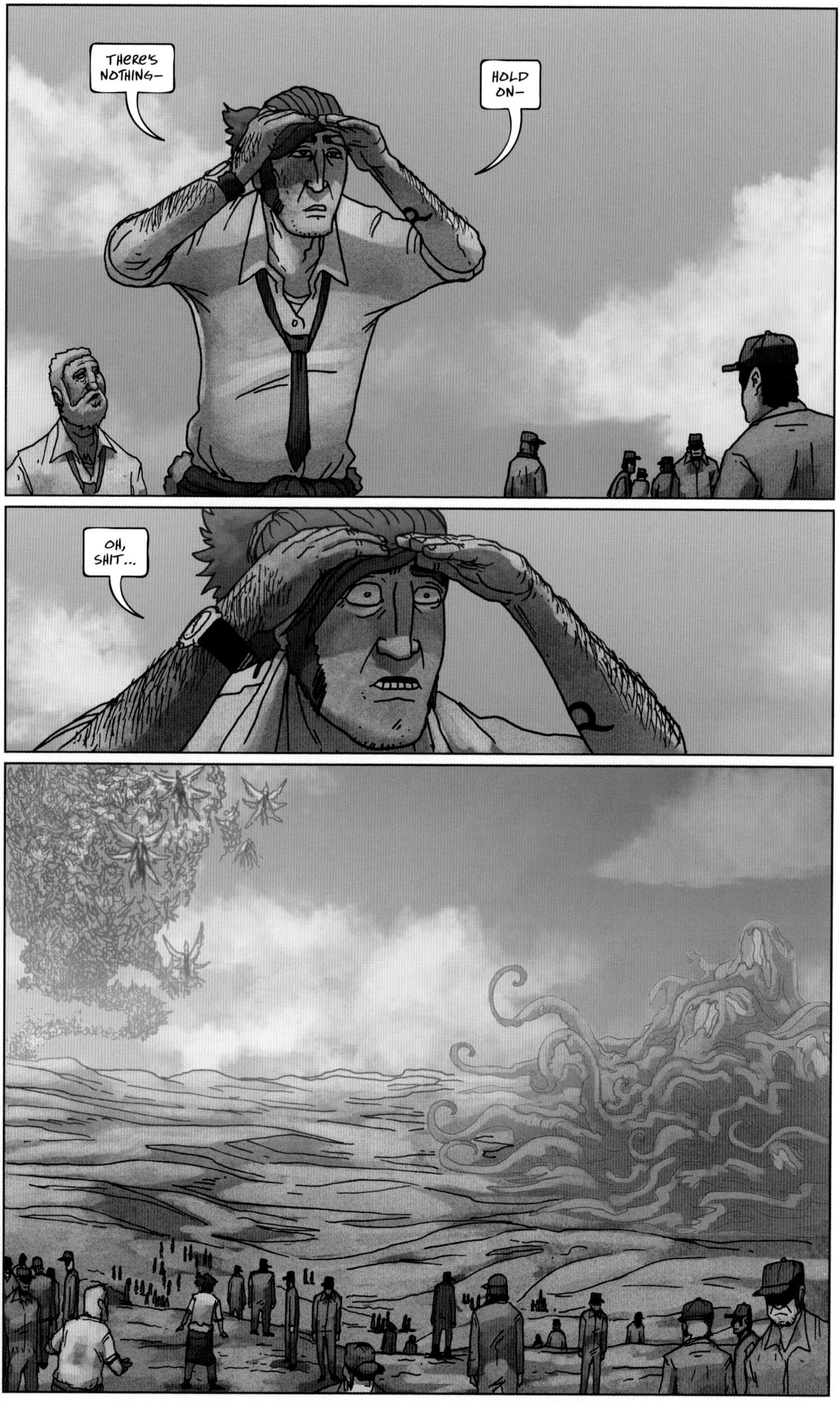
THERE'S NOTHING—
HOLD ON—
OH, SHIT...

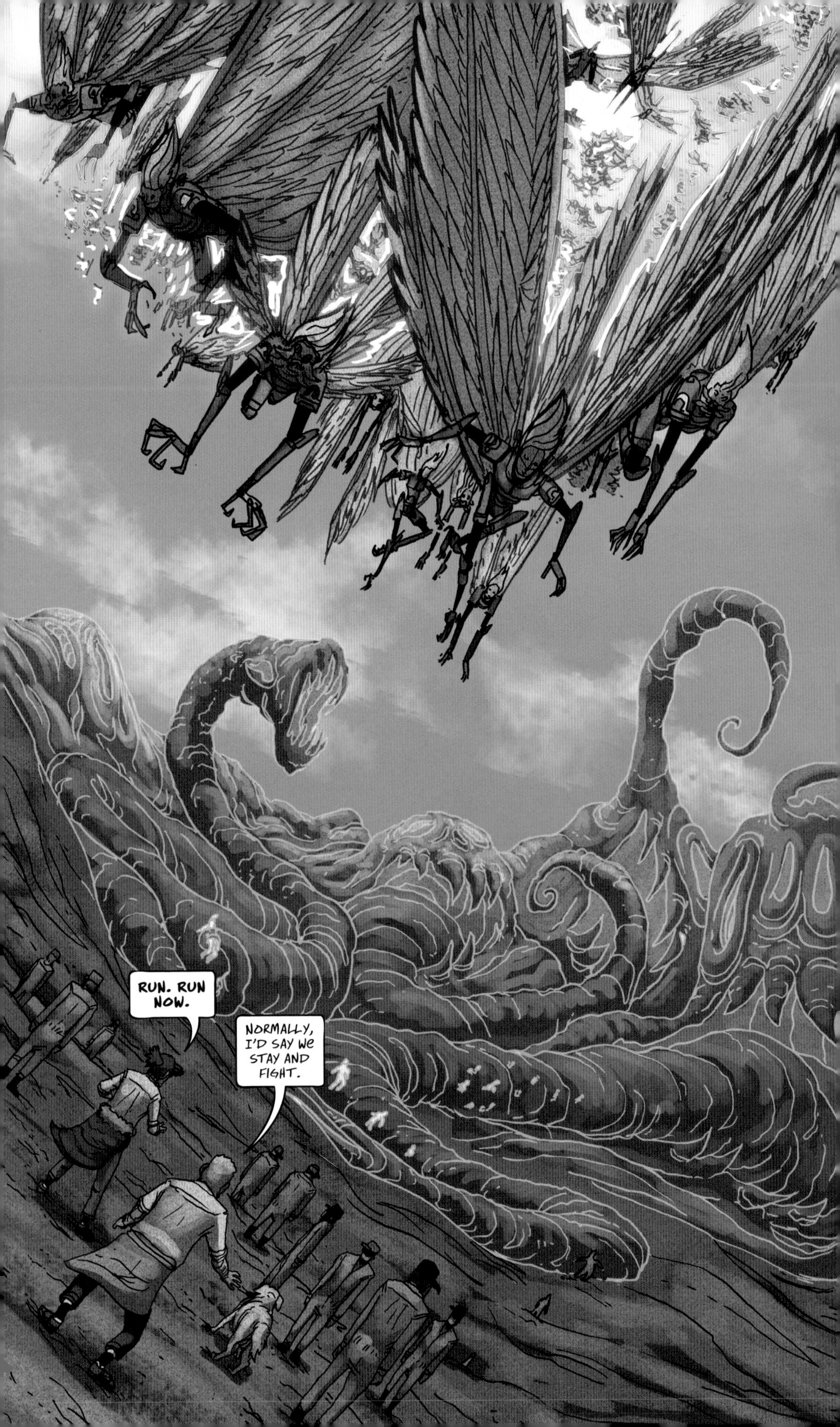
RUN. RUN NOW.
NORMALLY, I'D SAY WE STAY AND FIGHT.

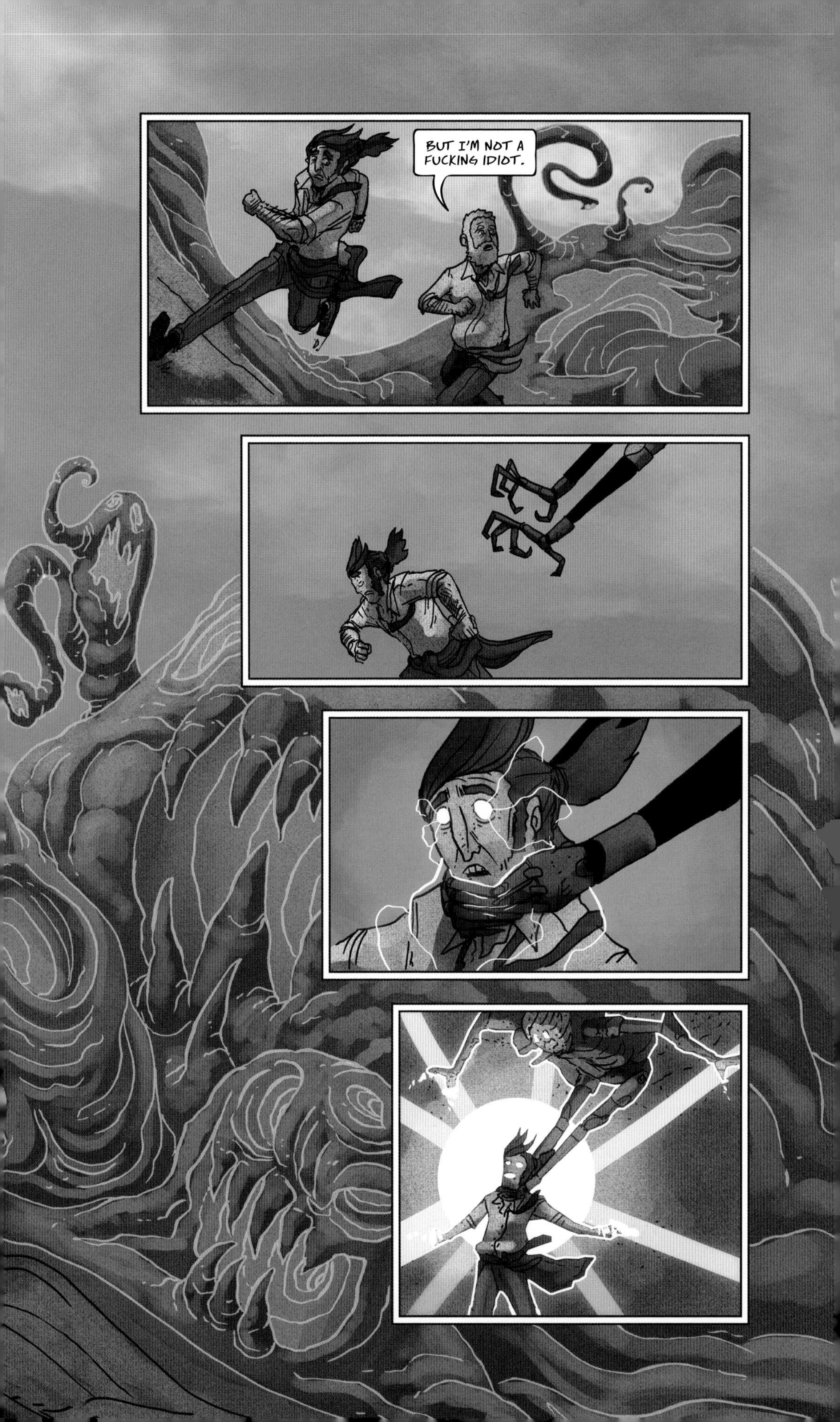
BUT I'M NOT A FUCKING IDIOT.

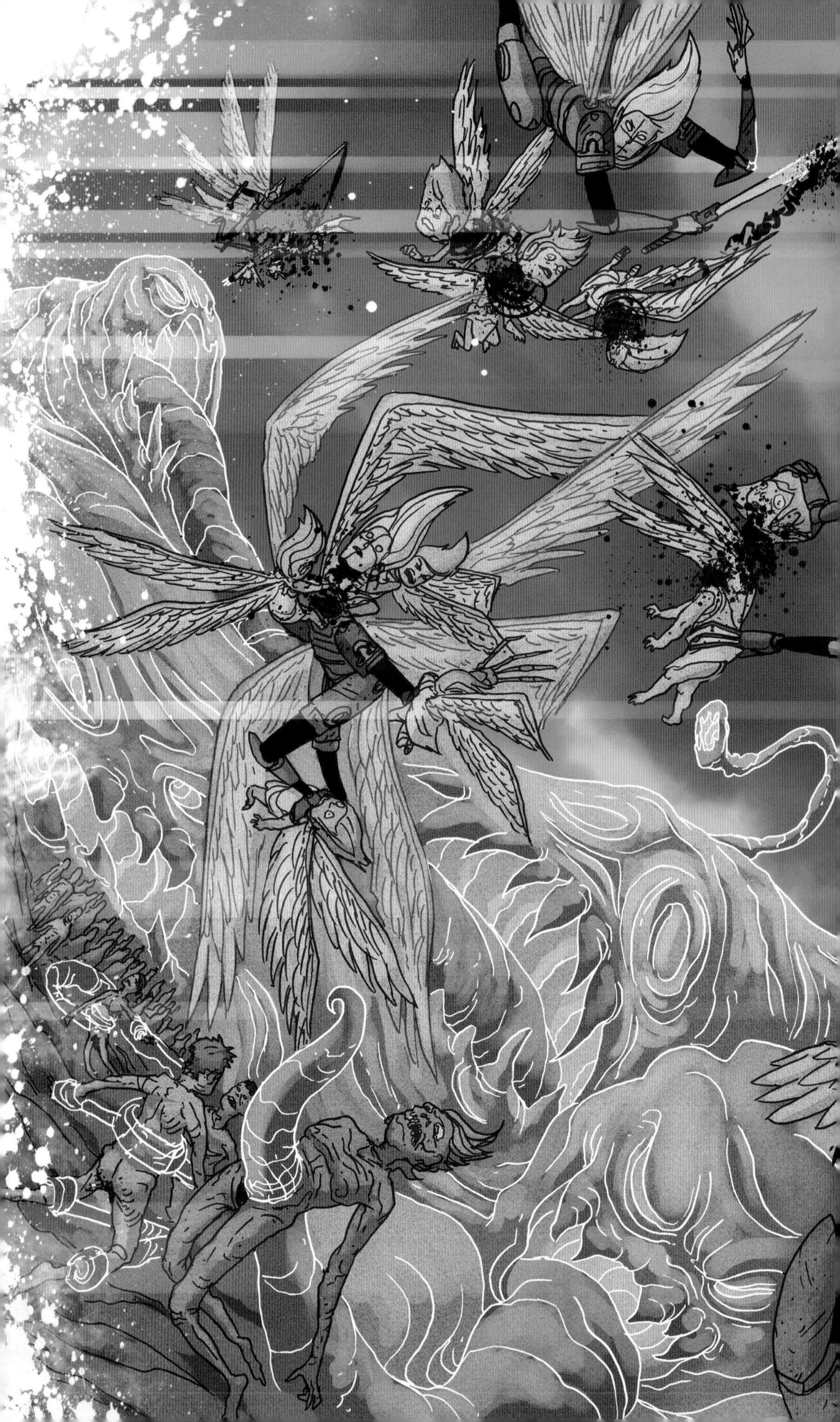

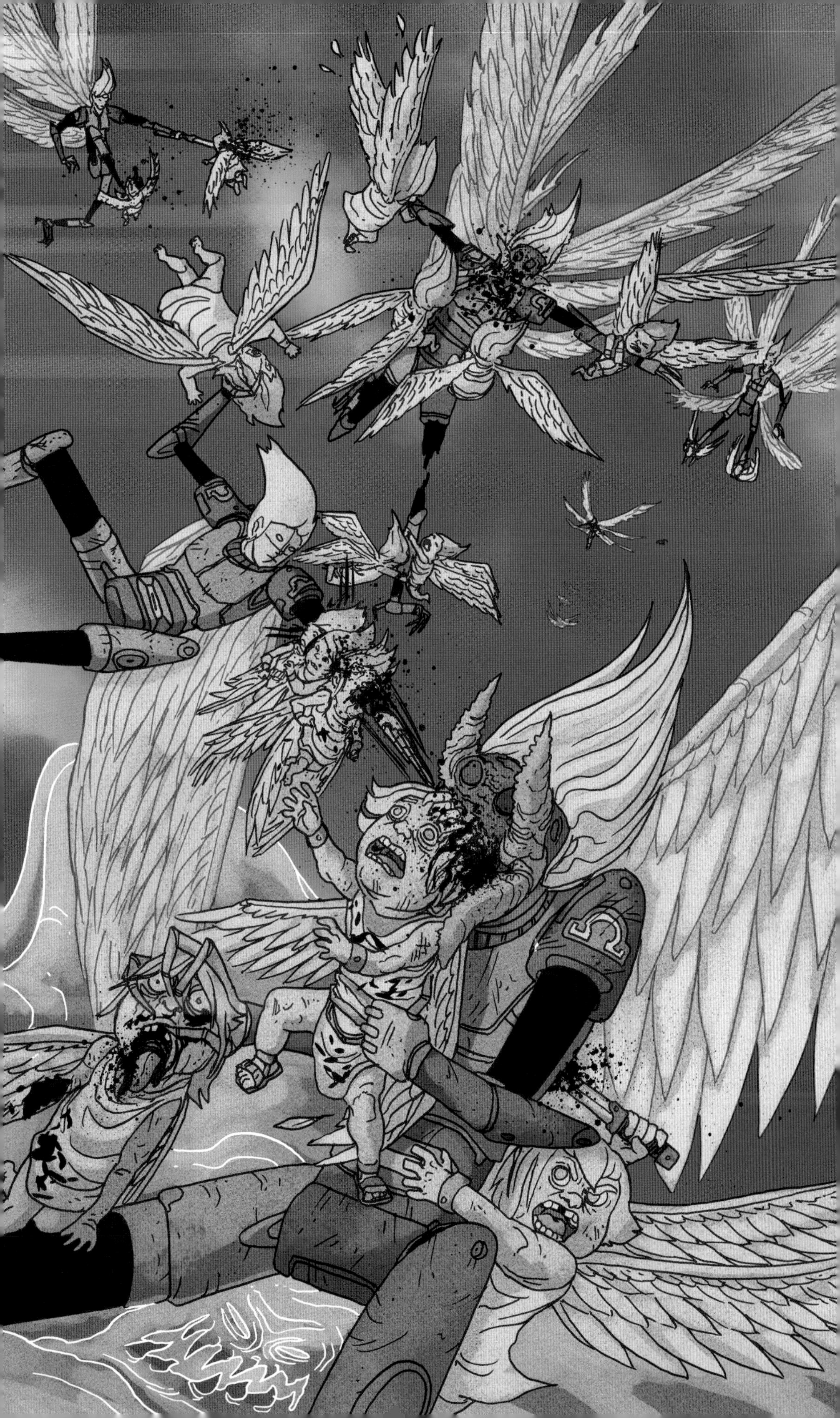

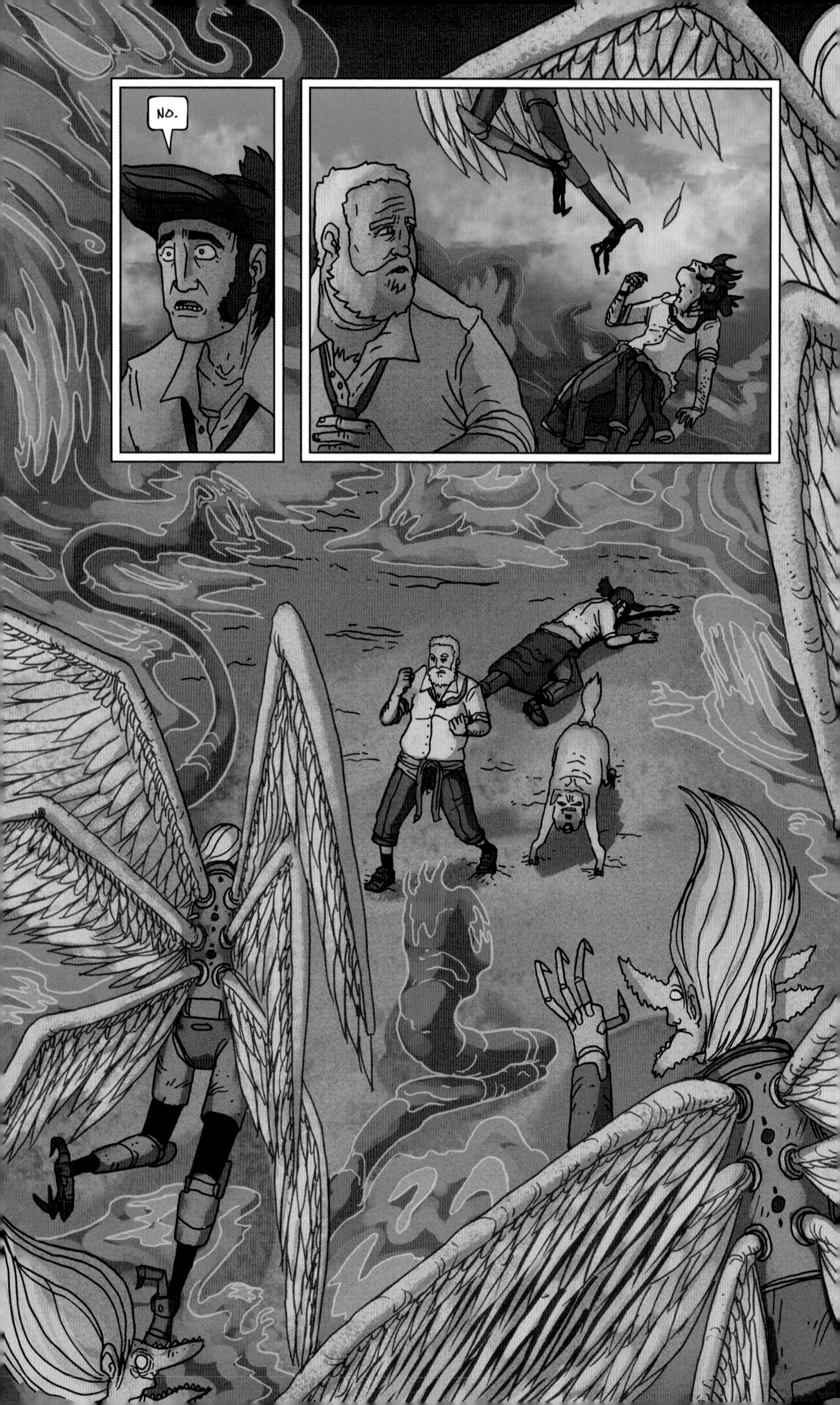
NO.

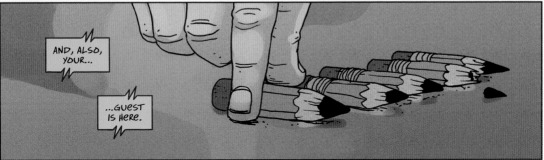

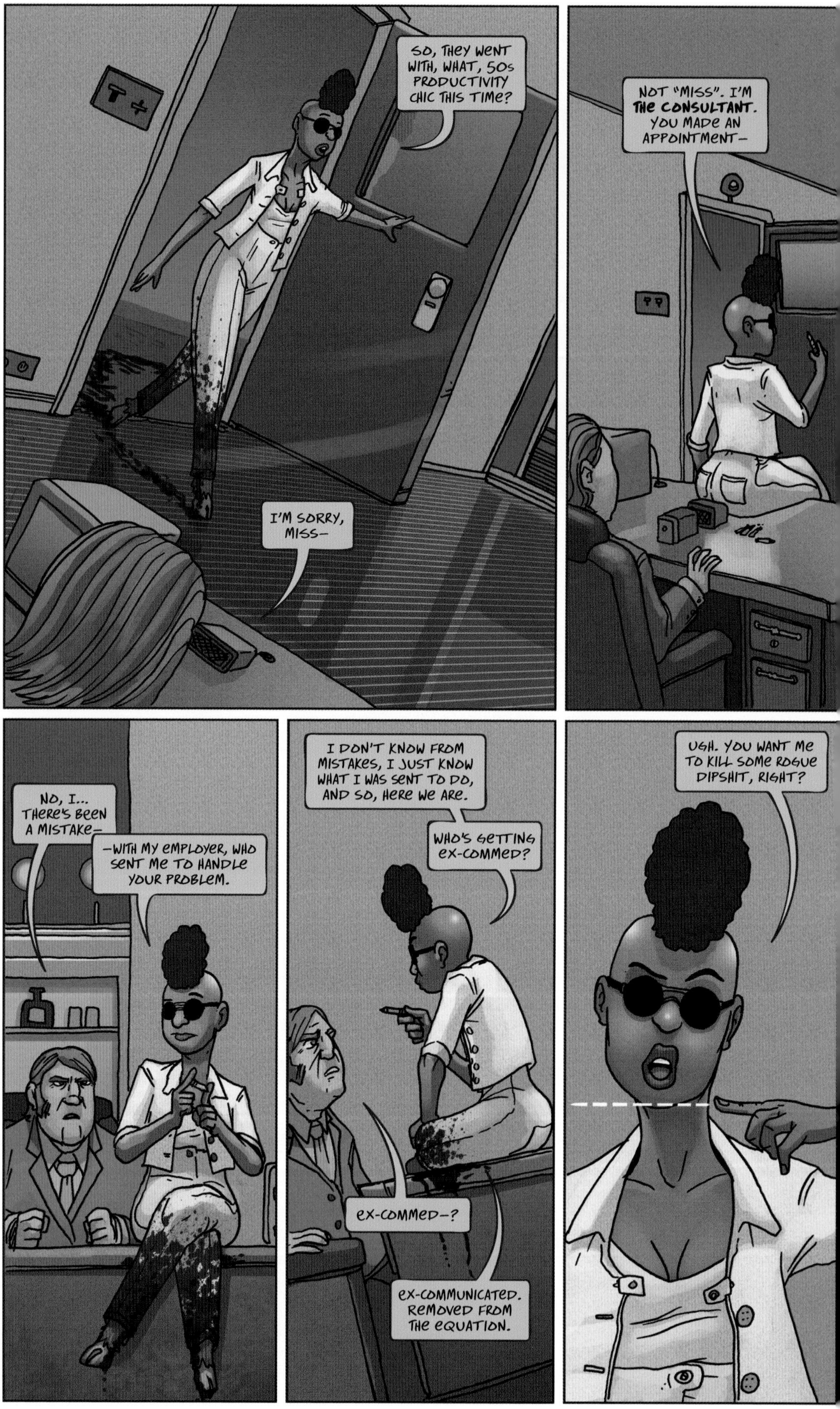
SO, THEY WENT WITH, WHAT, 50s PRODUCTIVITY CHIC THIS TIME?
I'M SORRY, MISS—
NOT "MISS". I'M THE CONSULTANT. YOU MADE AN APPOINTMENT—
NO, I... THERE'S BEEN A MISTAKE—
—WITH MY EMPLOYER, WHO SENT ME TO HANDLE YOUR PROBLEM.
I DON'T KNOW FROM MISTAKES, I JUST KNOW WHAT I WAS SENT TO DO, AND SO, HERE WE ARE.
WHO'S GETTING EX-COMMED?
EX-COMMED—?
EX-COMMUNICATED. REMOVED FROM THE EQUATION.
UGH. YOU WANT ME TO KILL SOME ROGUE DIPSHIT, RIGHT?

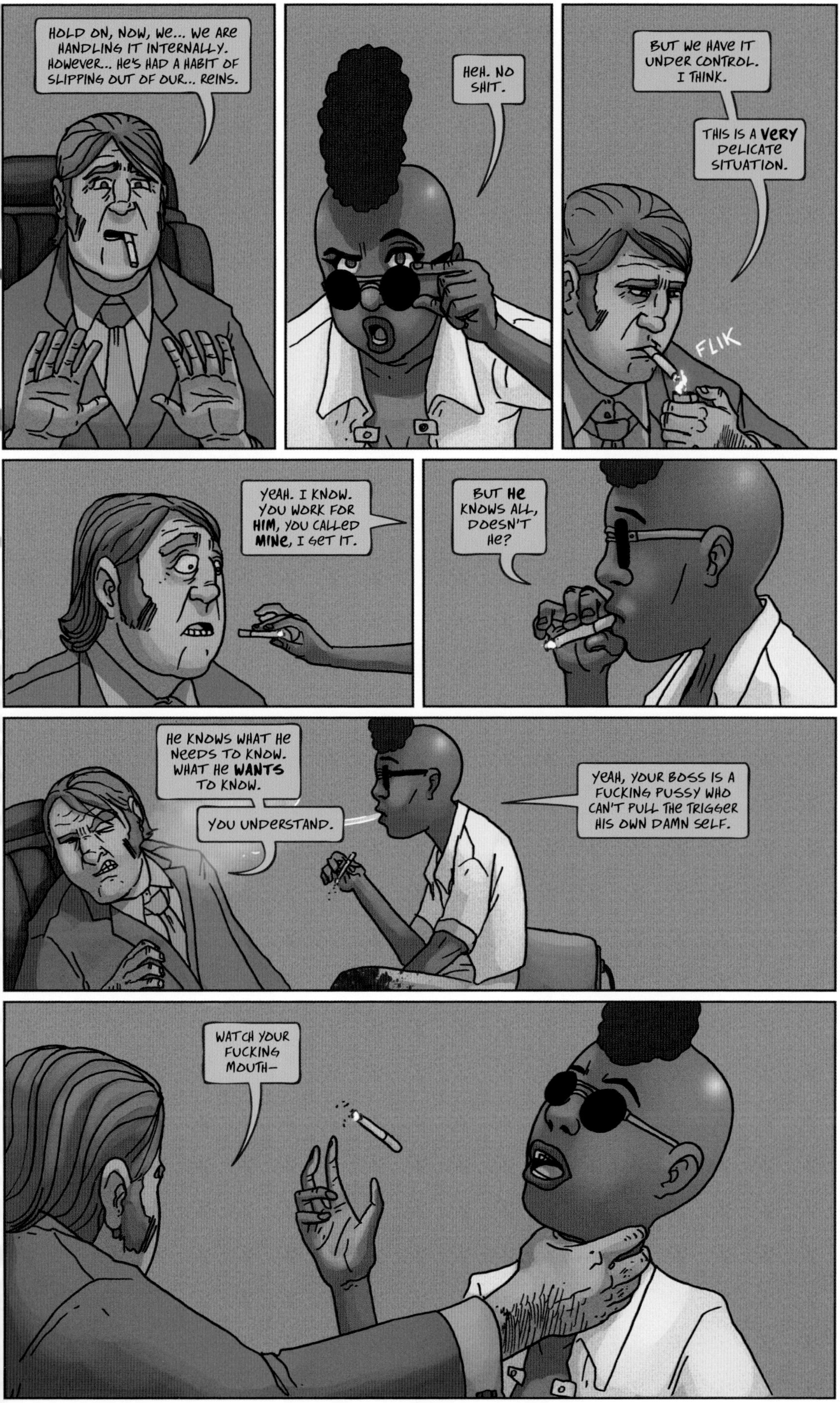
HOLD ON, NOW, WE... WE ARE HANDLING IT INTERNALLY. HOWEVER... HE'S HAD A HABIT OF SLIPPING OUT OF OUR... REINS.
HEH. NO SHIT.
BUT WE HAVE IT UNDER CONTROL. I THINK.
THIS IS A VERY DELICATE SITUATION.
FLIK
YEAH. I KNOW. YOU WORK FOR HIM, YOU CALLED MINE, I GET IT.
BUT HE KNOWS ALL, DOESN'T HE?
HE KNOWS WHAT HE NEEDS TO KNOW. WHAT HE WANTS TO KNOW.
YOU UNDERSTAND.
YEAH, YOUR BOSS IS A FUCKING PUSSY WHO CAN'T PULL THE TRIGGER HIS OWN DAMN SELF.
WATCH YOUR FUCKING MOUTH—

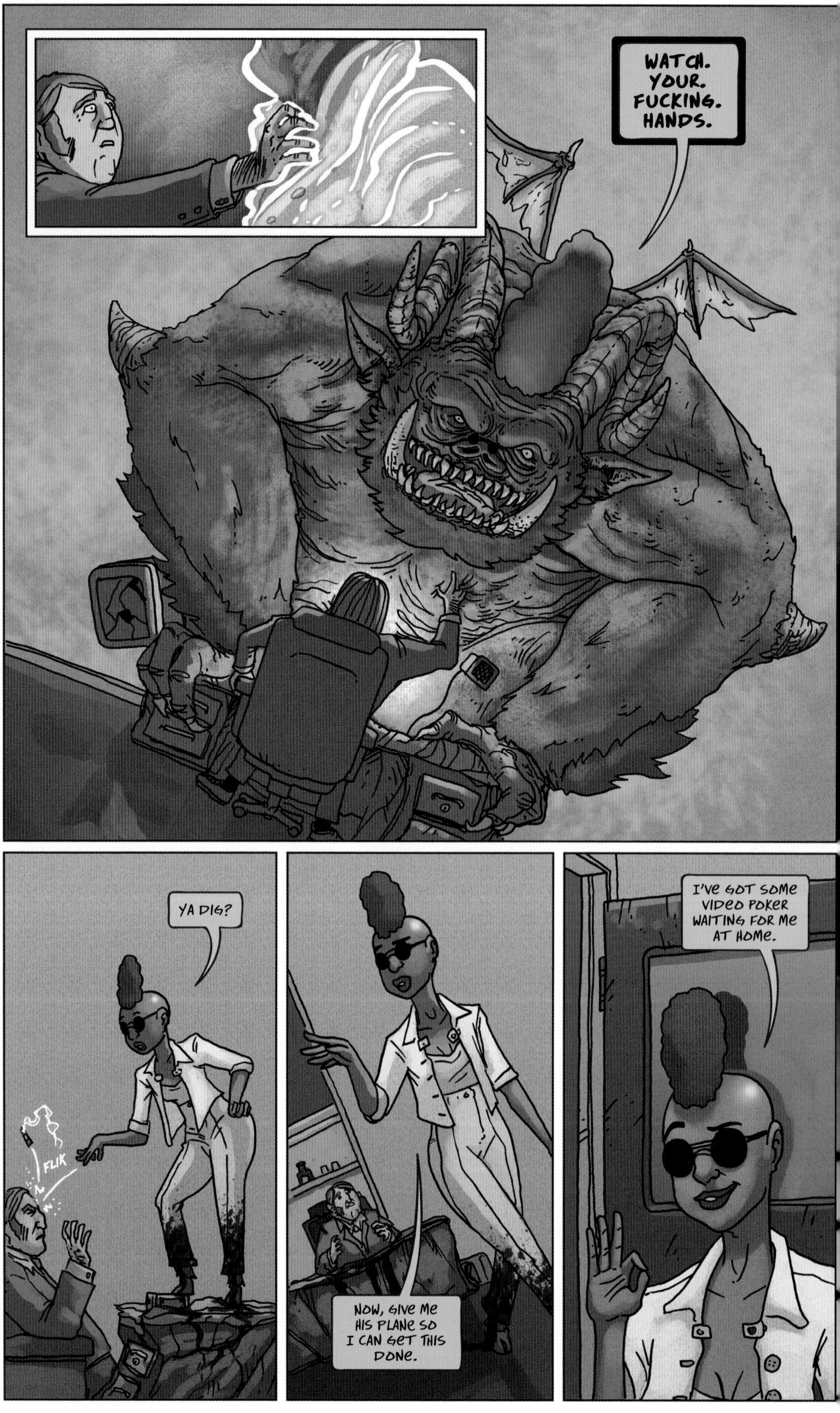
WATCH.
YOUR.
FUCKING.
HANDS.
YA DIG?
FLIK
NOW, GIVE ME HIS PLANE SO I CAN GET THIS DONE.
I'VE GOT SOME VIDEO POKER WAITING FOR ME AT HOME.

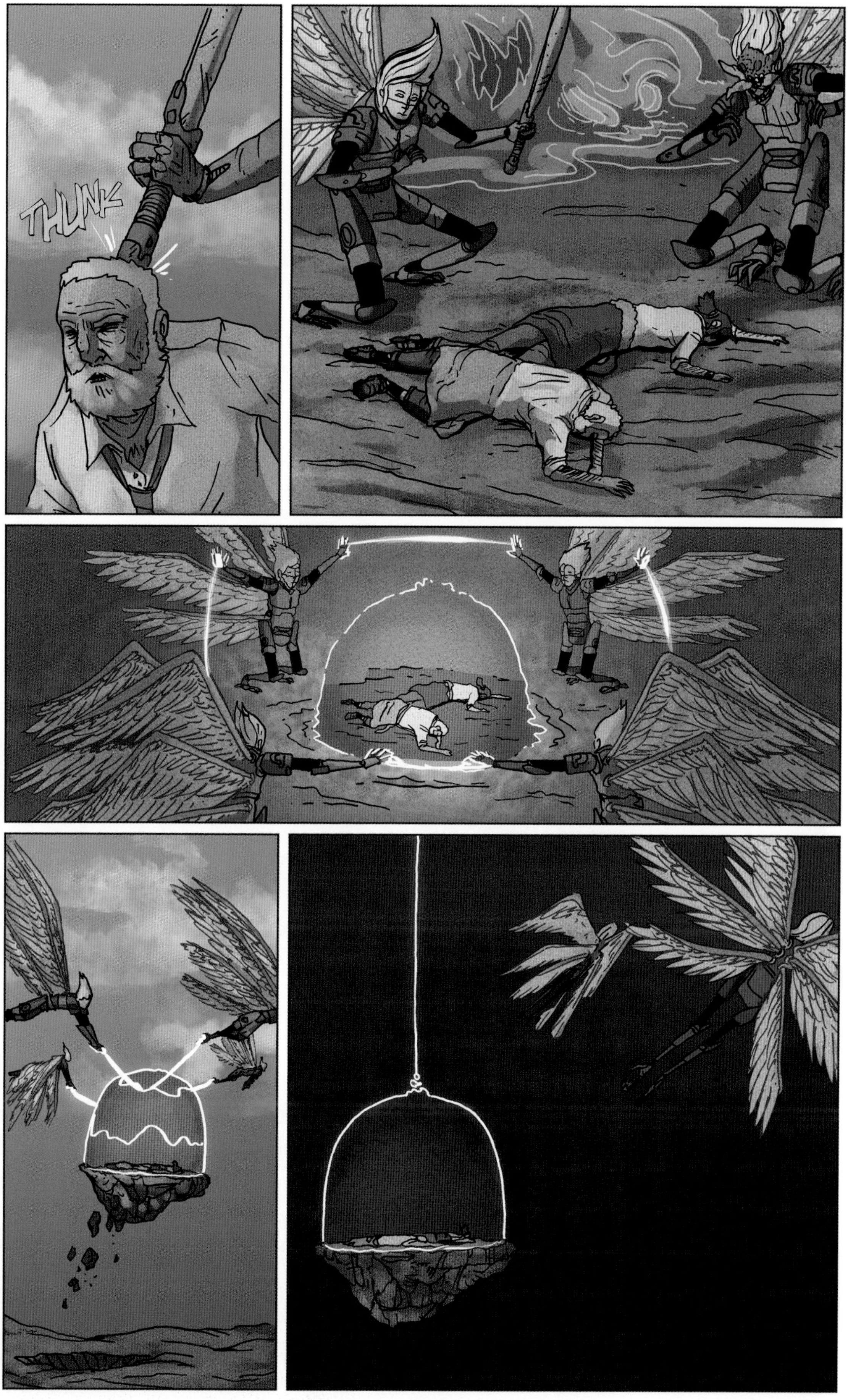
THUNK

C'MON, JUDE, WAKE UP, MY BOY.

I'M GOING TO NEED SOME HELP—

I DON'T THINK THAT'LL WORK.

I CAN'T SEE YOU, COME INTO THE LIGHT.

NO. I'M FINE, THANKS.

WHAT... WHAT IS THIS PLACE?

I THINK IT'S HELL.

I DON'T THINK IT IS. I'M NOT IN PAIN. ARE YOU IN PAIN?

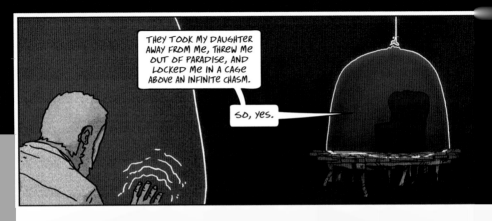

THEY TOOK MY DAUGHTER AWAY FROM ME, THREW ME OUT OF PARADISE, AND LOCKED ME IN A CAGE ABOVE AN INFINITE CHASM.

SO, YES.

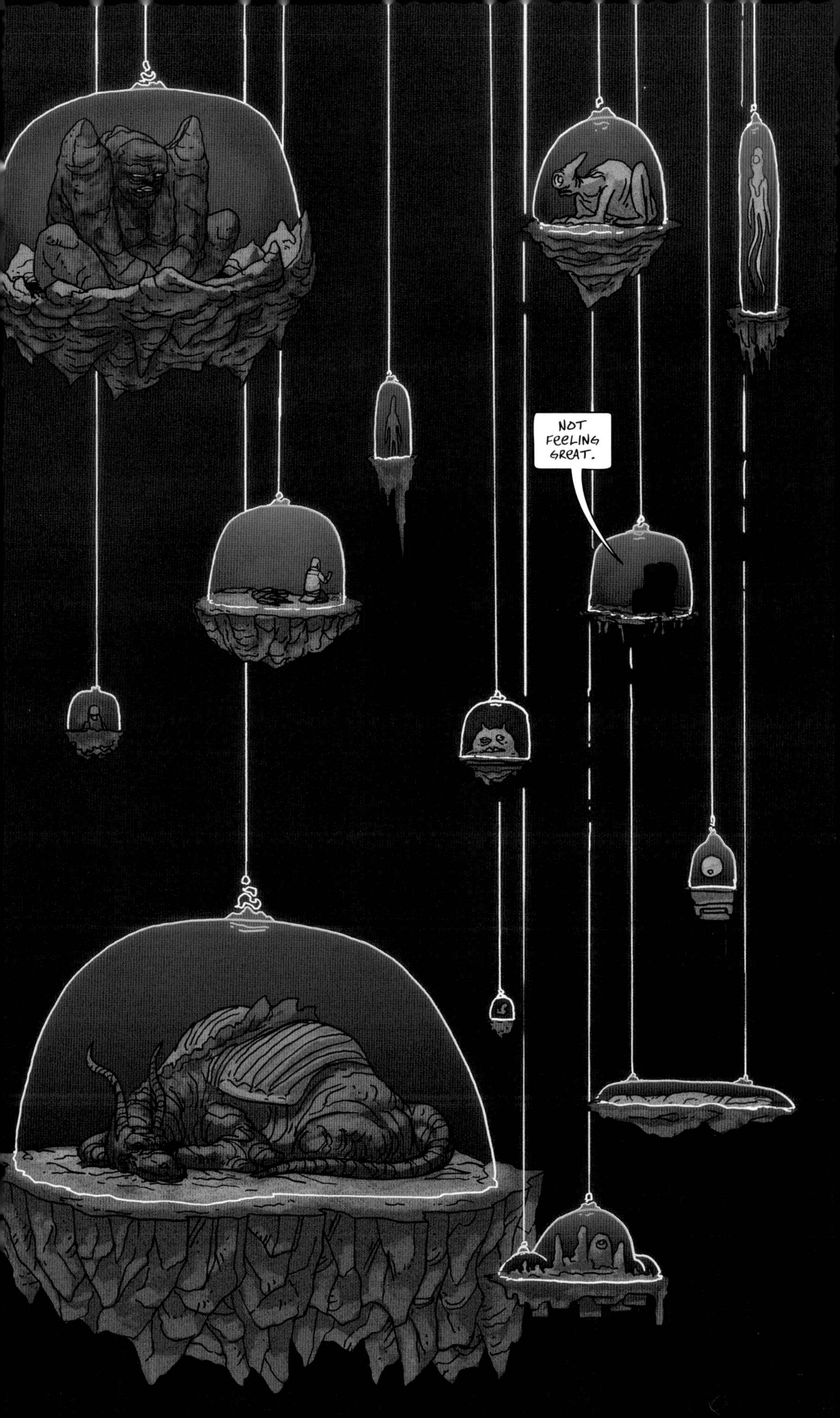
NOT FEELING GREAT.

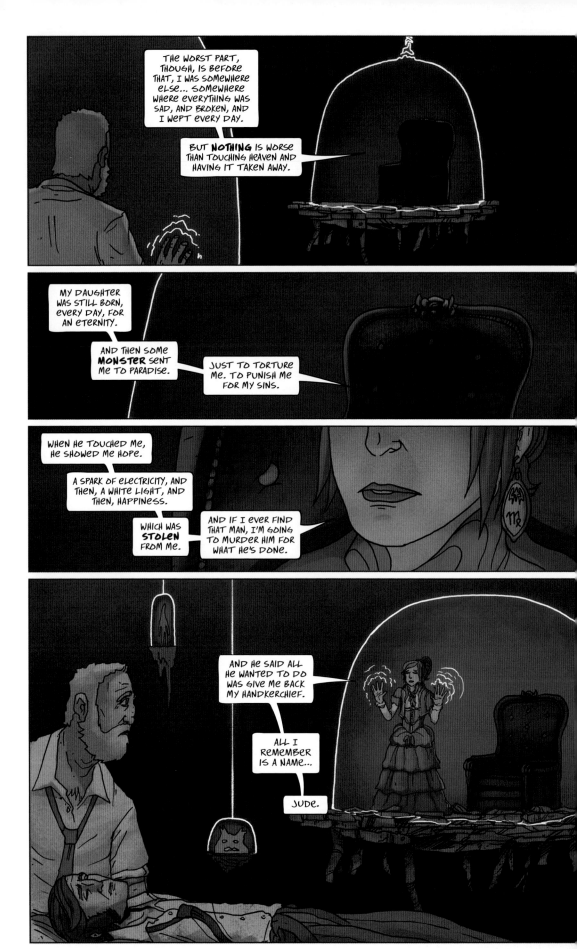

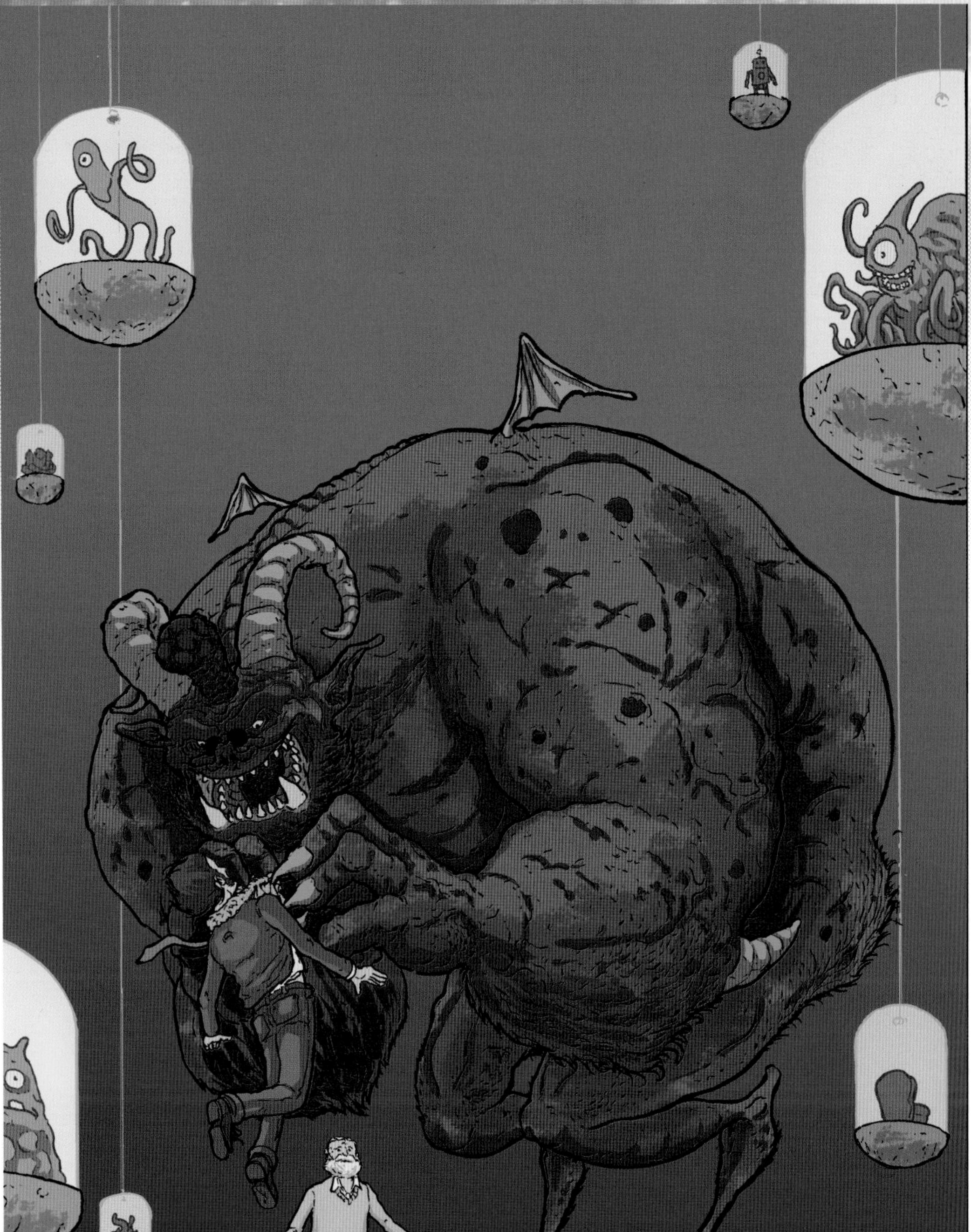

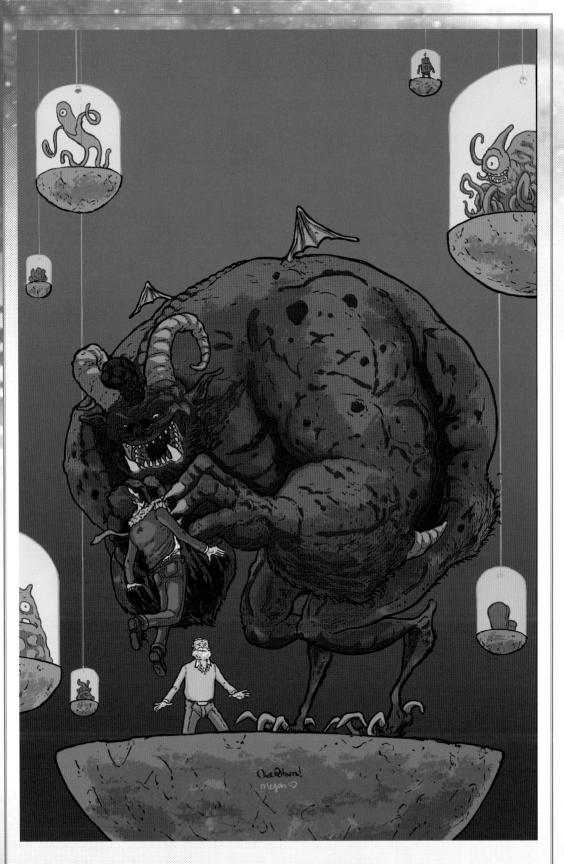

Chapter Five

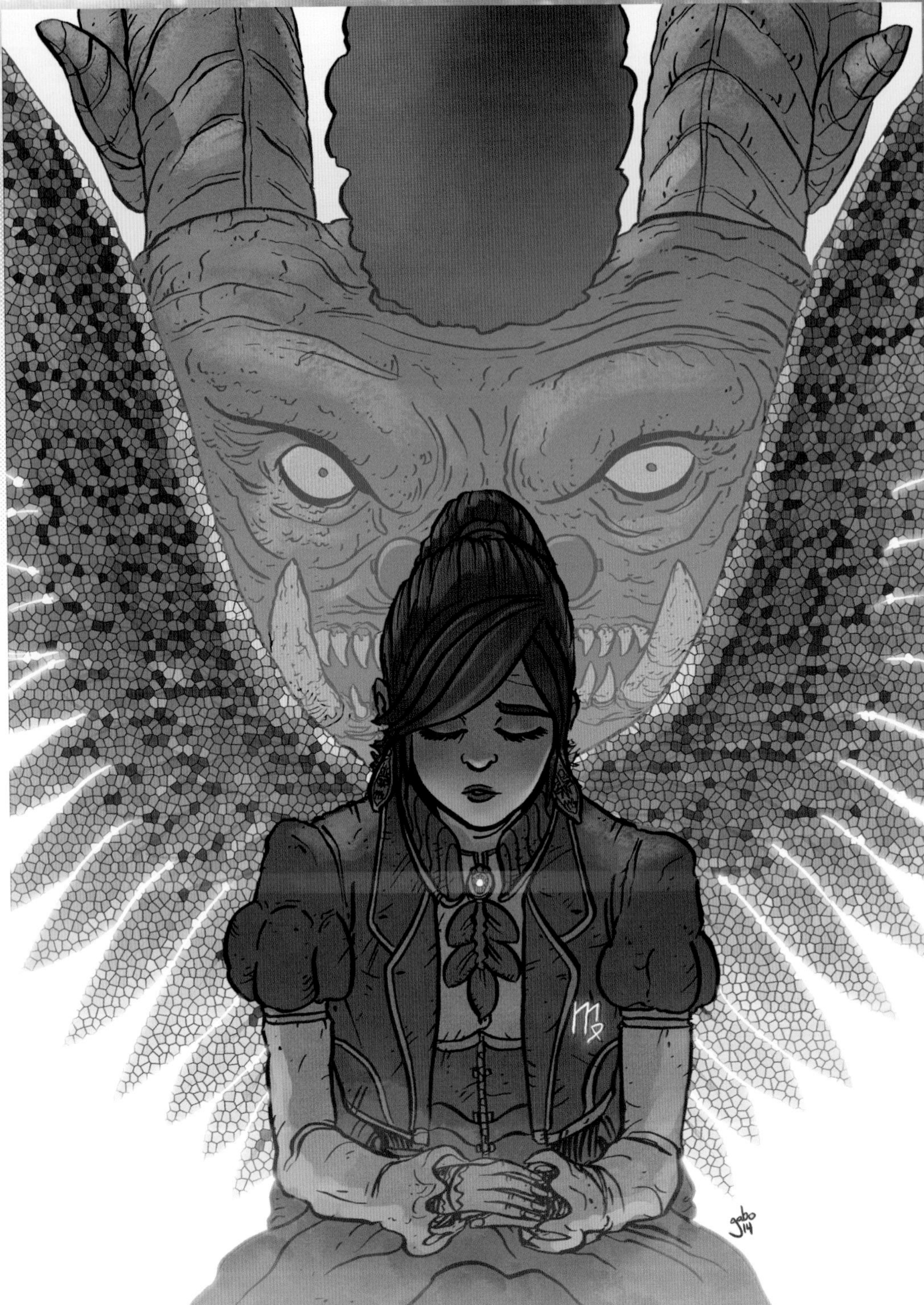

THE LIFE
AFTER

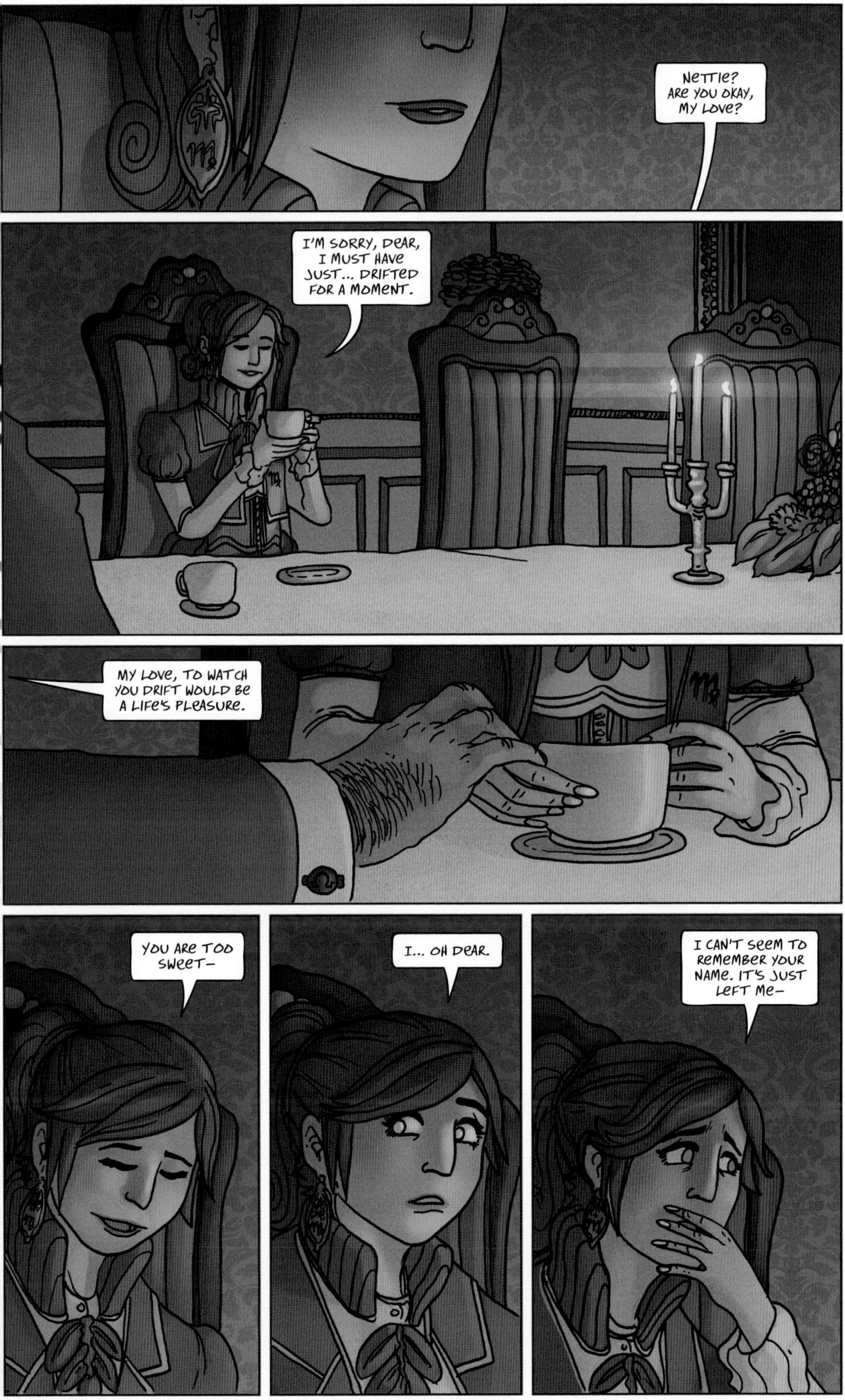
NETTIE? ARE YOU OKAY, MY LOVE?
I'M SORRY, DEAR, I MUST HAVE JUST... DRIFTED FOR A MOMENT.
MY LOVE, TO WATCH YOU DRIFT WOULD BE A LIFE'S PLEASURE.
YOU ARE TOO SWEET—
I... OH DEAR.
I CAN'T SEEM TO REMEMBER YOUR NAME. IT'S JUST LEFT ME—

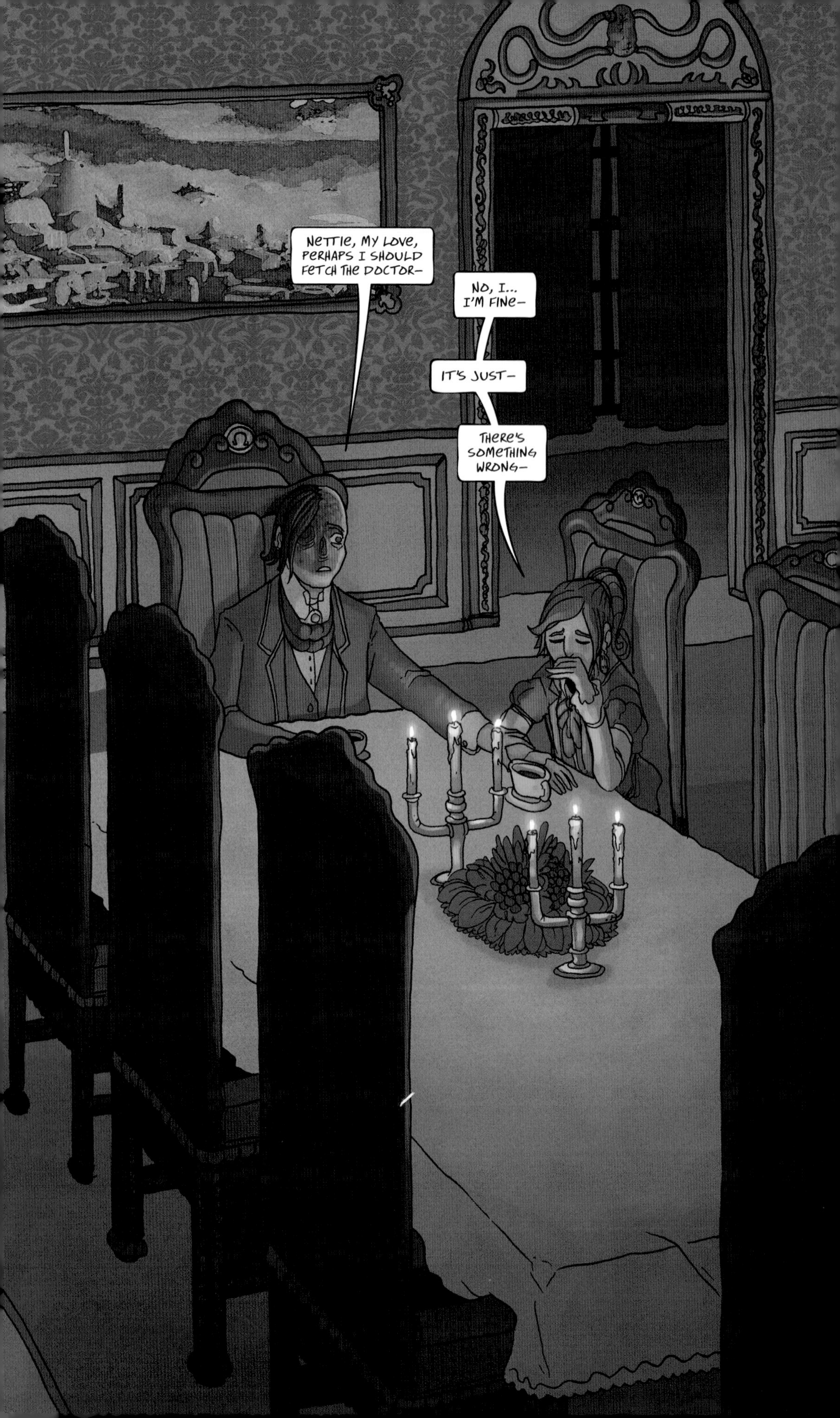

NETTIE, MY LOVE, PERHAPS I SHOULD FETCH THE DOCTOR–
NO, I... I'M FINE–
IT'S JUST–
THERE'S SOMETHING WRONG–

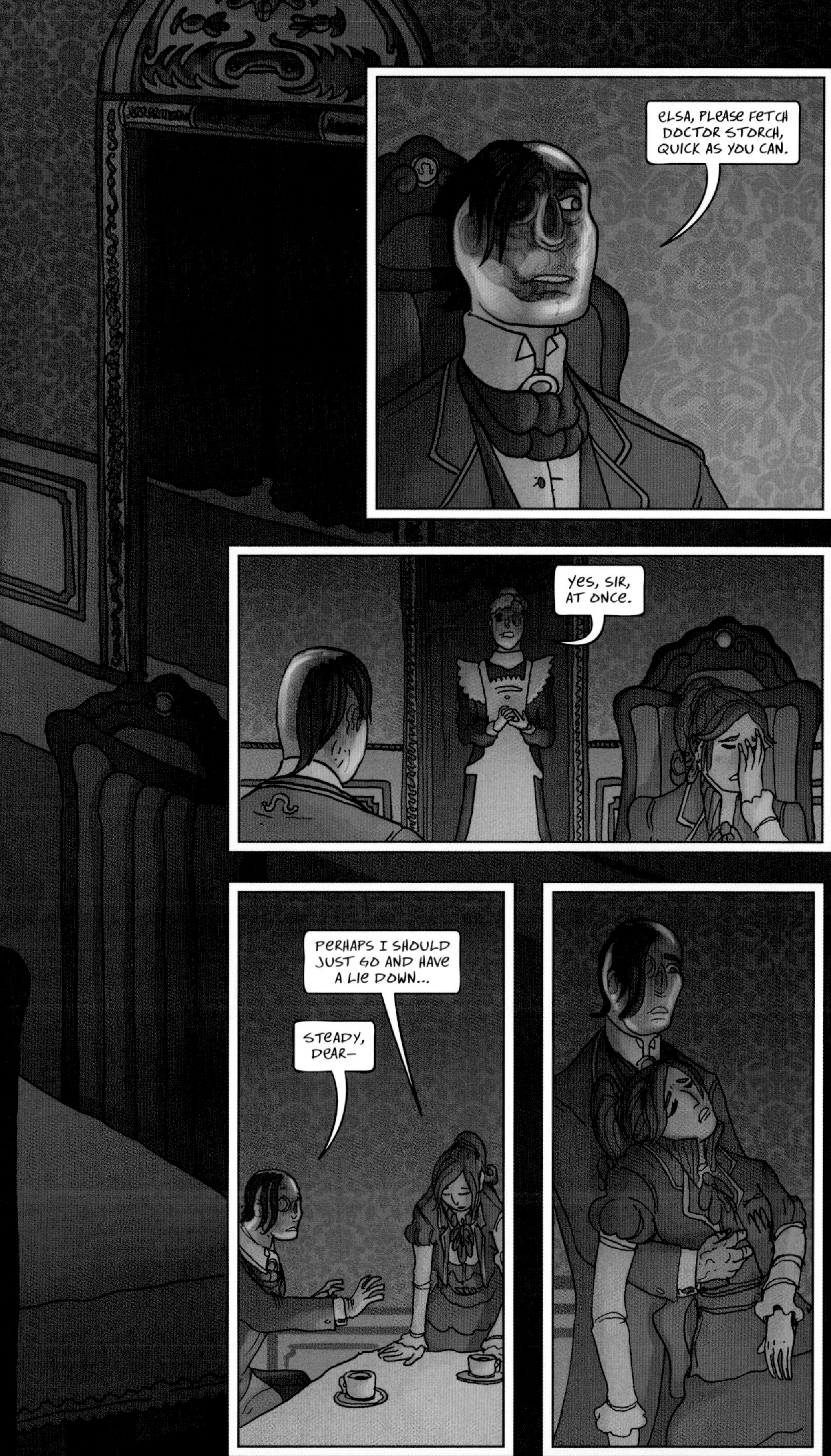
ELSA, PLEASE FETCH DOCTOR STORCH, QUICK AS YOU CAN.
YES, SIR, AT ONCE.
PERHAPS I SHOULD JUST GO AND HAVE A LIE DOWN...
STEADY, DEAR–

I HOPE I'M NOT INTERRUPTING...

DOCTOR, THANK GOODNESS YOU'VE ARRIVED—

YOU APPEAR WELL ENOUGH, LADY HENRIETTA, THAT I CAN EXAMINE THE WEE ONE FIRST, YES?

YOU'RE LOOKING AS BEAUTIFUL AS THE DAY I DELIVERED YOU, ESMERELDA—

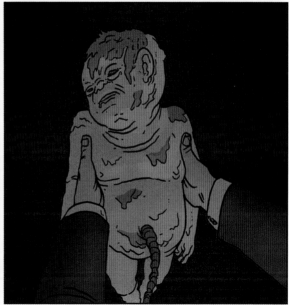

PLEASE, DOCTOR—

I... I KEEP SEEING THINGS.

WHAT KIND OF THINGS, NETTIE?

I...

I FEEL AS THOUGH I'M LOSING MY MIND—

STORCH M.D.

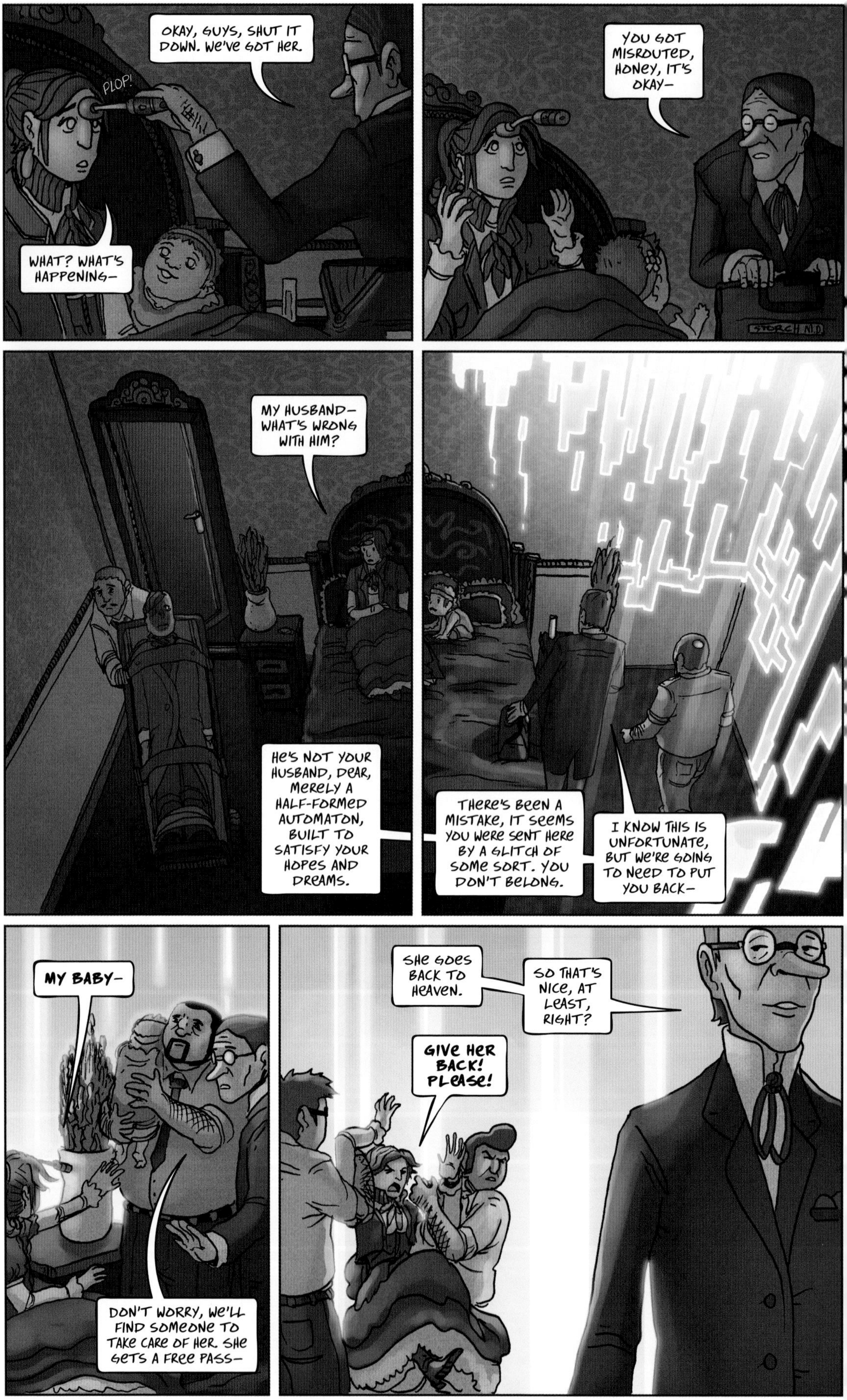
OKAY, GUYS, SHUT IT DOWN. WE'VE GOT HER.
PLOP!
WHAT? WHAT'S HAPPENING—
YOU GOT MISROUTED, HONEY, IT'S OKAY—
STORCH M.D.
MY HUSBAND—WHAT'S WRONG WITH HIM?
HE'S NOT YOUR HUSBAND, DEAR, MERELY A HALF-FORMED AUTOMATON, BUILT TO SATISFY YOUR HOPES AND DREAMS.
THERE'S BEEN A MISTAKE, IT SEEMS YOU WERE SENT HERE BY A GLITCH OF SOME SORT. YOU DON'T BELONG.
I KNOW THIS IS UNFORTUNATE, BUT WE'RE GOING TO NEED TO PUT YOU BACK—
MY BABY—
DON'T WORRY, WE'LL FIND SOMEONE TO TAKE CARE OF HER. SHE GETS A FREE PASS—
SHE GOES BACK TO HEAVEN.
SO THAT'S NICE, AT LEAST, RIGHT?
GIVE HER BACK! PLEASE!

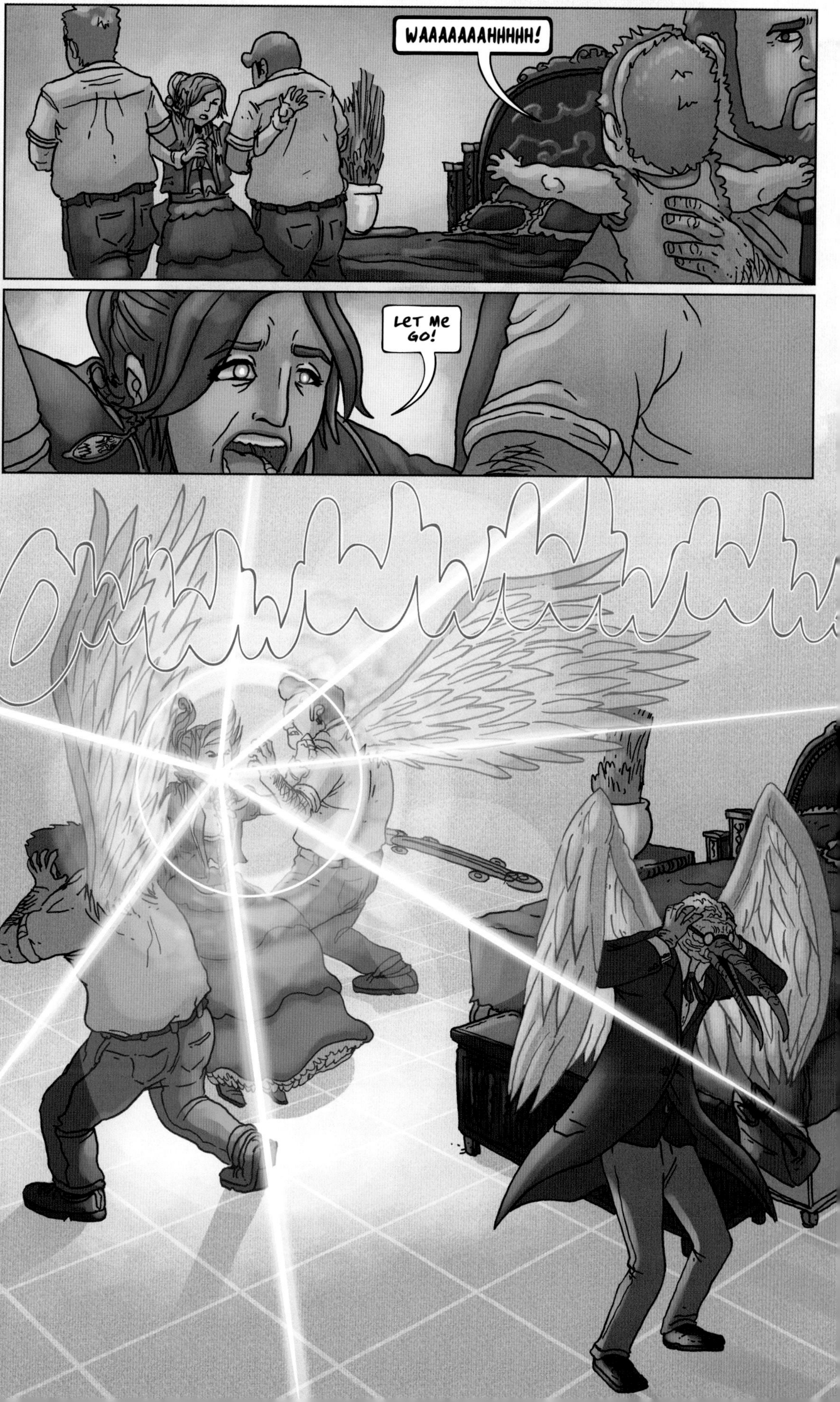
WAAAAAAAHHHHH!
LET ME GO!

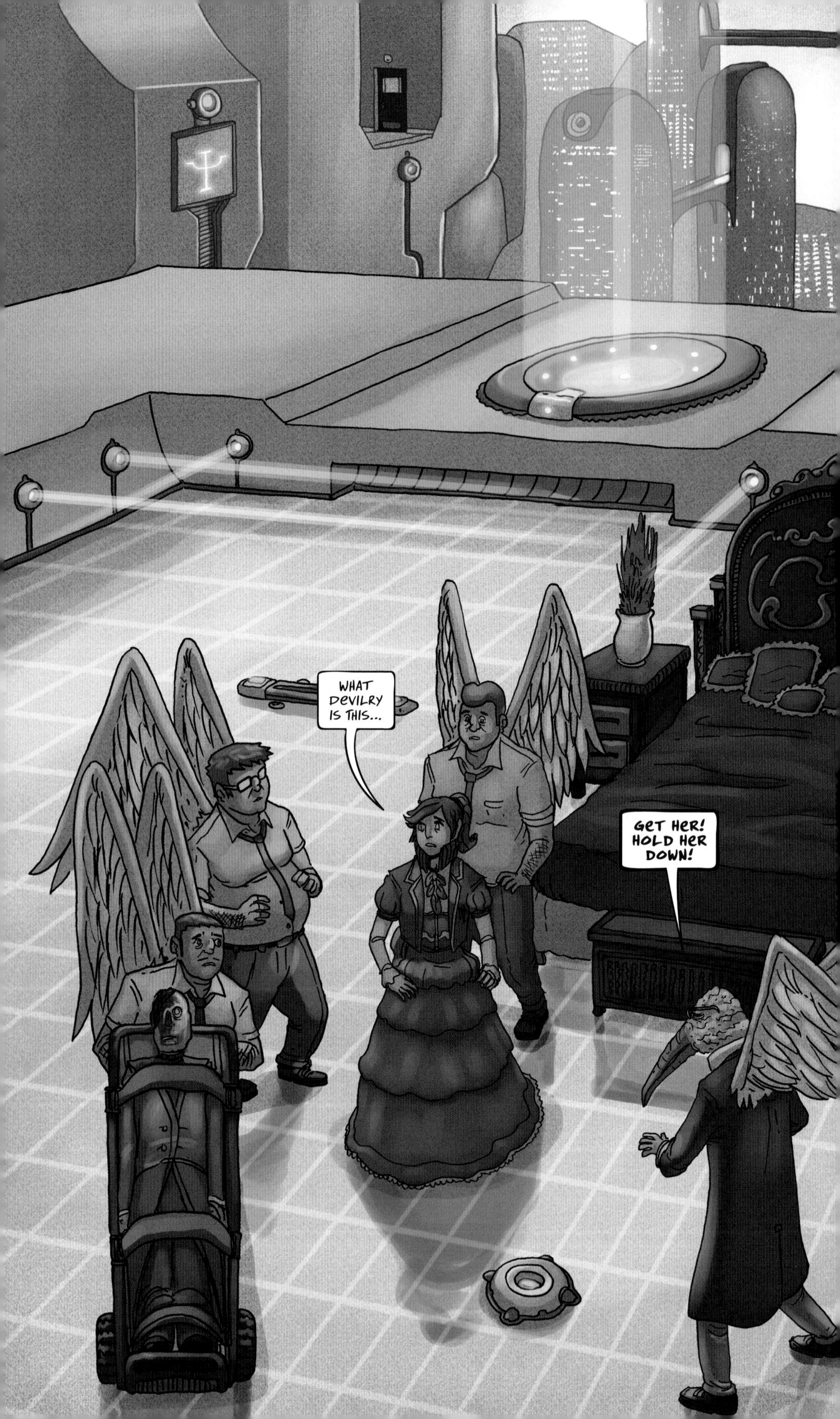
WHAT DEVILRY IS THIS...
GET HER! HOLD HER DOWN!

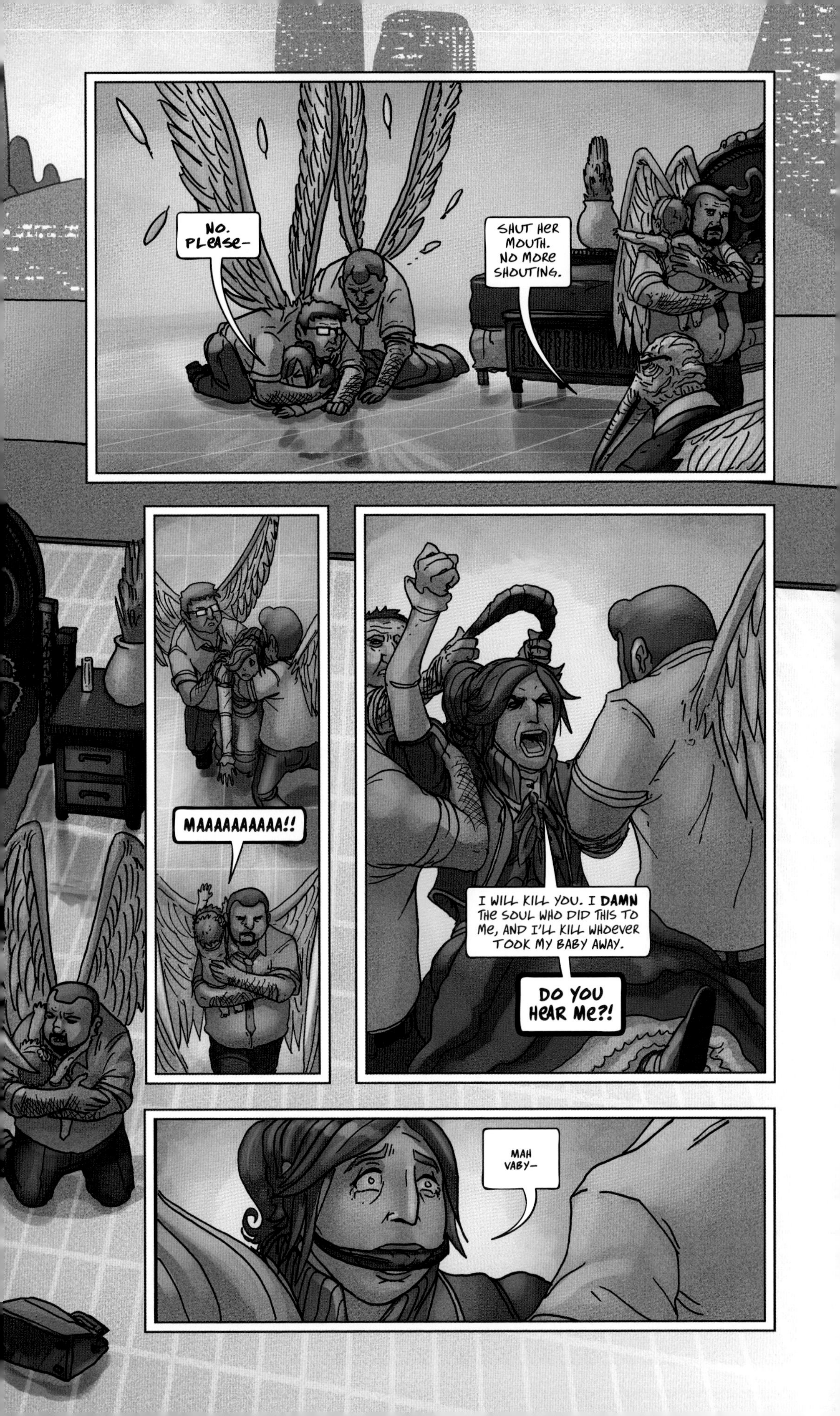

NO. PLEASE-
SHUT HER MOUTH. NO MORE SHOUTING.
MAAAAAAAAAA!!
I WILL KILL YOU. I DAMN THE SOUL WHO DID THIS TO ME, AND I'LL KILL WHOEVER TOOK MY BABY AWAY.
DO YOU HEAR ME?!
MAH VABY–

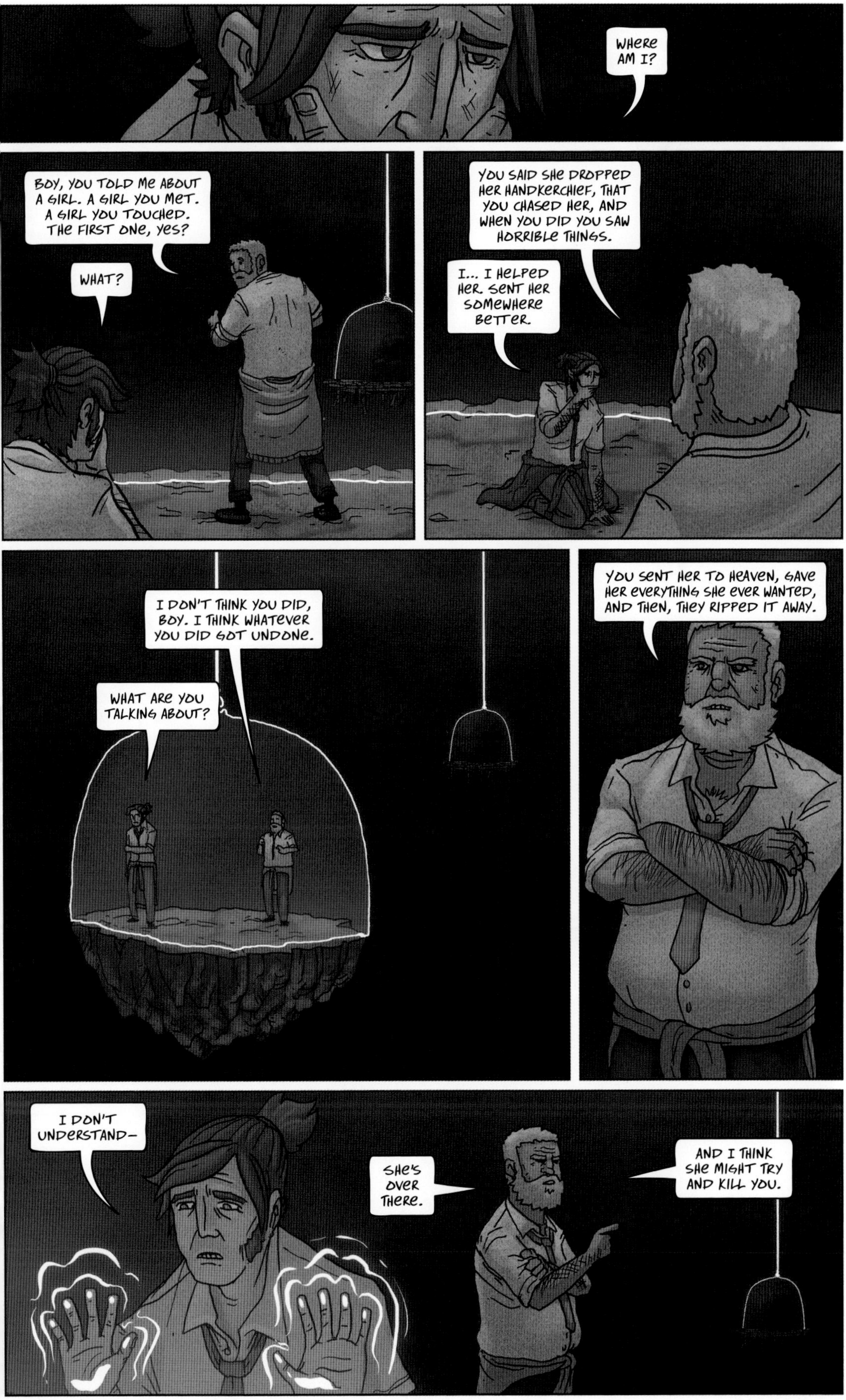
WHERE AM I?
BOY, YOU TOLD ME ABOUT A GIRL. A GIRL YOU MET. A GIRL YOU TOUCHED. THE FIRST ONE, YES?
WHAT?
YOU SAID SHE DROPPED HER HANDKERCHIEF, THAT YOU CHASED HER, AND WHEN YOU DID YOU SAW HORRIBLE THINGS.
I... I HELPED HER. SENT HER SOMEWHERE BETTER.
I DON'T THINK YOU DID, BOY. I THINK WHATEVER YOU DID GOT UNDONE.
WHAT ARE YOU TALKING ABOUT?
YOU SENT HER TO HEAVEN, GAVE HER EVERYTHING SHE EVER WANTED, AND THEN, THEY RIPPED IT AWAY.
I DON'T UNDERSTAND–
SHE'S OVER THERE.
AND I THINK SHE MIGHT TRY AND KILL YOU.

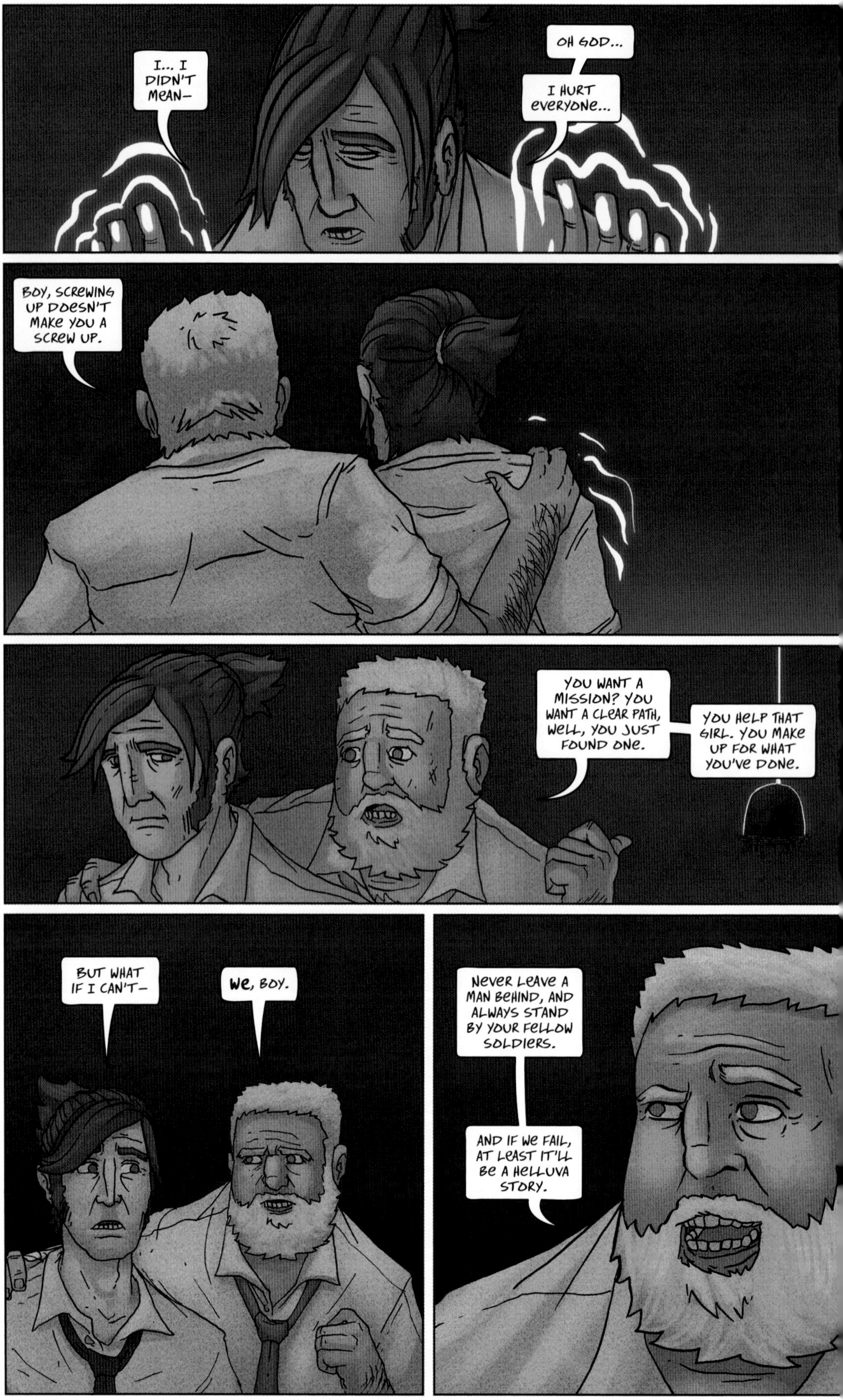

I... I DIDN'T MEAN—
OH GOD...
I HURT EVERYONE...
BOY, SCREWING UP DOESN'T MAKE YOU A SCREW UP.
YOU WANT A MISSION? YOU WANT A CLEAR PATH, WELL, YOU JUST FOUND ONE.
YOU HELP THAT GIRL. YOU MAKE UP FOR WHAT YOU'VE DONE.
BUT WHAT IF I CAN'T—
WE, BOY.
NEVER LEAVE A MAN BEHIND, AND ALWAYS STAND BY YOUR FELLOW SOLDIERS.
AND IF WE FAIL, AT LEAST IT'LL BE A HELLUVA STORY.

UH, SIR?

WE'VE MANAGED TO CAPTURE THE... UH... ERRANT SOULS.

THE INITIAL THREE, ANYWAYS.

OH. REALLY? AND YOU HAVE THEM...

IN THE ETERNAL PIT, SIR. WE'RE TRYING TO GET THE SYSTEM TO REINSERT THEM, BUT IT SAYS WE NEED TO UPGRADE TO AN 8-BIT ENCRYPTION OR SOMETHING—

LEAVE THEM FOR NOW.

THANK YOU, JONES.

I'M PLAWSKY, SIR.

RIGHT, OF COURSE.

LIKE IT MATTERS.

MISS? THIS IS FOREMAN...

119

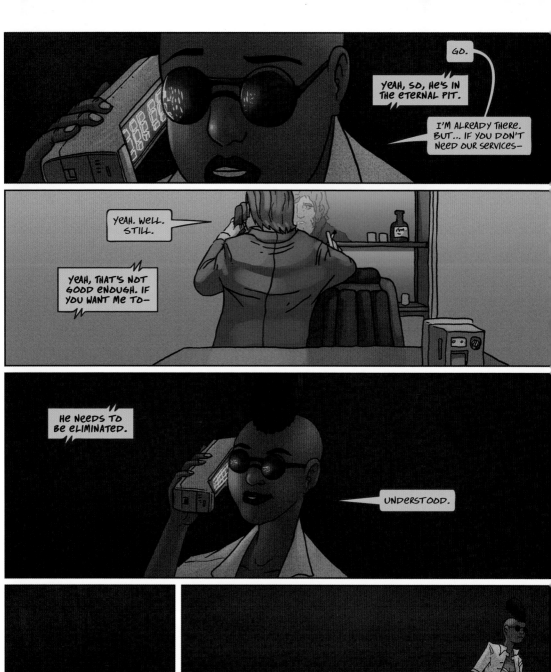

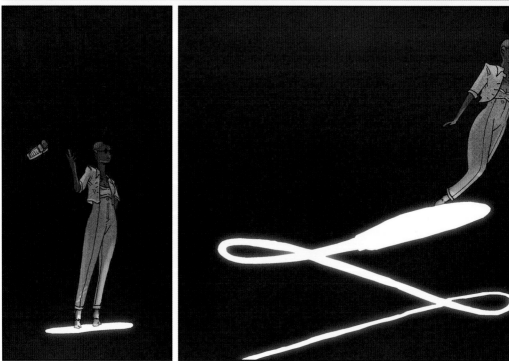

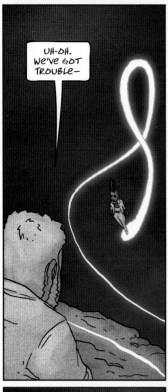

UH-OH. WE'VE GOT TROUBLE—

YOU'RE HIM, HUH?

THAT'S RIGHT. ERNEST HEMING—

NOT YOU, BEARD-O.

HIM.

I DON'T KNOW **WHO** EXACTLY YOU ARE, MISTER, BUT I'VE NEVER SEEN BOTH SIDES SO KEEN TO KILL A SOUL BEFORE.

SO WHAT DO YOU SAY YOU JUST COME WITH ME, AND I'LL EAT YOU UP REAL QUICK.

I'LL... I'LL FIGHT BACK. EVEN IF I HAVE TO HIT A GIRL—

HAHAHAH HAHAAHAH HAHAHA HA HA!

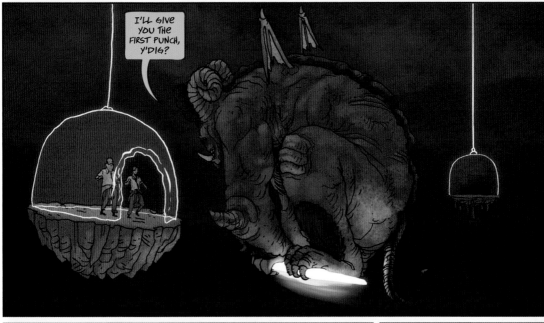

I'LL GIVE YOU THE FIRST PUNCH, Y'DIG?

WHAT'S WRONG, CASSIUS CLAY?

ZZIZZIZZIZZIZZI

122

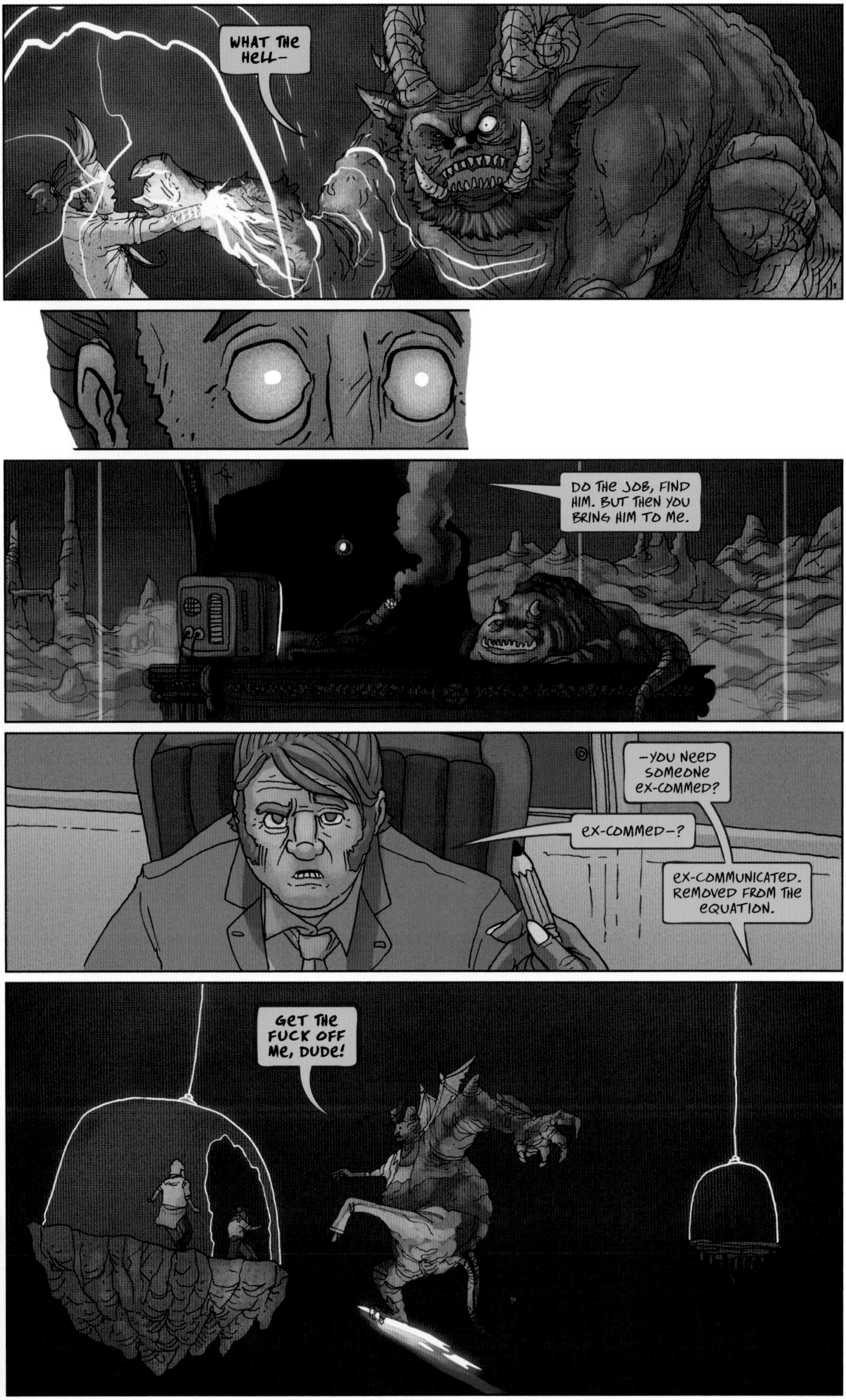
WHAT THE HELL-
DO THE JOB, FIND HIM. BUT THEN YOU BRING HIM TO ME.
-YOU NEED SOMEONE EX-COMMED?
EX-COMMED-?
EX-COMMUNICATED. REMOVED FROM THE EQUATION.
GET THE FUCK OFF ME, DUDE!

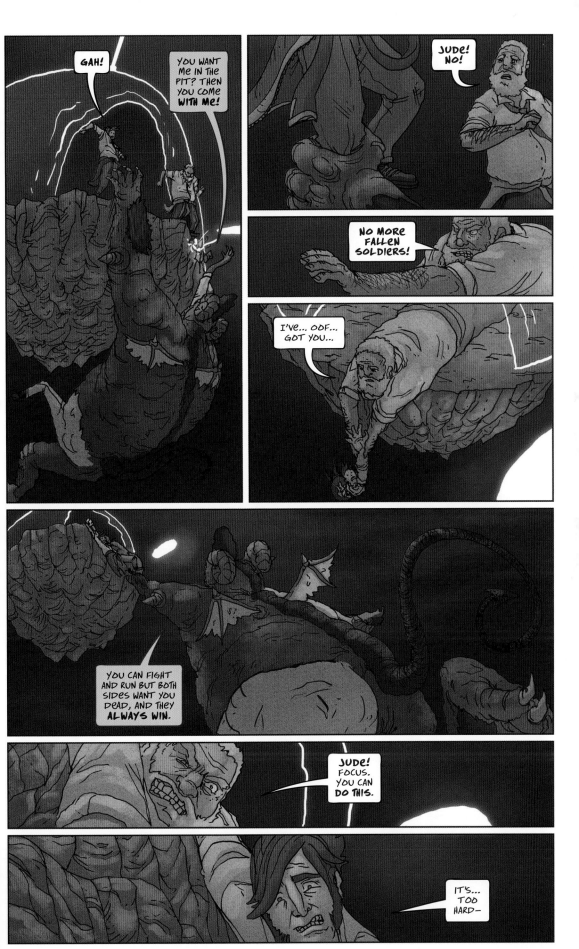

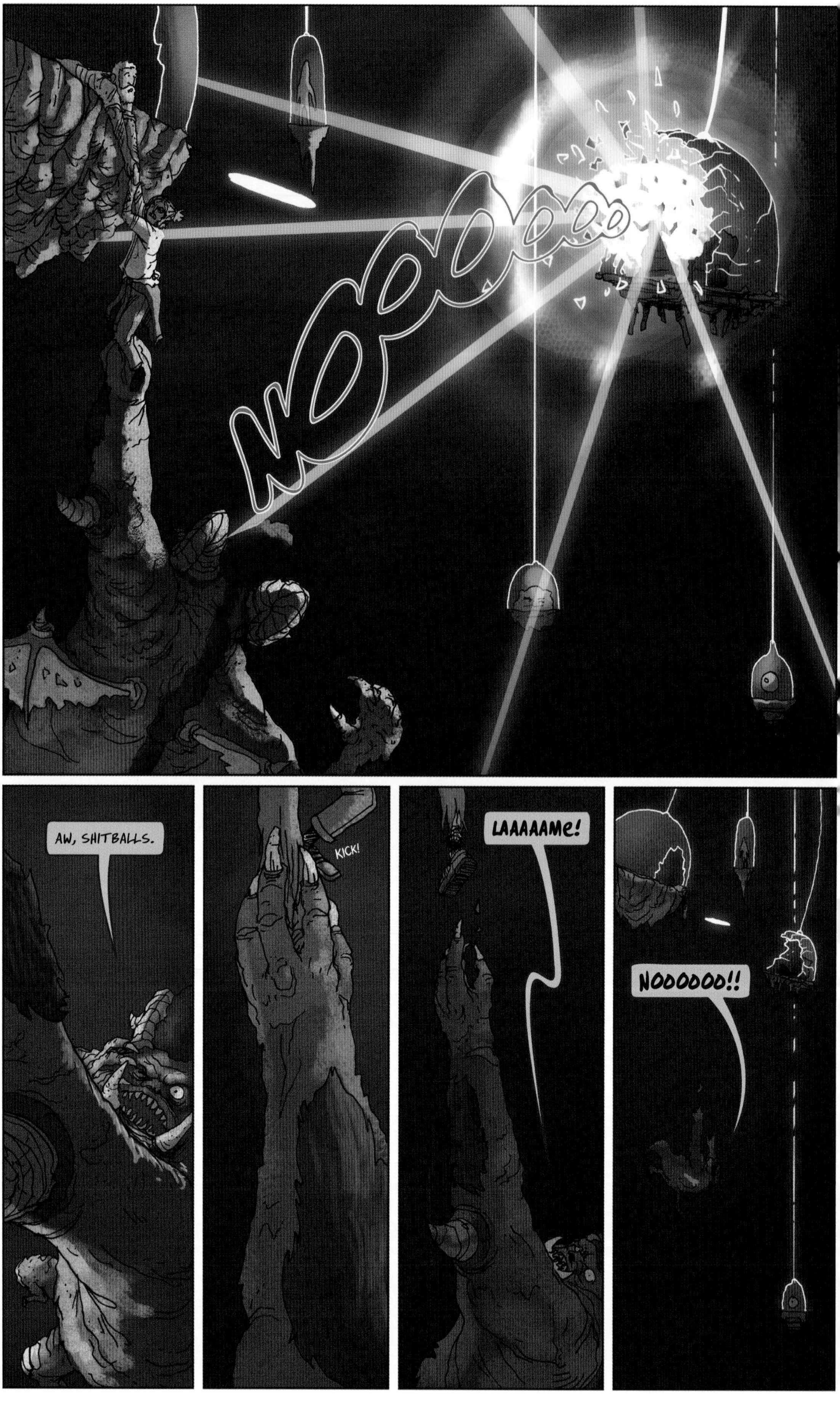
NOOOOOOO
AW, SHITBALLS.
KICK!
LAAAAAME!
NOOOOOO!!

127

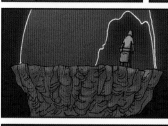

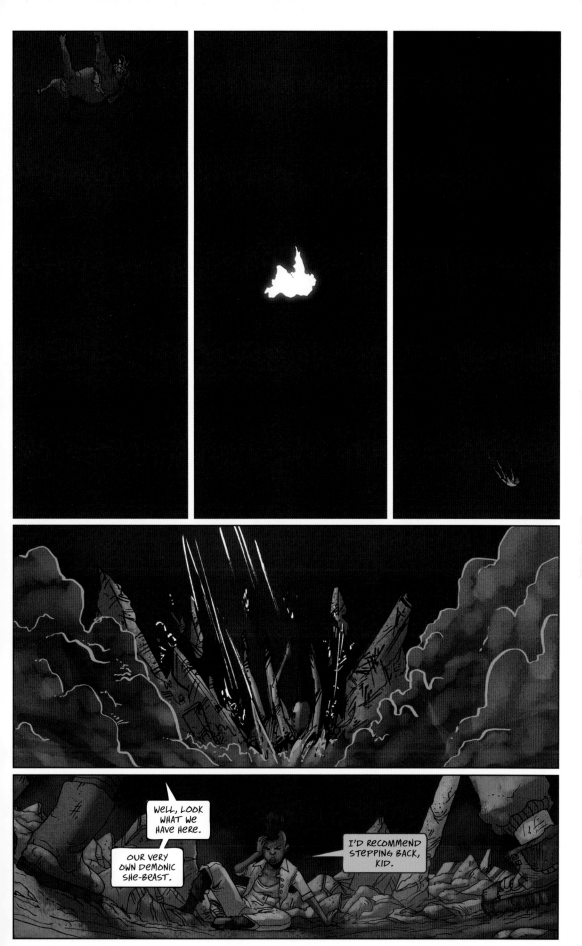

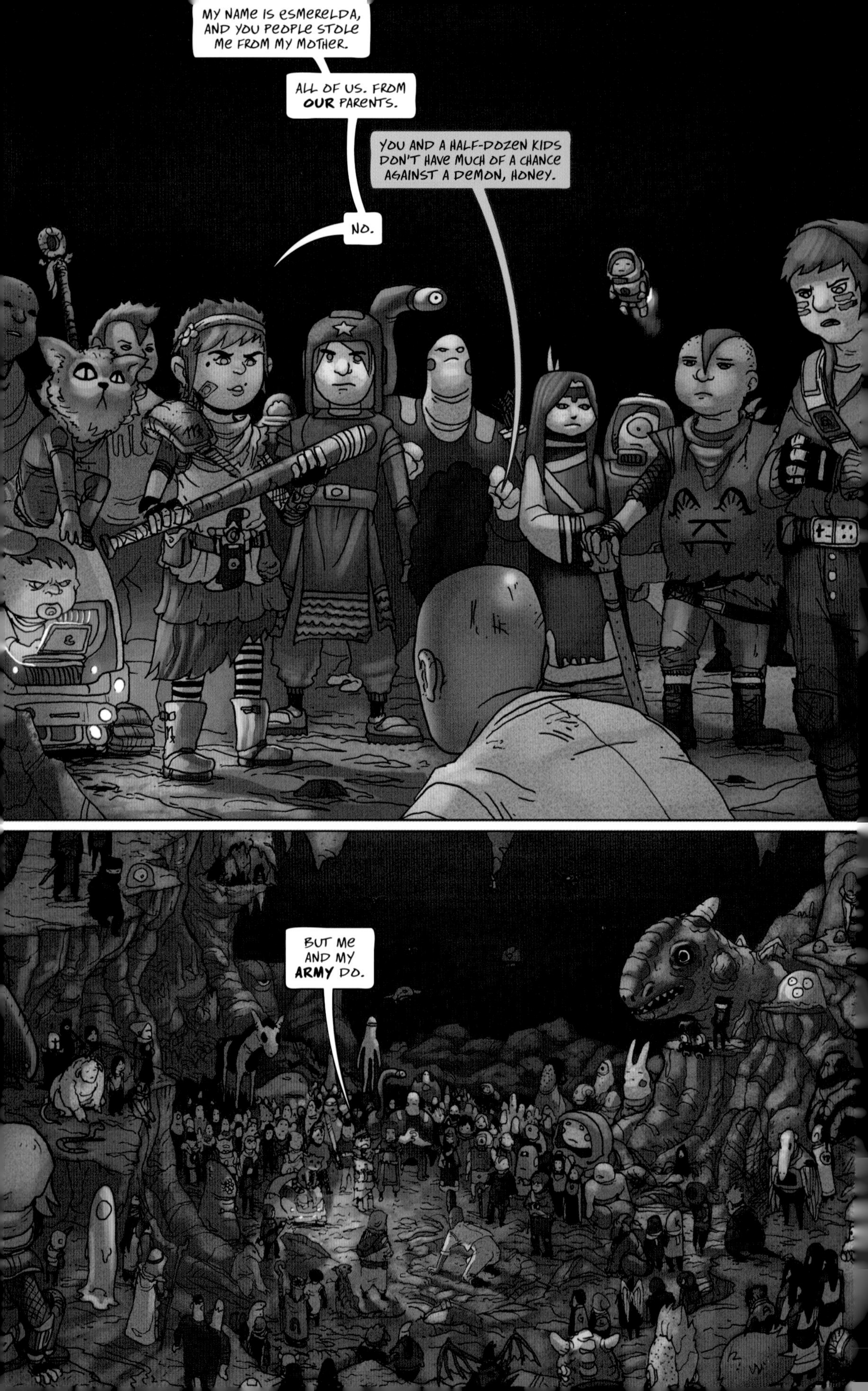
My name is Esmerelda, and you people stole me from my mother.
All of us. From **our** parents.
You and a half-dozen kids don't have much of a chance against a demon, honey.
No.
But me and my **army** do.

THE LIFE AFTER

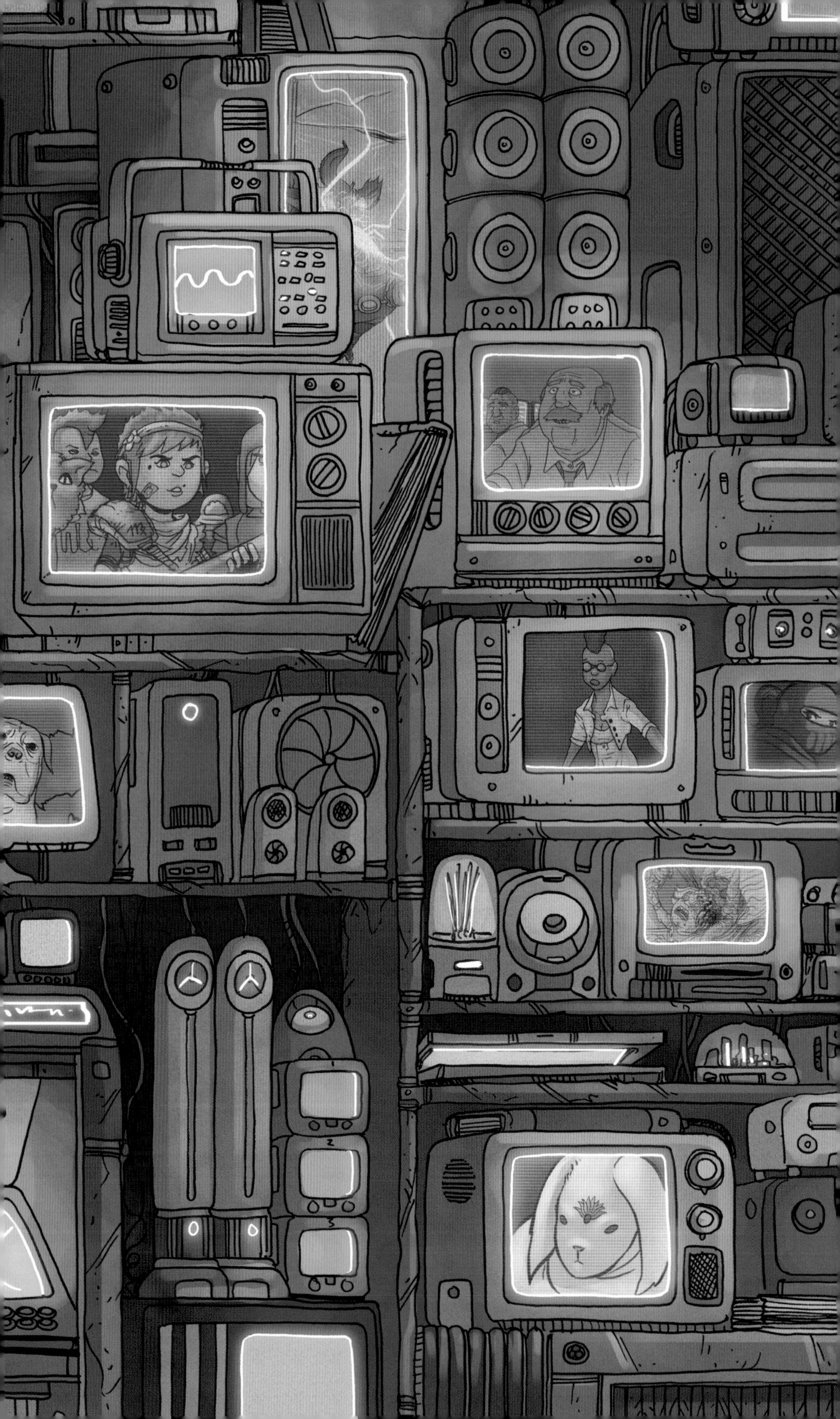

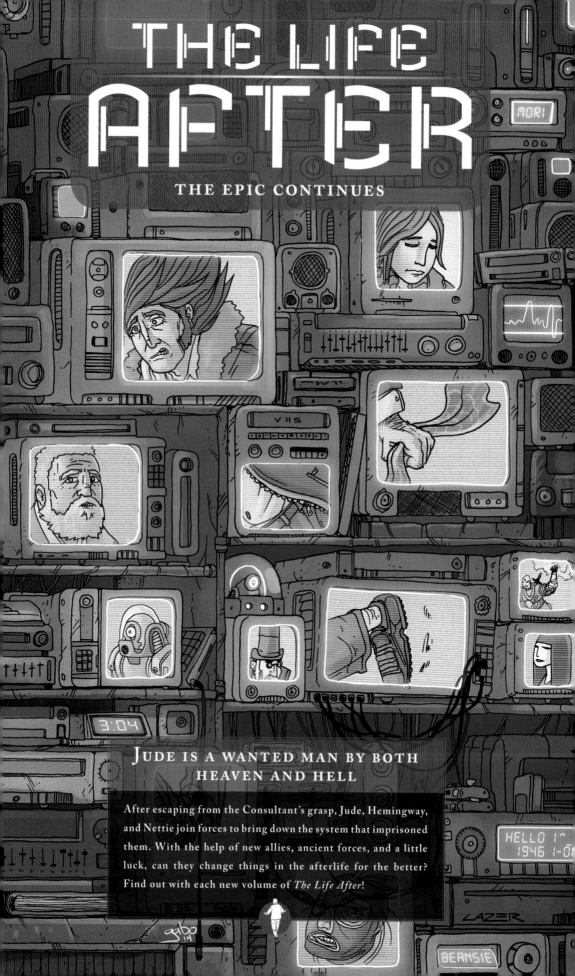

JOSHUA HALE FIALKOV

Joshua Hale Fialkov is the Harvey-, Eisner-, and Emmy-nominated creator of graphic novels, including *The Bunker*, *Punks*, *Tumor*, *Echoes*, and *Elk's Run*. He has written *The Ultimates* for Marvel and *I, Vampire* for DC Comics. He lives in Los Angeles with his wife, author Christina Rice, their daughter, who will remain anonymous (and adorable), their dogs Cole and Olaf. Their cat Smokey has moved on to afterlife 3480-B6, where she's likely playing with her also late sister, The Bandit.

GABO

The Chicago-based Mexican-American known as Gabo eats a bowl of layouts for breakfast, sips ink soup for lunch and has a fatty gouache steak for dinner. He was a 2015 Russ Manning Promising Newcomer award nominee, and in the past has earned an Eisner and Harvey award for his color work.

In his downtime he is the series artist on *Albert the Alien* (Thrillbent) and is the father of the world's best comic book battle website, EnterVoid.com.

He currently resides in the backwoods of Wisconsin with five other like-minded artists. Together they come together and form VONNHAUS.

ALSO BY JOSHUA HALE FIALKOV AND ONI PRESS...

THE LIFE AFTER
JOSHUA HALE FIALKOV • GABO
2

THE LIFE AFTER, VOLUME TWO
By Joshua Hale Fialkov and Gabo
144 pages, softcover, color
ISBN 978-1-62010-254-1

THE LIFE AFTER
JOSHUA HALE FIALKOV • GABO
3
EXODUS

THE LIFE AFTER, VOLUME THREE
By Joshua Hale Fialkov and Gabo
144 pages, softcover, color
ISBN 978-1-62010-321-0

ELK'S RUN
A TALE OF SMALL TOWN HORROR
JOSHUA HALE FIALKOV
NOEL TUAZON
SCOTT KEATING

ELK'S RUN: TENTH ANNIVERSARY EDITION
By Joshua Hale Fialkov, Noel Tuazon, and Scott Keating
248 pages, hardcover, color
ISBN 978-1-62010-279-4

TUMOR
JOSHUA HALE FIALKOV & NOEL TUAZON

TUMOR
By Joshua Hale Fialkov and Noel Tuazon
248 pages, hardcover, B&W
ISBN 978-1-62010-326-5

CHECK OUT OUR OTHER ONI PRESS SQUARE ONE TITLES, EACH ONLY $10!

AVAILABLE NOW:
Letter 44, Volume One

AVAILABLE SUMMER AND FALL 2017:
The Bunker, Volume One
The Sixth Gun, Volume One
Courtney Crumrin, Volume One: The Night Things
Stumptown, Volume One

ONI PRESS

For more information on these and other fine Oni Press comic books and graphic novels visit www.onipress.com.
To find a comic specialty store in your area visit www.comicshops.us.

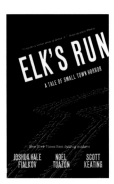